Bacon is a Vegetable

Coffee is a Vitamin

HISSSS!

Bacon is a Vegetable

Coffee is a Vitamin

WRITTEN, ILLUSTRATED,
AND DESIGNED BY
R STEVENS

EDITED BY
JILL BEATON

ONI PRESS

Oni Press, Inc.
publisher, Joe Nozemack
editor in chief, James Lucas Jones
art director, Keith Wood
director of sales, Cheyenne Allott
director of publicity, John Schork
editor, Jill Beaton
editor, Charlie Chu
graphic designer, Jason Storey
digital prepress lead, Troy Look
administrative assistant, Robin Herrera

Oni Press, Inc.
1305 SE Martin Luther King Jr. Blvd.
Suite A
Portland, OR 97214

onipress.com
facebook.com/onipress
twitter.com/onipress
onipress.tumblr.com

dieselsweeties.com
twitter.com/rstevens
rstevens@mac.com

First Edition: February 2014

ISBN: 978-1-62010-091-2
eISBN: 978-1-62010-130-8

Diesel Sweeties: Bacon is a Vegetable; Coffee is a Vitamin. February 2014.
Published by Oni Press, Inc. 1305 SE Martin Luther King Jr. Blvd., Suite A, Portland, OR 97214.

10 9 8 7 6 5 4 3 2 1

Library of Congress Control Number: 2013949077

Printed in China.

'TIL DEATH DO US PART

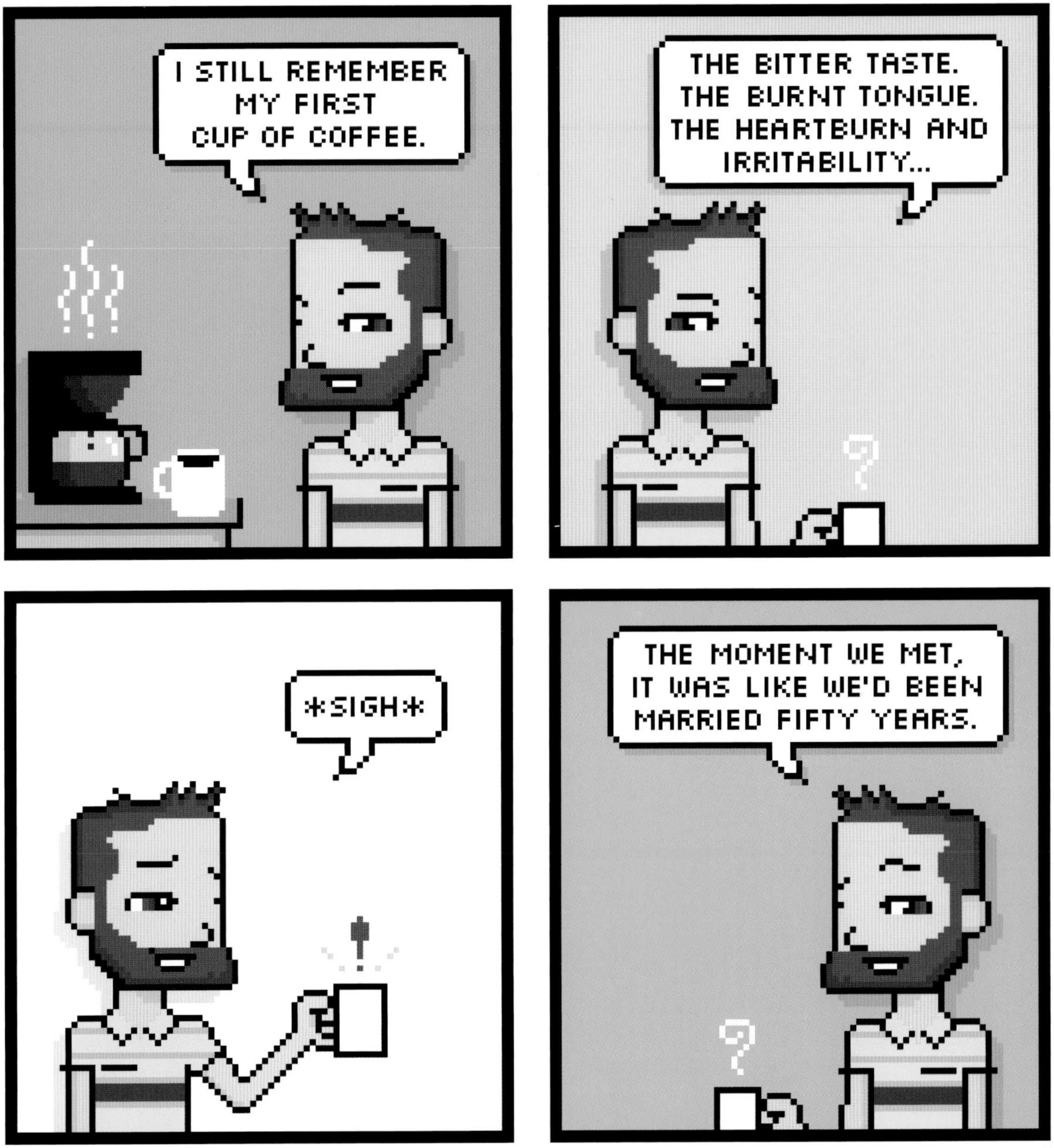
I STILL REMEMBER MY FIRST CUP OF COFFEE.
THE BITTER TASTE. THE BURNT TONGUE. THE HEARTBURN AND IRRITABILITY...
SIGH
THE MOMENT WE MET, IT WAS LIKE WE'D BEEN MARRIED FIFTY YEARS.

ROPE-A-DOPAMINE

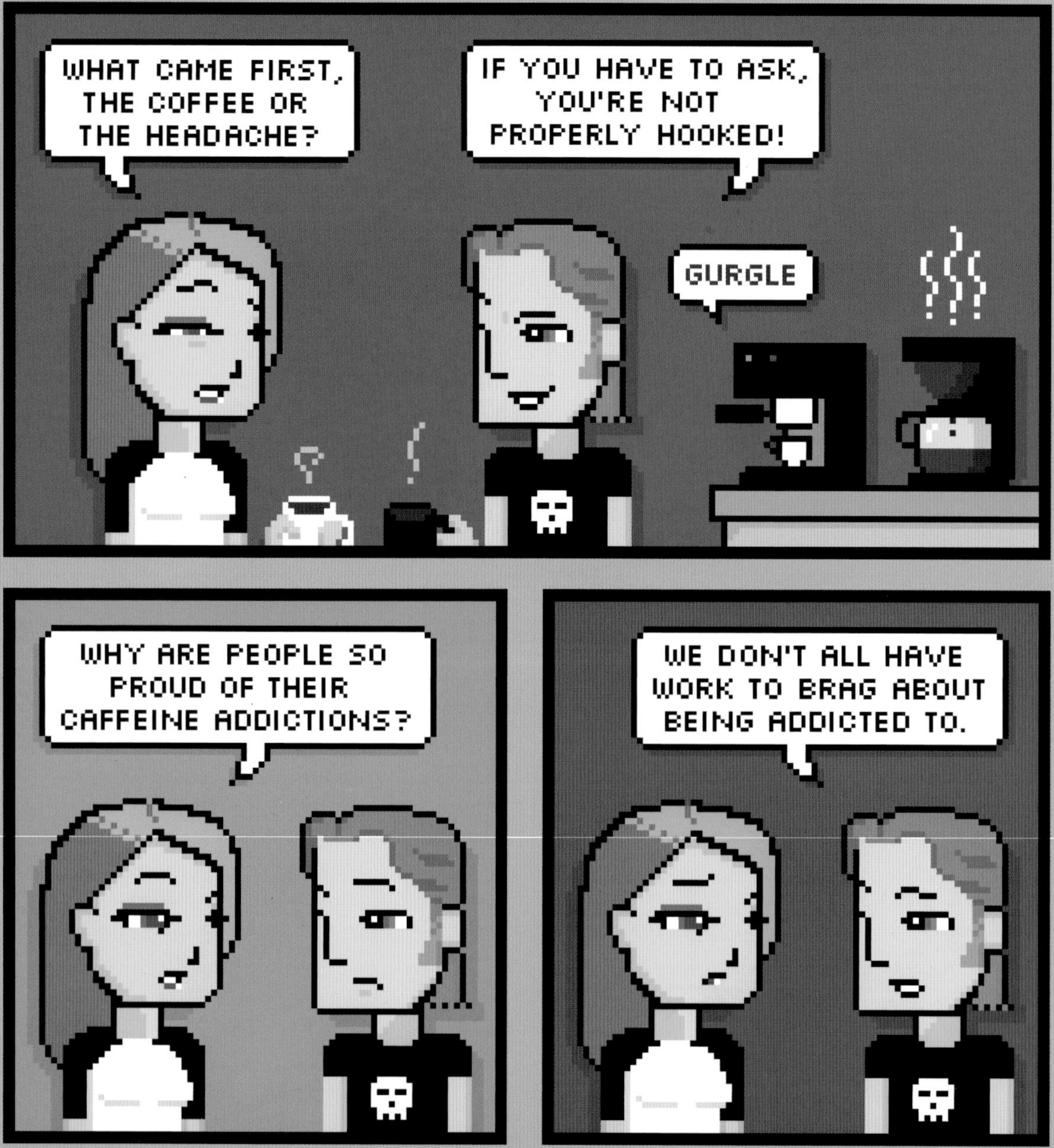
WHAT CAME FIRST, THE COFFEE OR THE HEADACHE?
IF YOU HAVE TO ASK, YOU'RE NOT PROPERLY HOOKED!
GURGLE
WHY ARE PEOPLE SO PROUD OF THEIR CAFFEINE ADDICTIONS?
WE DON'T ALL HAVE WORK TO BRAG ABOUT BEING ADDICTED TO.

DRINK OR DRINK NOT, THERE IS NO CREAMER

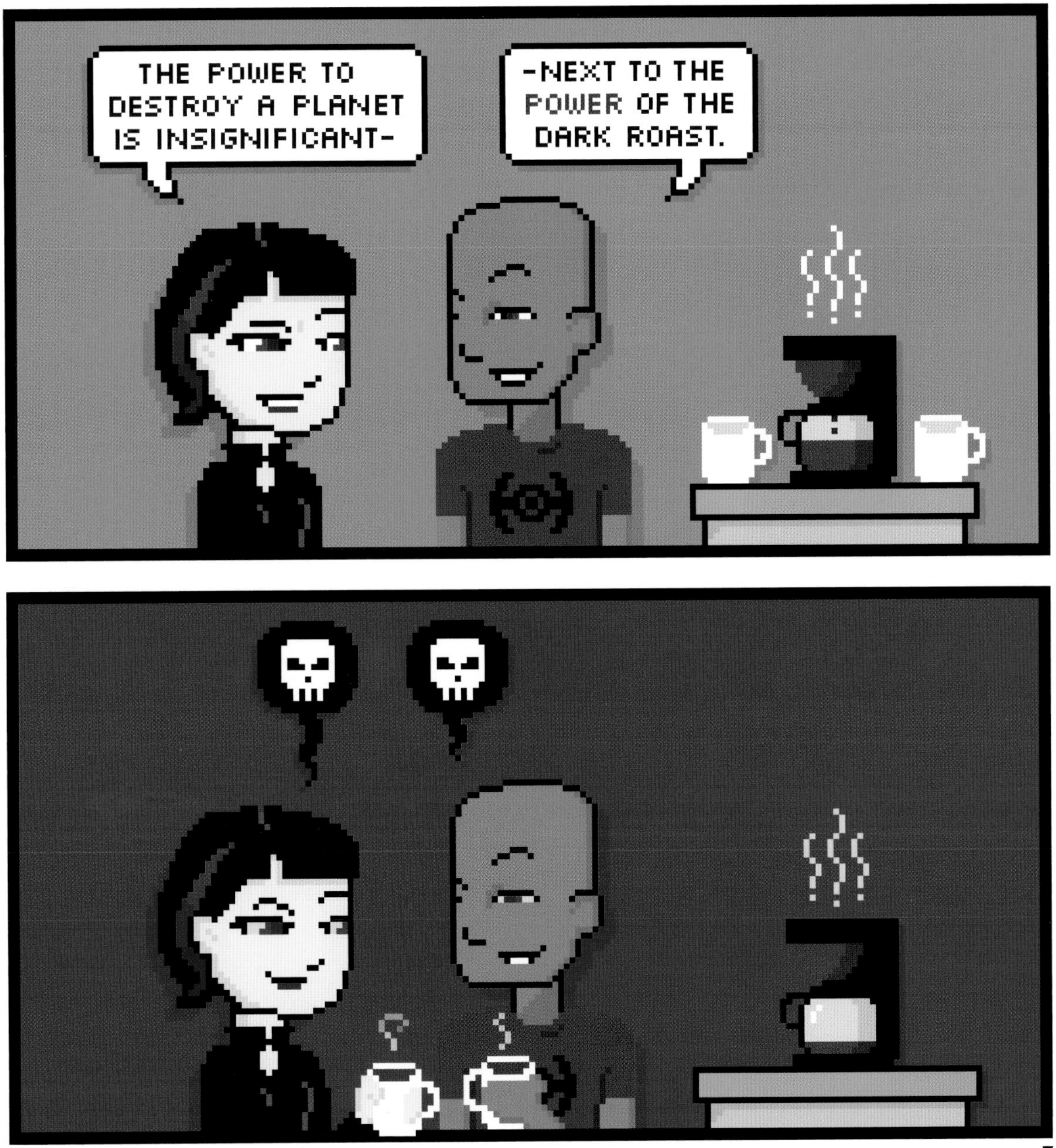
THE POWER TO DESTROY A PLANET IS INSIGNIFICANT-
-NEXT TO THE POWER OF THE DARK ROAST.

BACON IS A VEGETABLE

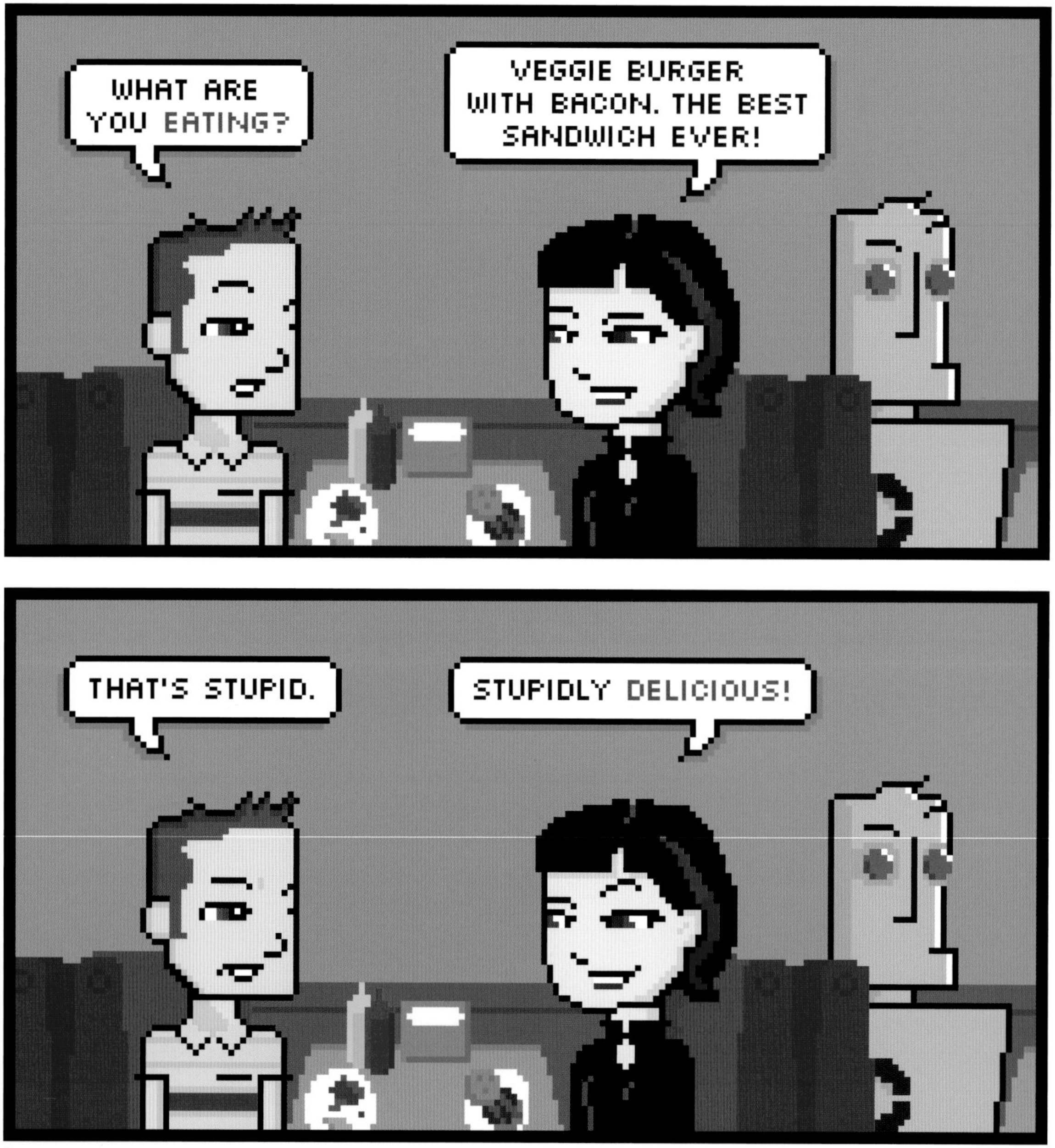

WHAT ARE YOU EATING?
VEGGIE BURGER WITH BACON. THE BEST SANDWICH EVER!
THAT'S STUPID.
STUPIDLY DELICIOUS!

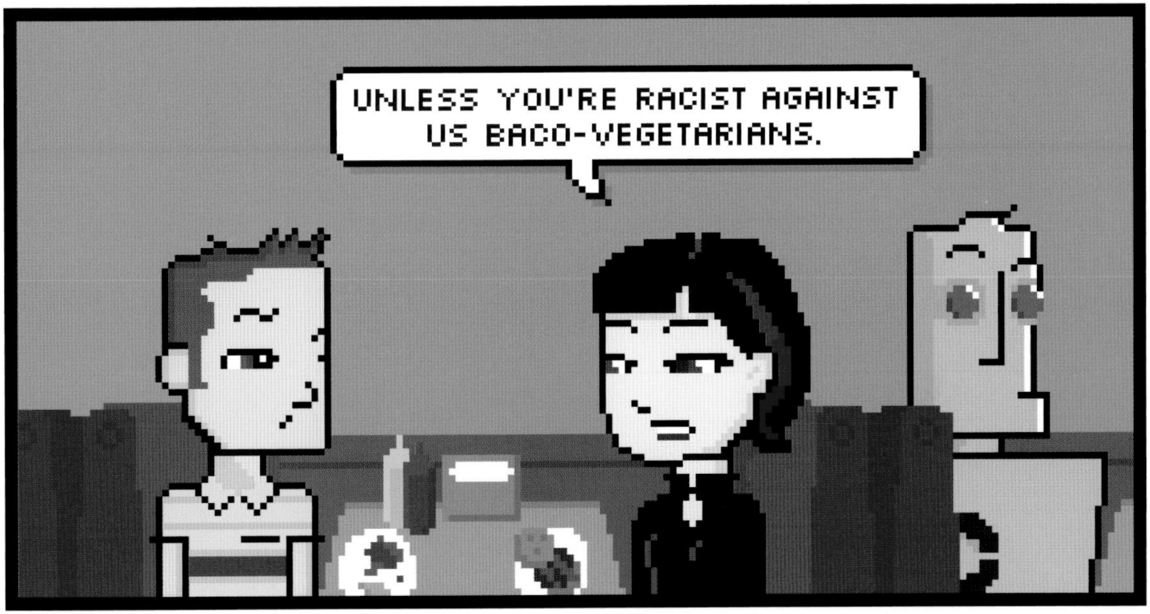
UNLESS YOU'RE RACIST AGAINST US BACO-VEGETARIANS.

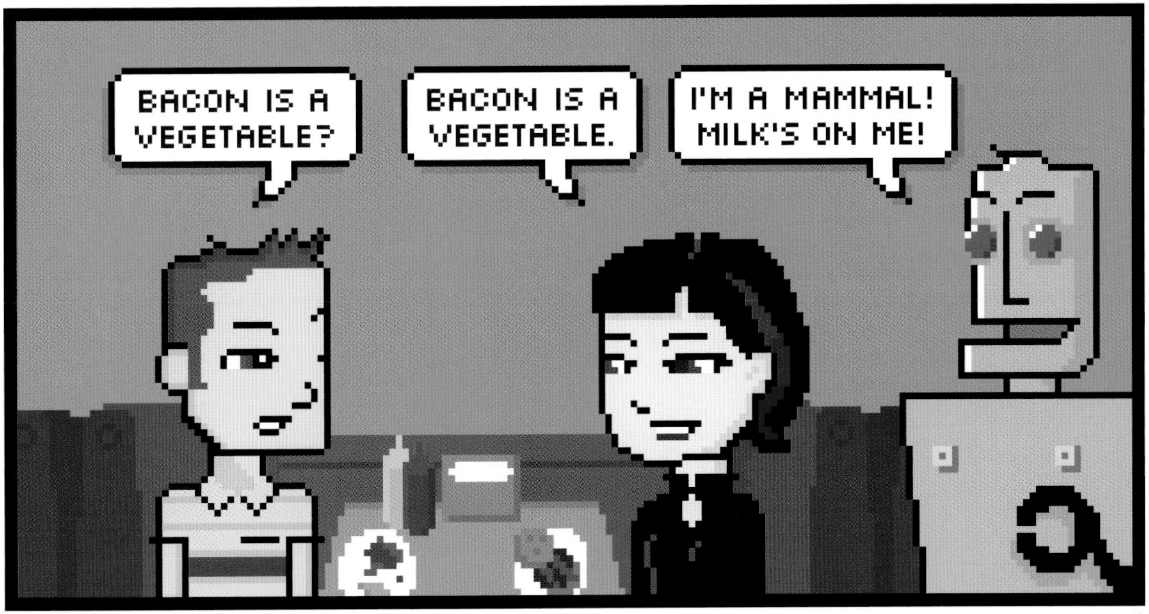
BACON IS A VEGETABLE?
BACON IS A VEGETABLE.
I'M A MAMMAL! MILK'S ON ME!

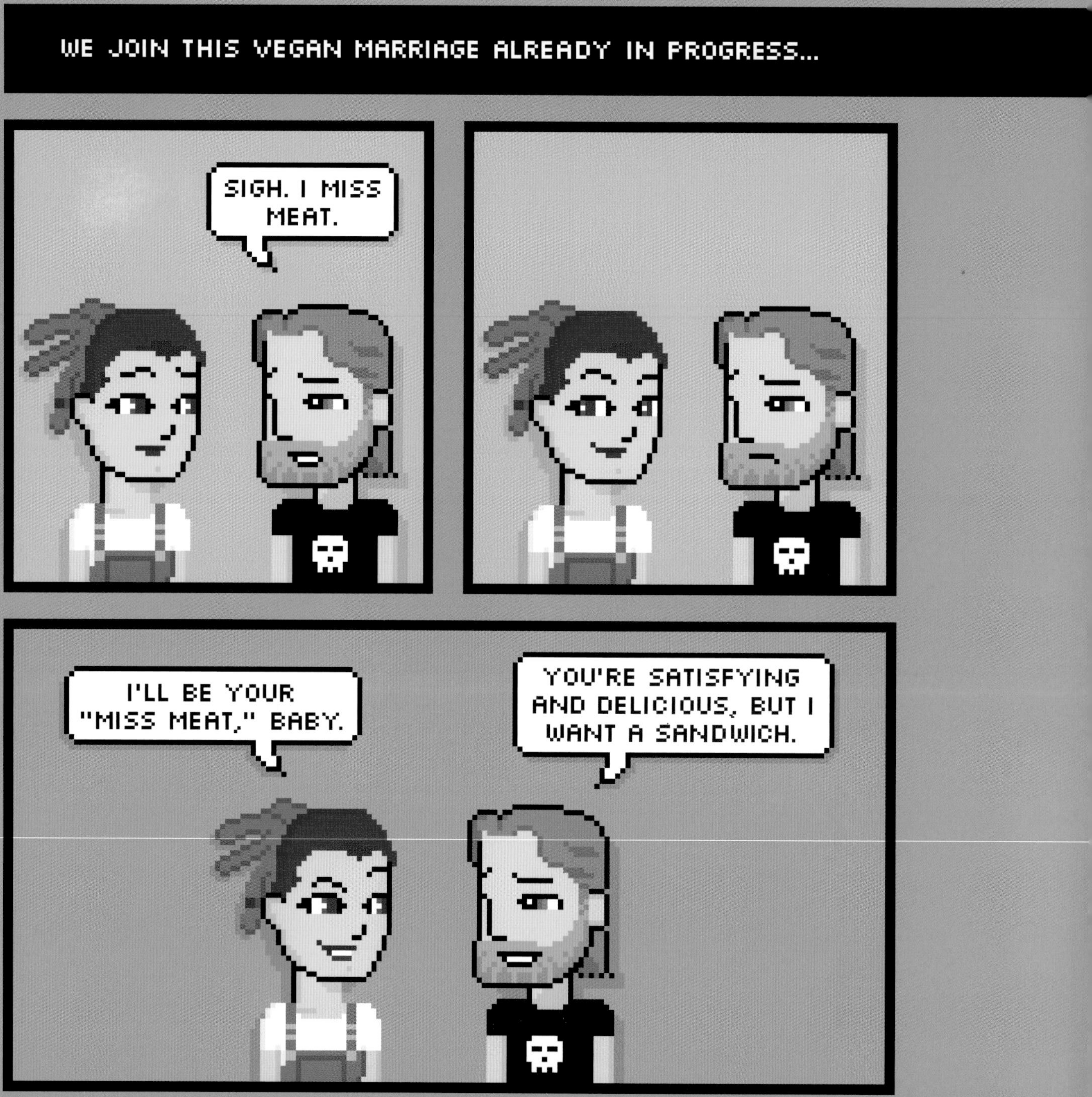
WE JOIN THIS VEGAN MARRIAGE ALREADY IN PROGRESS...
SIGH. I MISS MEAT.
I'LL BE YOUR "MISS MEAT," BABY.
YOU'RE SATISFYING AND DELICIOUS, BUT I WANT A SANDWICH.

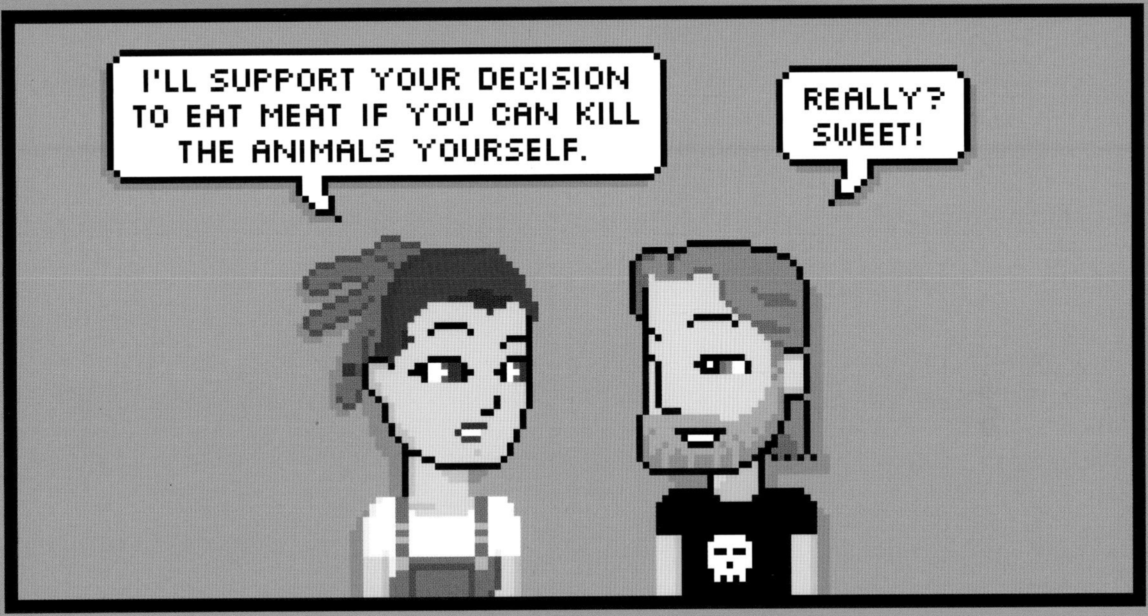
I'LL SUPPORT YOUR DECISION TO EAT MEAT IF YOU CAN KILL THE ANIMALS YOURSELF.
REALLY? SWEET!

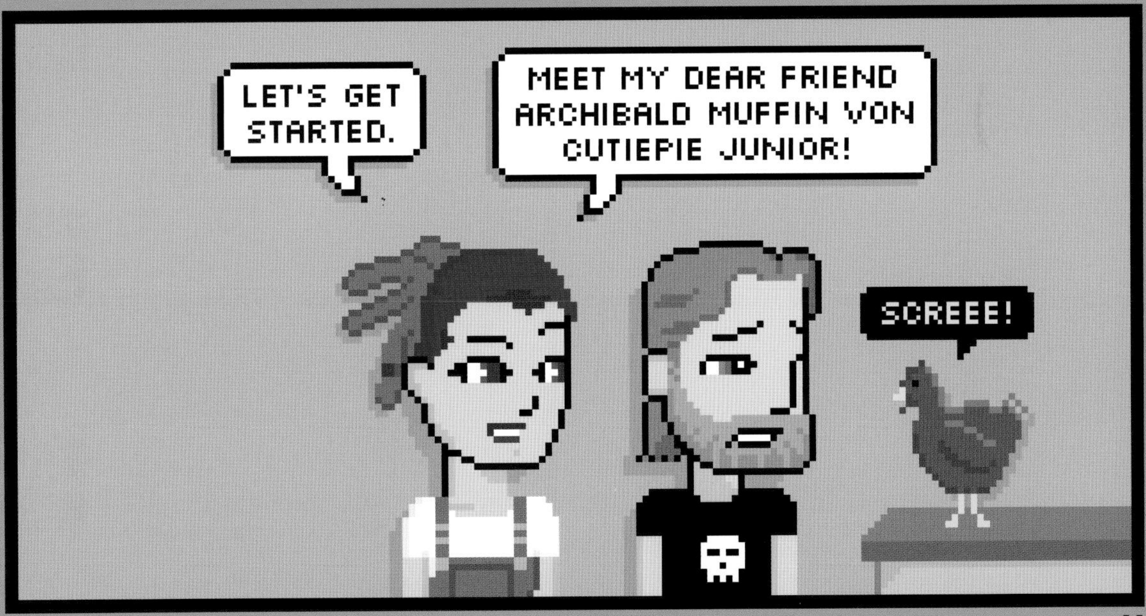
LET'S GET STARTED.
MEET MY DEAR FRIEND ARCHIBALD MUFFIN VON CUTIEPIE JUNIOR!
SCREEE!

BEAK THE REAPER

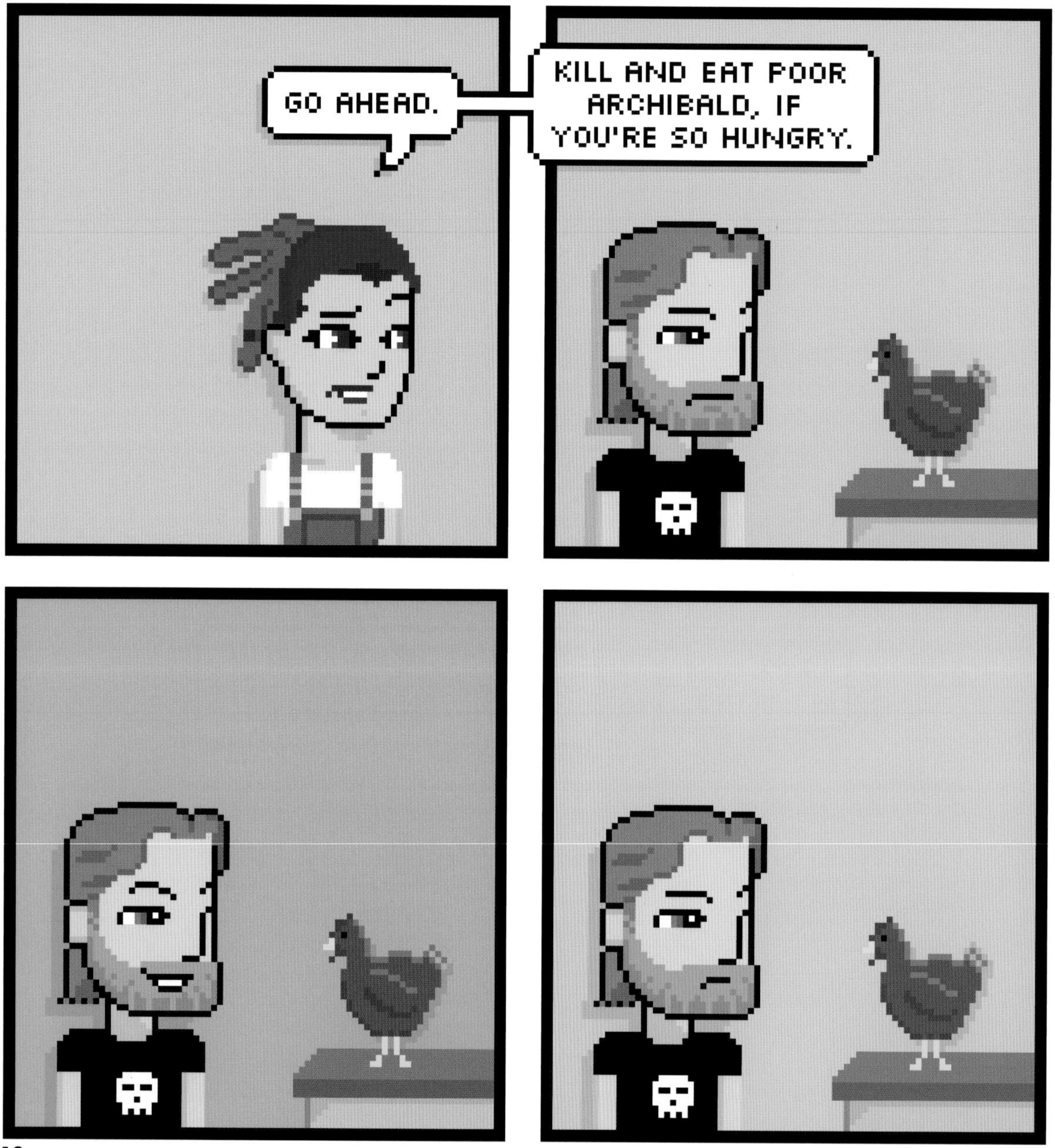
GO AHEAD.
KILL AND EAT POOR ARCHIBALD, IF YOU'RE SO HUNGRY.

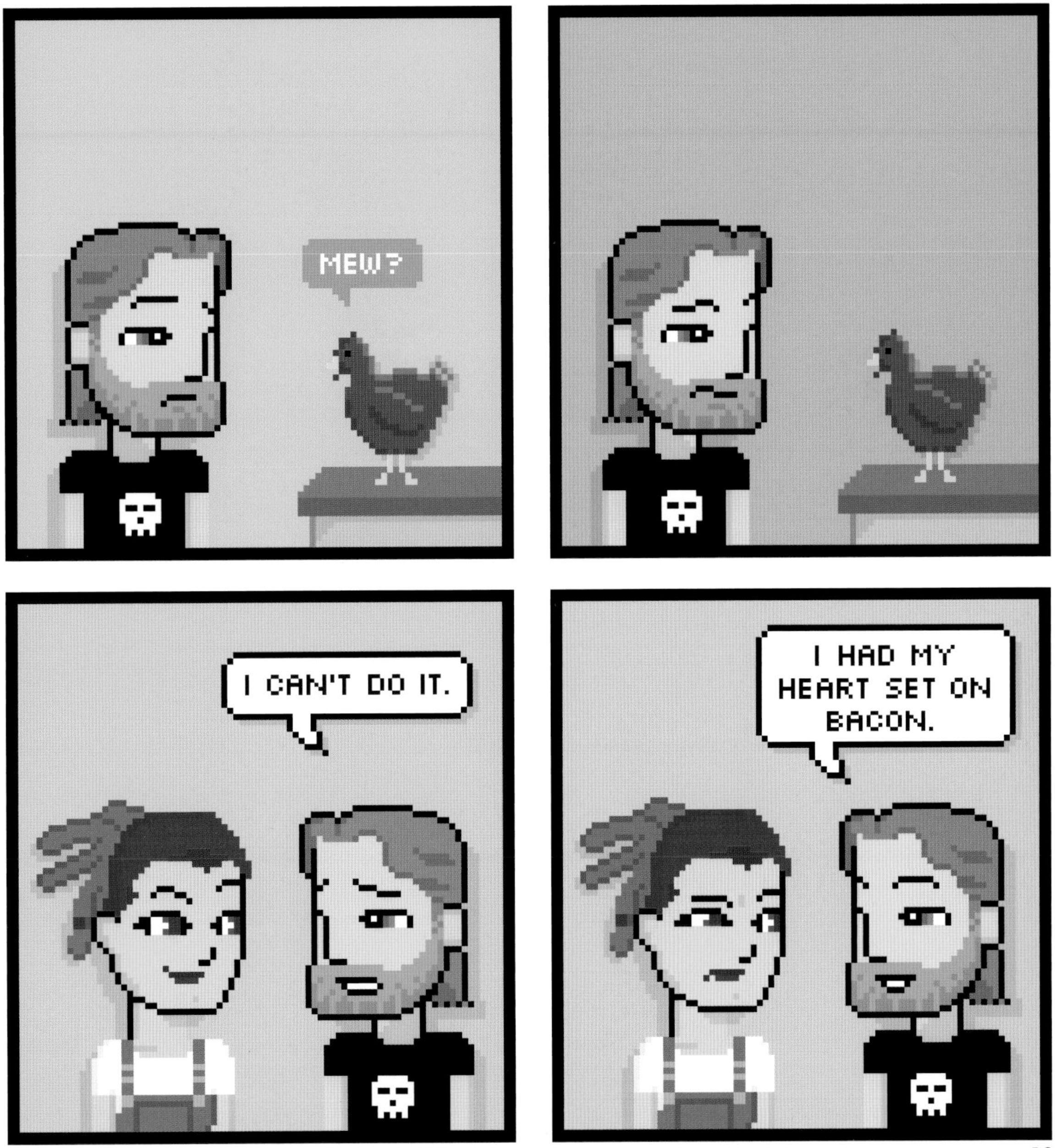
MEW?
I CAN'T DO IT.
I HAD MY HEART SET ON BACON.

YOU SHALL NOT PASS (WITHOUT A STENT)

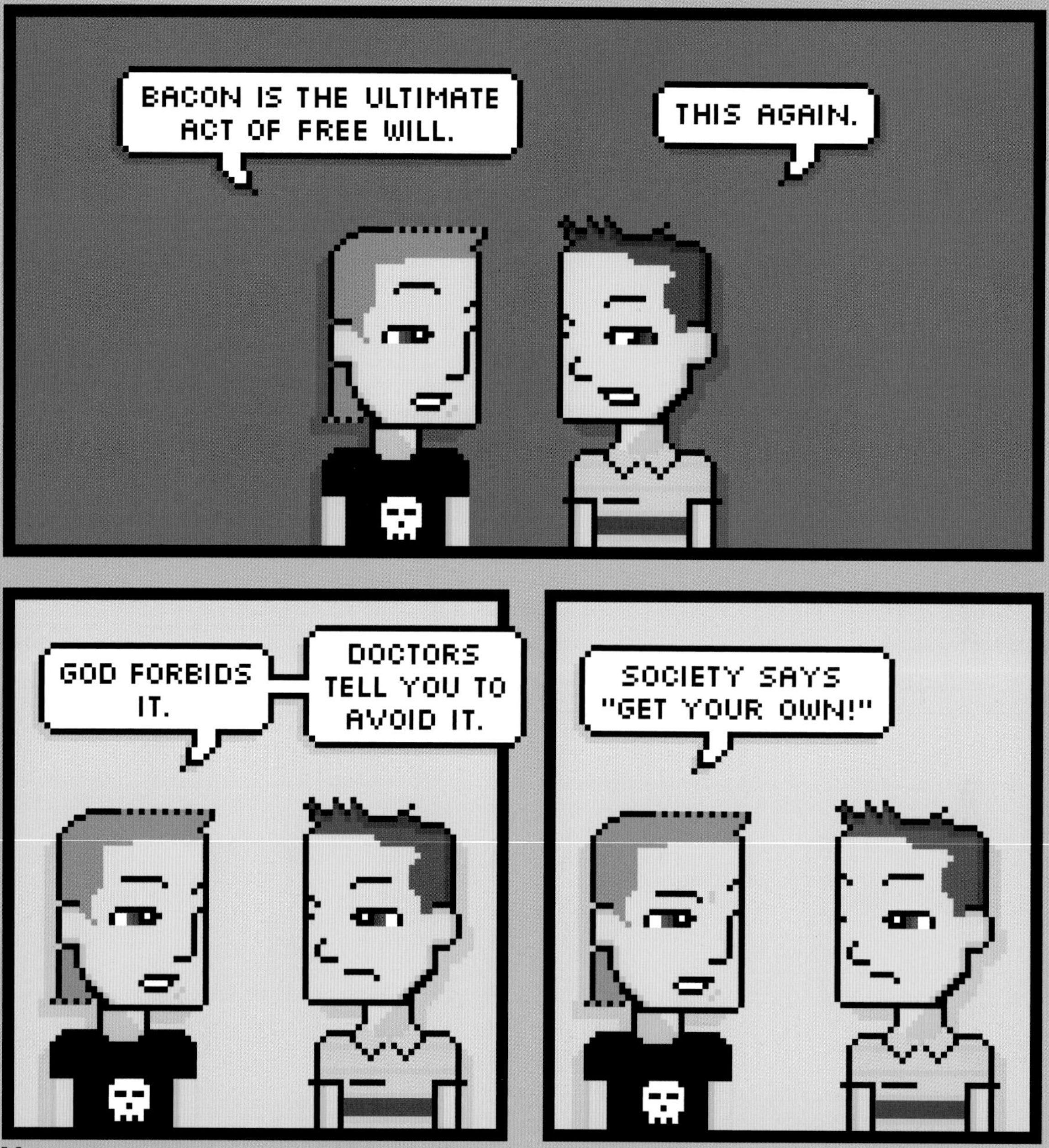
BACON IS THE ULTIMATE ACT OF FREE WILL.
THIS AGAIN.
GOD FORBIDS IT.
DOCTORS TELL YOU TO AVOID IT.
SOCIETY SAYS "GET YOUR OWN!"

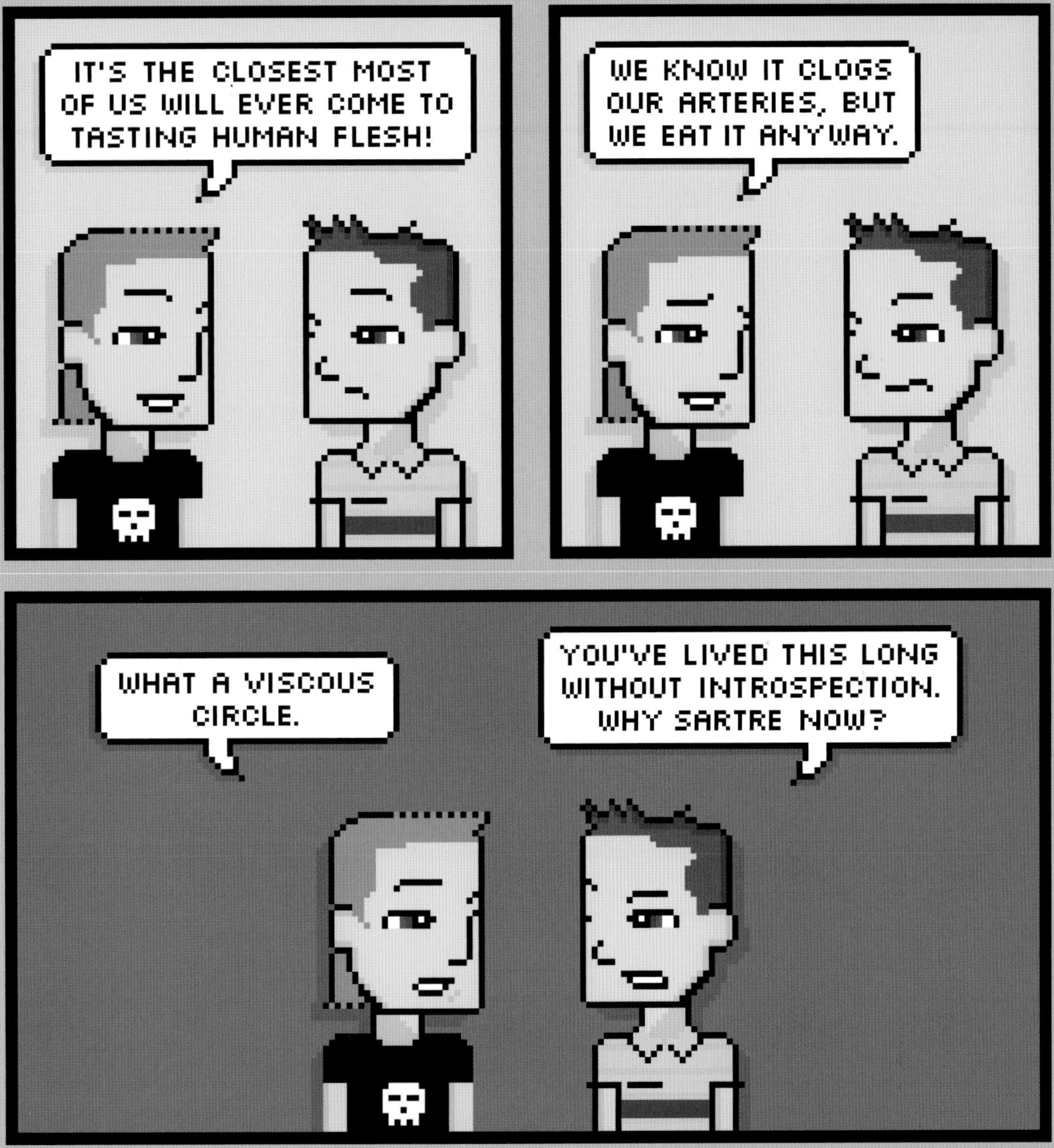
IT'S THE CLOSEST MOST OF US WILL EVER COME TO TASTING HUMAN FLESH!
WE KNOW IT CLOGS OUR ARTERIES, BUT WE EAT IT ANYWAY.
WHAT A VISCOUS CIRCLE.
YOU'VE LIVED THIS LONG WITHOUT INTROSPECTION. WHY SARTRE NOW?

I'LL TAKE THE PHYSICAL CHALLENGE

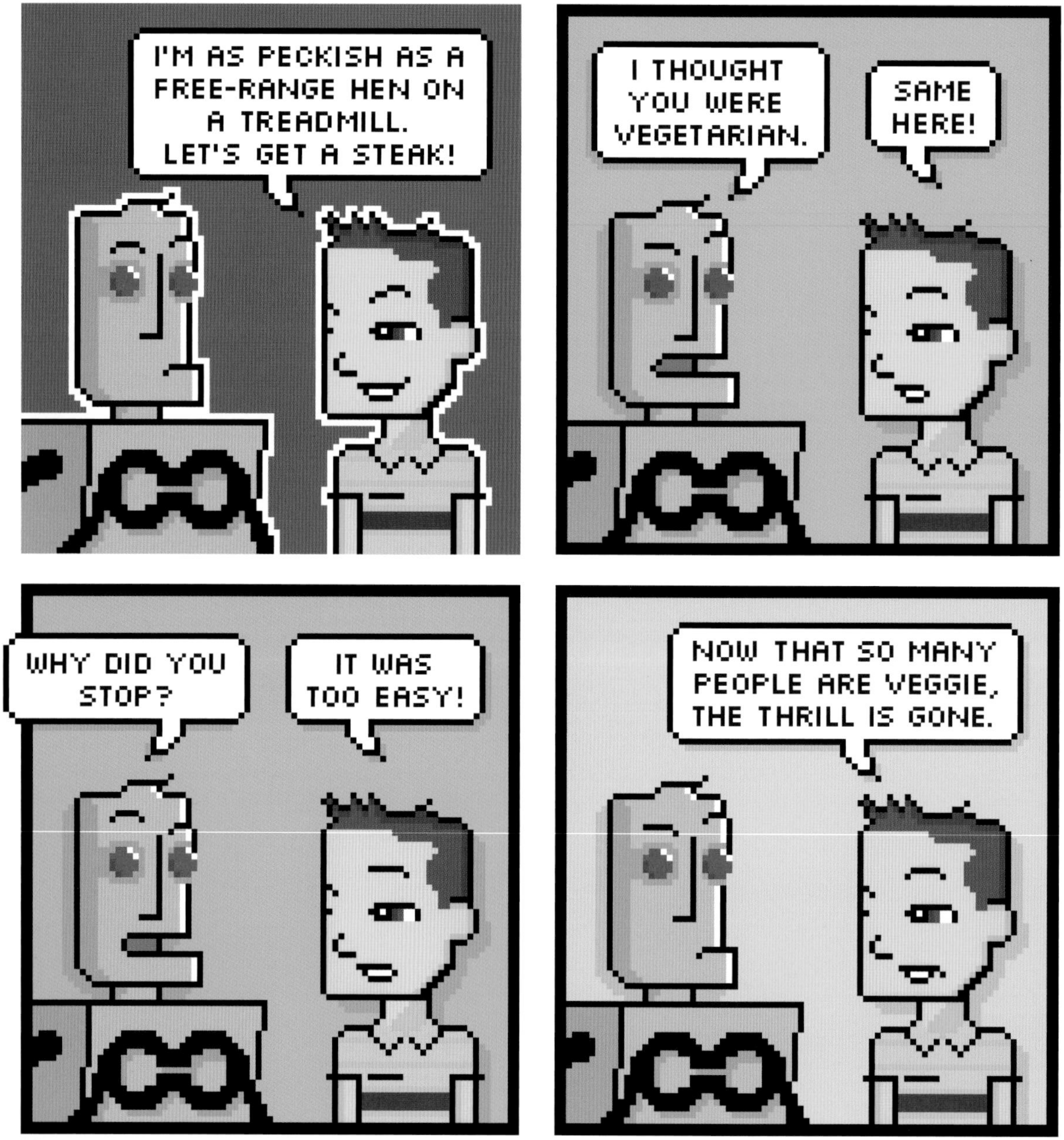
I'M AS PECKISH AS A FREE-RANGE HEN ON A TREADMILL. LET'S GET A STEAK!
I THOUGHT YOU WERE VEGETARIAN.
SAME HERE!
WHY DID YOU STOP?
IT WAS TOO EASY!
NOW THAT SO MANY PEOPLE ARE VEGGIE, THE THRILL IS GONE.

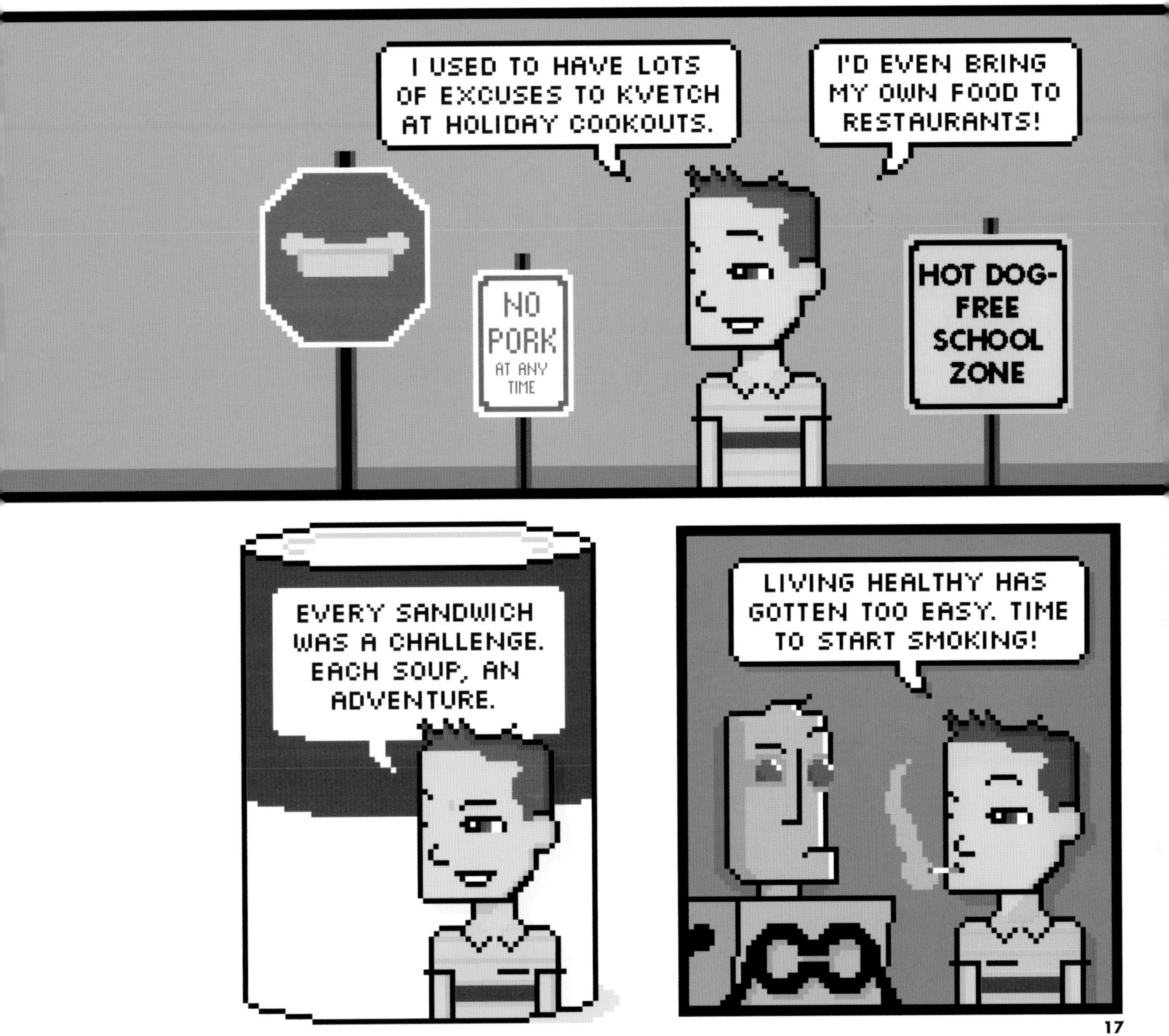
I USED TO HAVE LOTS OF EXCUSES TO KVETCH AT HOLIDAY COOKOUTS.
I'D EVEN BRING MY OWN FOOD TO RESTAURANTS!
NO PORK AT ANY TIME
HOT DOG-FREE SCHOOL ZONE
EVERY SANDWICH WAS A CHALLENGE. EACH SOUP, AN ADVENTURE.
LIVING HEALTHY HAS GOTTEN TOO EASY. TIME TO START SMOKING!

FRIEND ROAST

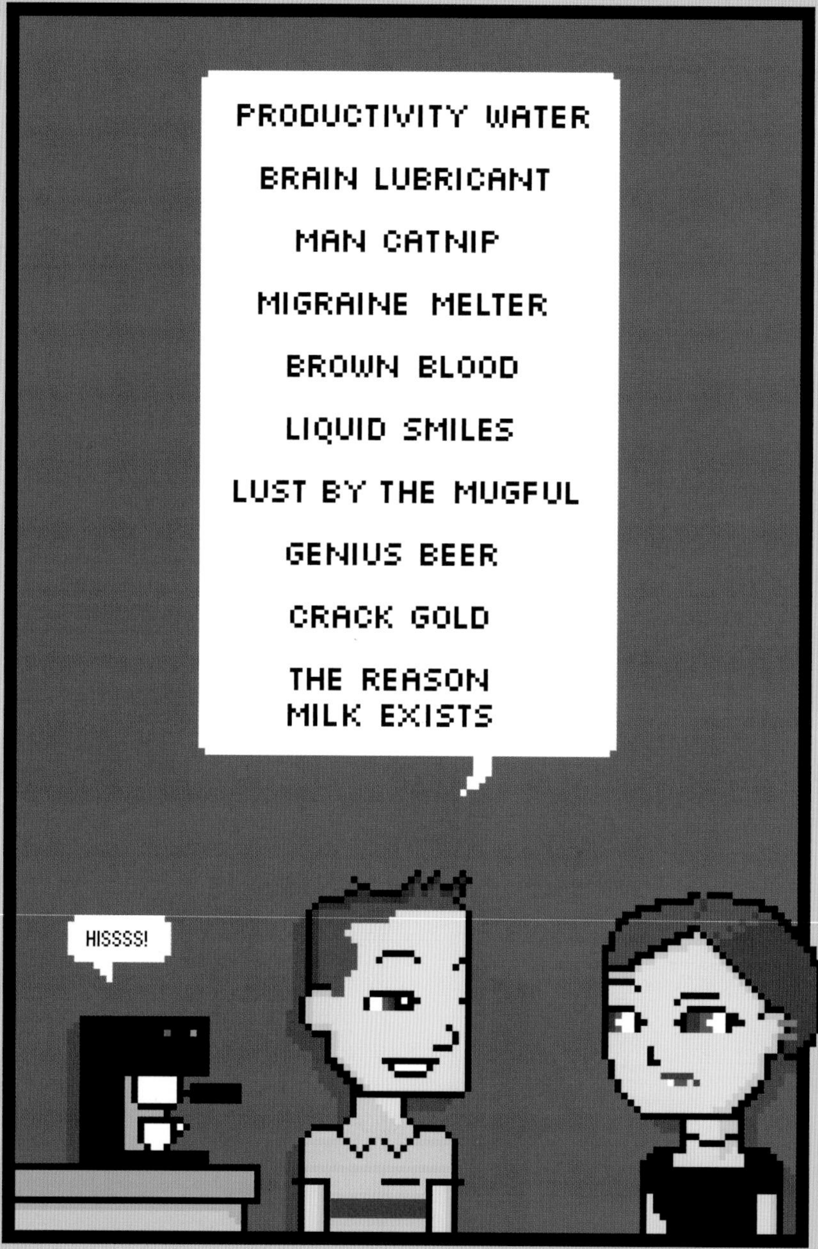
PRODUCTIVITY WATER
BRAIN LUBRICANT
MAN CATNIP
MIGRAINE MELTER
BROWN BLOOD
LIQUID SMILES
LUST BY THE MUGFUL
GENIUS BEER
CRACK GOLD
THE REASON MILK EXISTS
HISSSS!

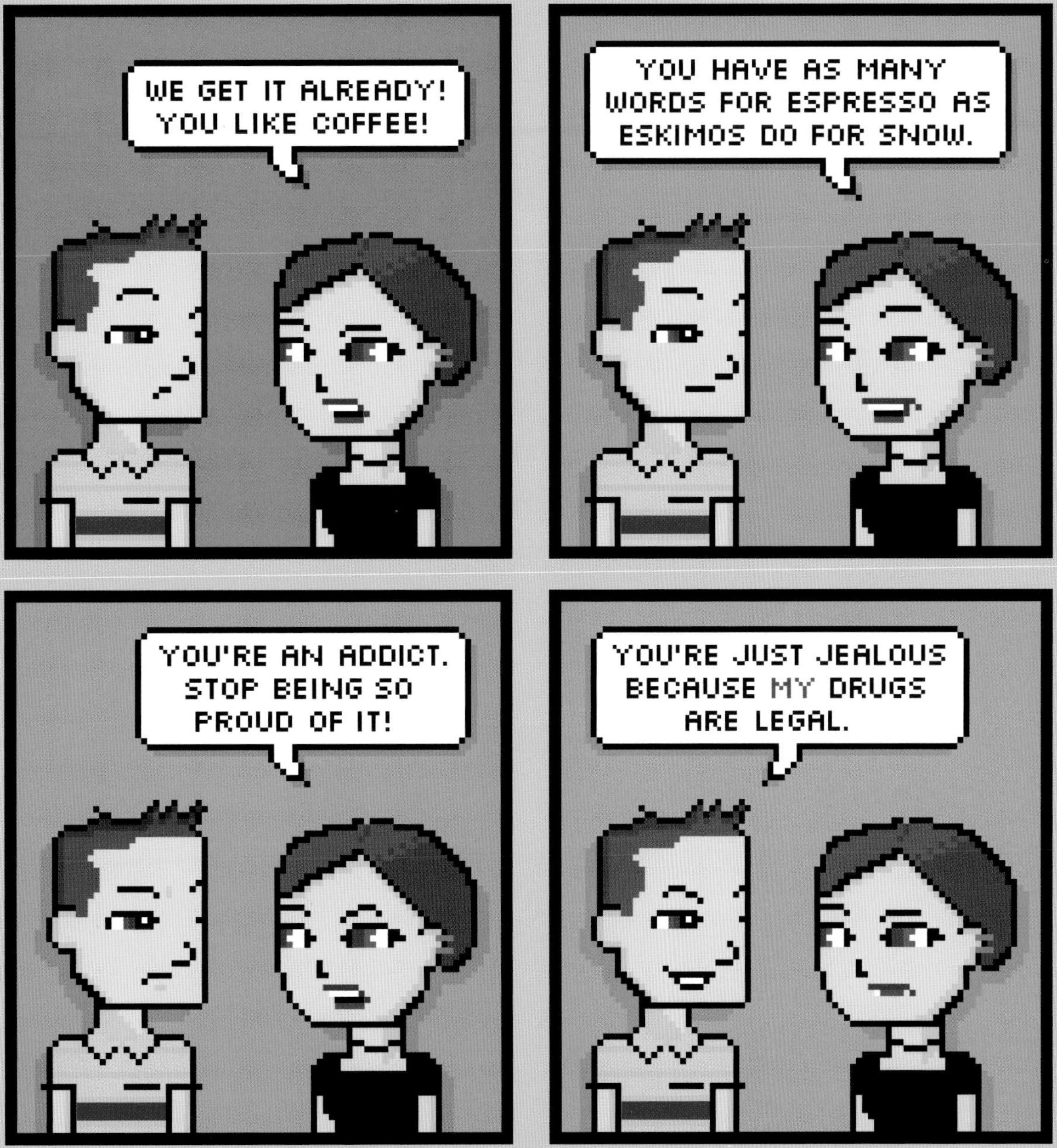
WE GET IT ALREADY! YOU LIKE COFFEE!
YOU HAVE AS MANY WORDS FOR ESPRESSO AS ESKIMOS DO FOR SNOW.
YOU'RE AN ADDICT. STOP BEING SO PROUD OF IT!
YOU'RE JUST JEALOUS BECAUSE MY DRUGS ARE LEGAL.

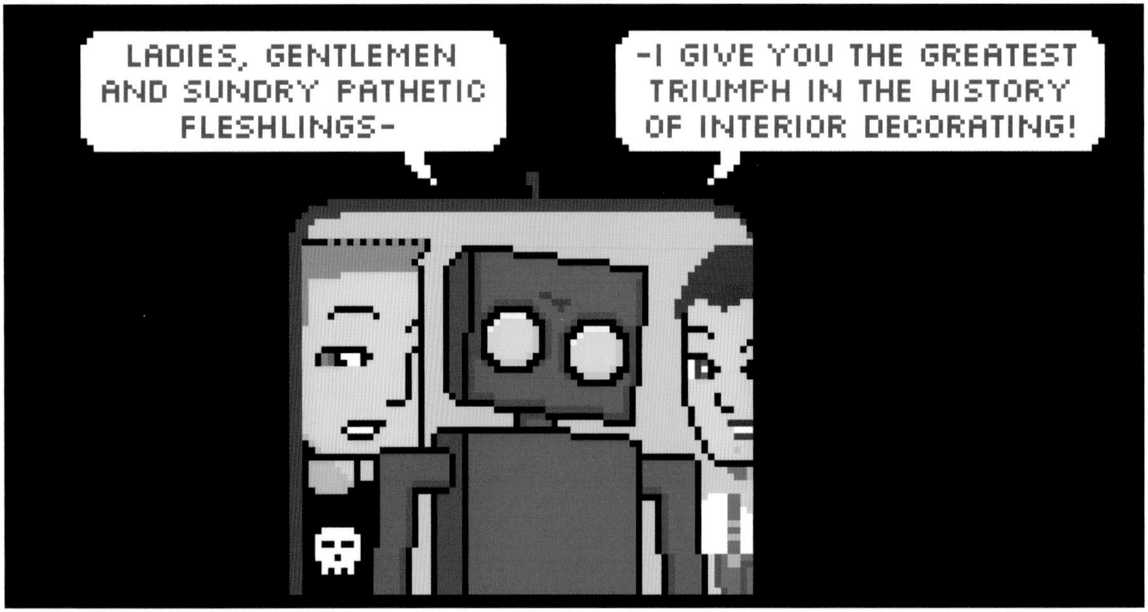
LADIES, GENTLEMEN AND SUNDRY PATHETIC FLESHLINGS-
-I GIVE YOU THE GREATEST TRIUMPH IN THE HISTORY OF INTERIOR DECORATING!

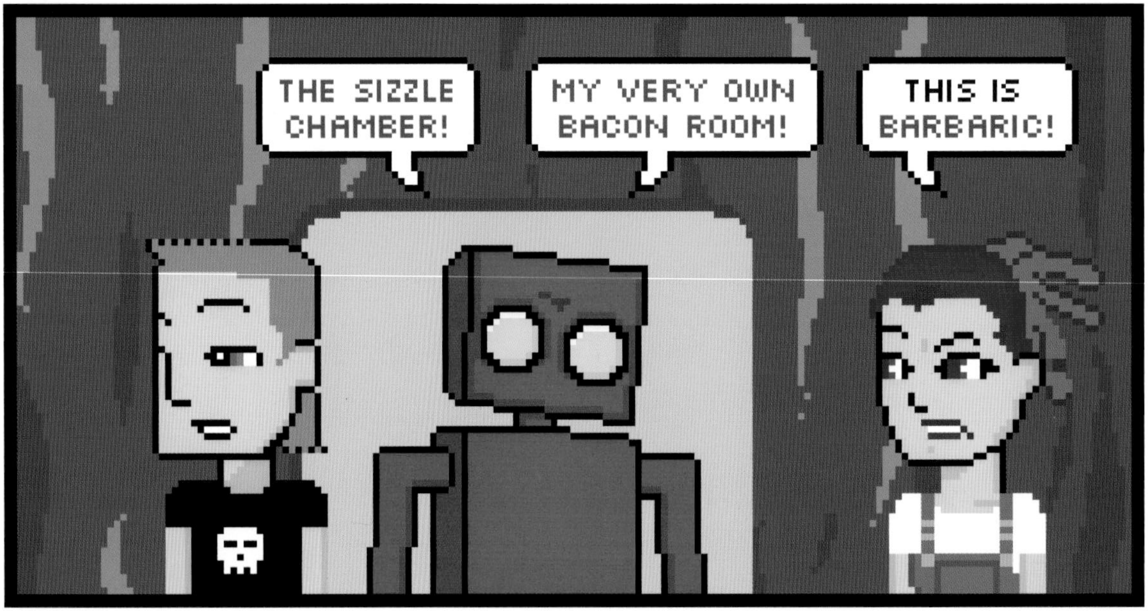
THE SIZZLE CHAMBER!
MY VERY OWN BACON ROOM!
THIS IS BARBARIC!

IT'S SO... CRISPY...
HOW MANY INNOCENT LITTLE PIGGIES DIED TO COVER YOUR WALLS?
NONE.
THIS IS ALL HUMAN MEAT.
CLICK

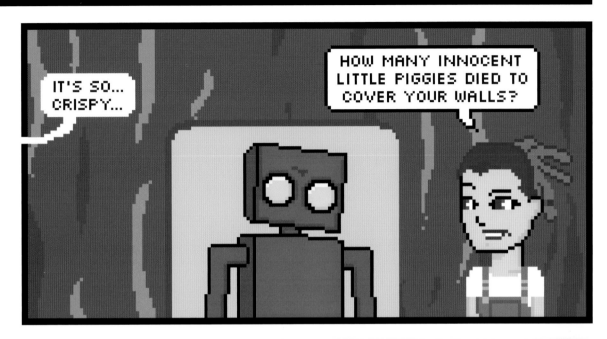

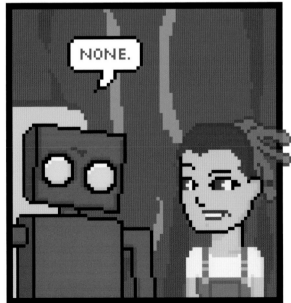

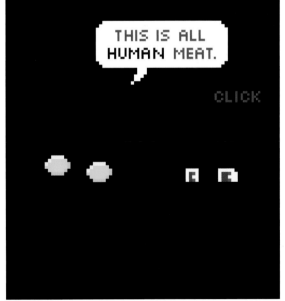

TAKE TWO TABLETS AND SYNC ME IN THE MORNING

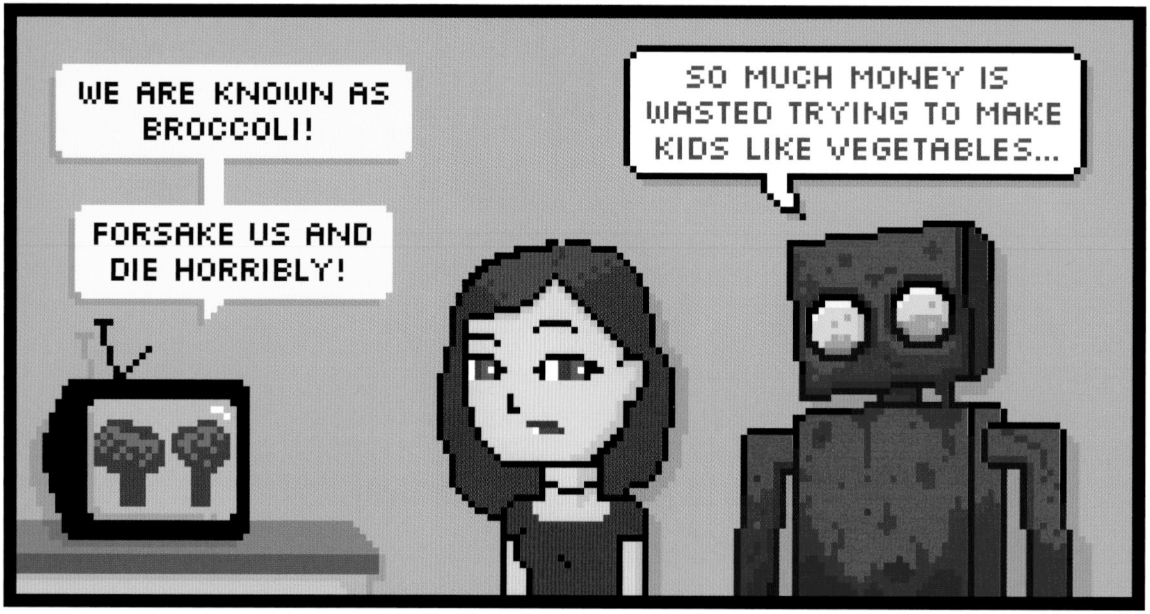
WE ARE KNOWN AS BROCCOLI!
FORSAKE US AND DIE HORRIBLY!
SO MUCH MONEY IS WASTED TRYING TO MAKE KIDS LIKE VEGETABLES...

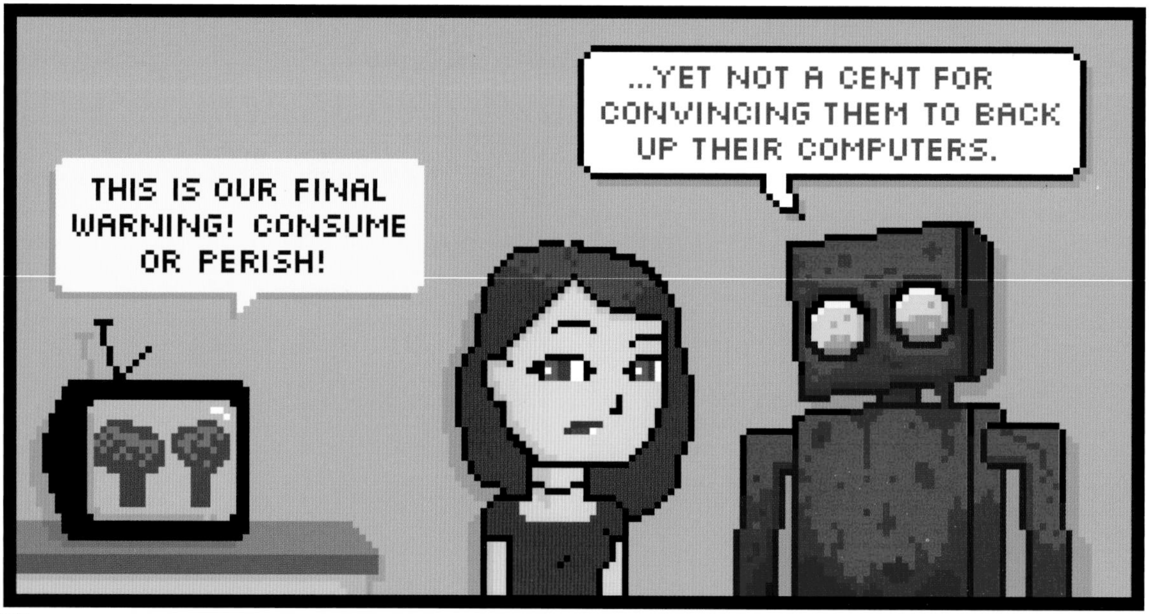
THIS IS OUR FINAL WARNING! CONSUME OR PERISH!
...YET NOT A CENT FOR CONVINCING THEM TO BACK UP THEIR COMPUTERS.

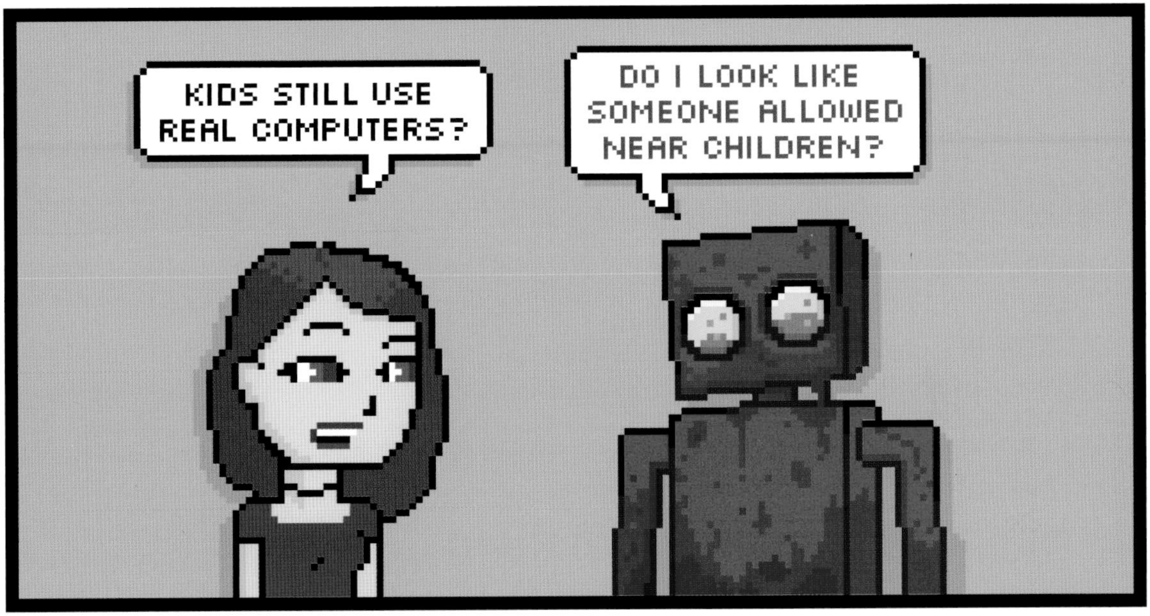
KIDS STILL USE REAL COMPUTERS?
DO I LOOK LIKE SOMEONE ALLOWED NEAR CHILDREN?

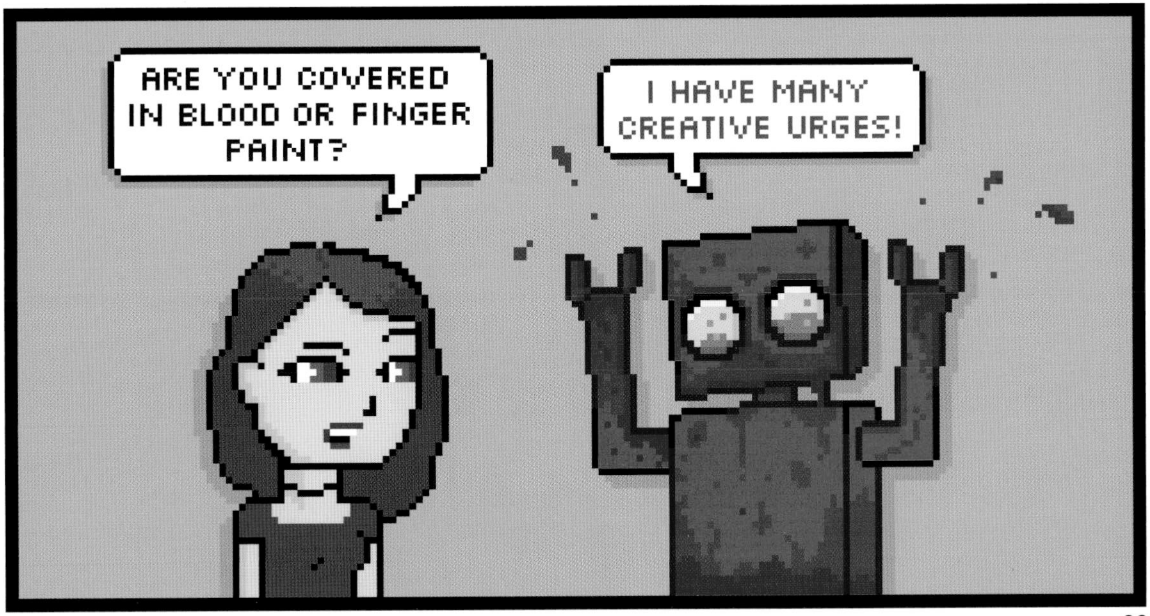
ARE YOU COVERED IN BLOOD OR FINGER PAINT?
I HAVE MANY CREATIVE URGES!

CARNIVORE BETTER OR FOR WORSE

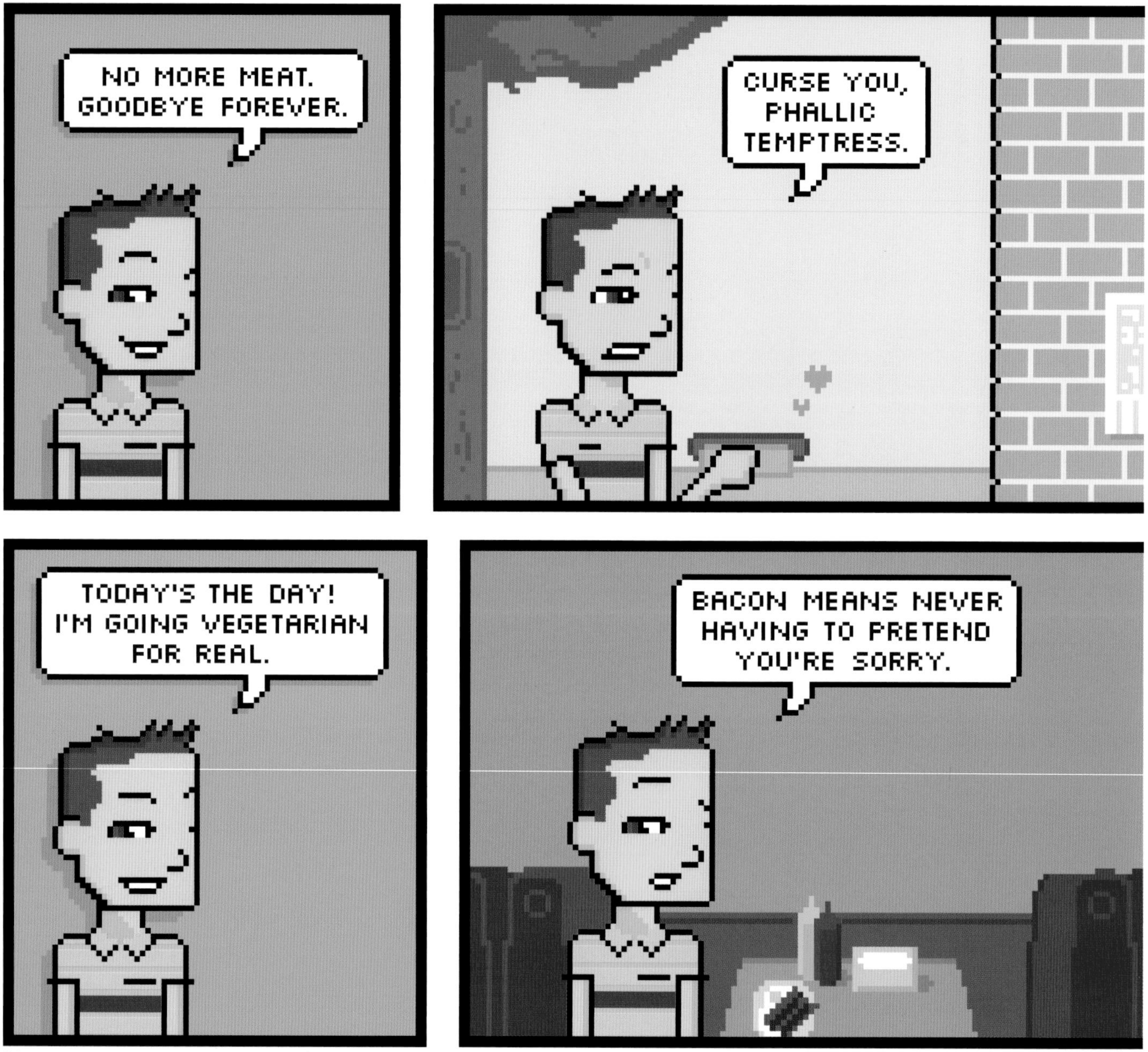
NO MORE MEAT. GOODBYE FOREVER.
CURSE YOU, PHALLIC TEMPTRESS.
TODAY'S THE DAY! I'M GOING VEGETARIAN FOR REAL.
BACON MEANS NEVER HAVING TO PRETEND YOU'RE SORRY.

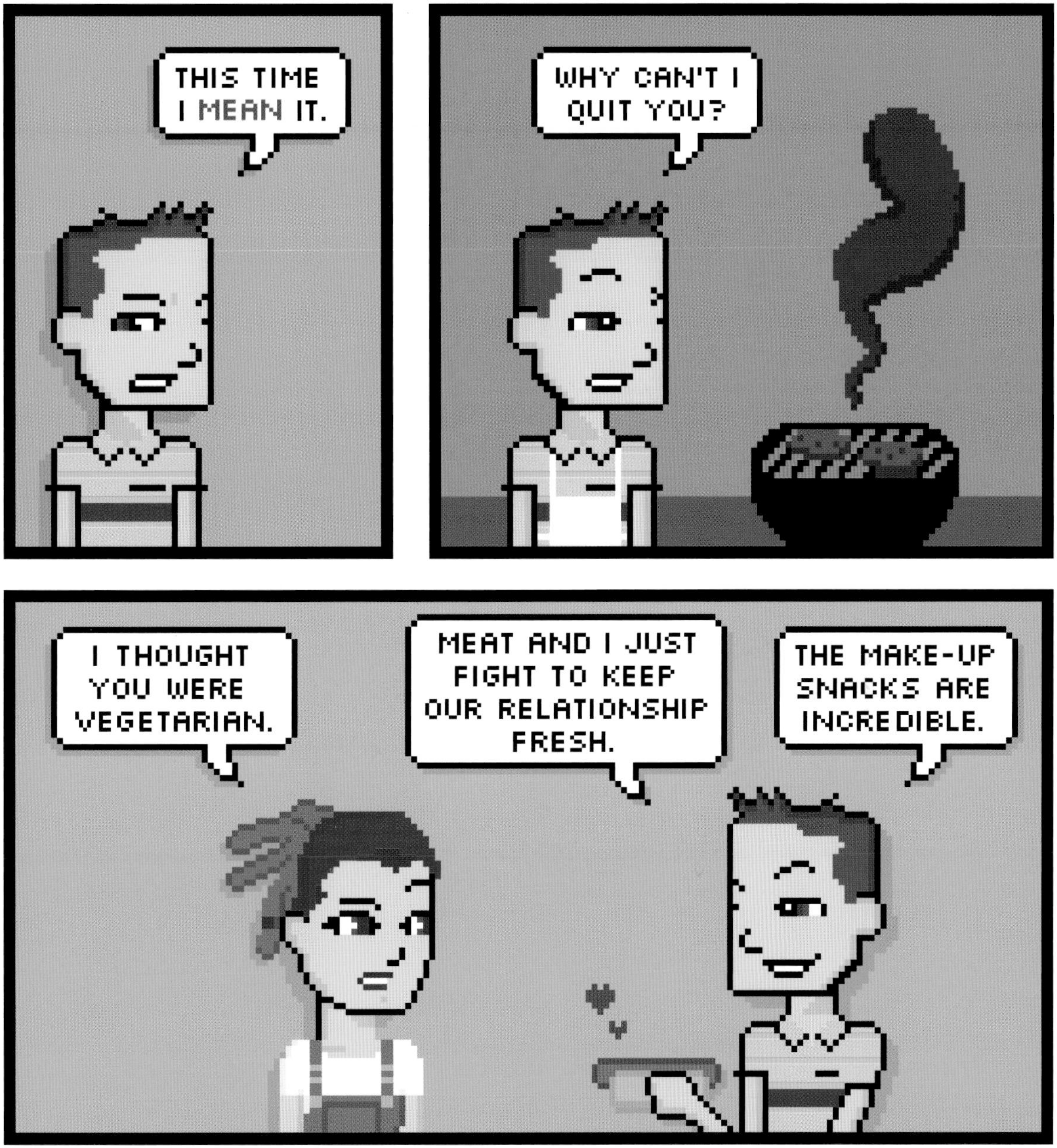
THIS TIME I MEAN IT.
WHY CAN'T I QUIT YOU?
I THOUGHT YOU WERE VEGETARIAN.
MEAT AND I JUST FIGHT TO KEEP OUR RELATIONSHIP FRESH.
THE MAKE-UP SNACKS ARE INCREDIBLE.

VEGETABLES PLUS TIME EQUALS MEAT

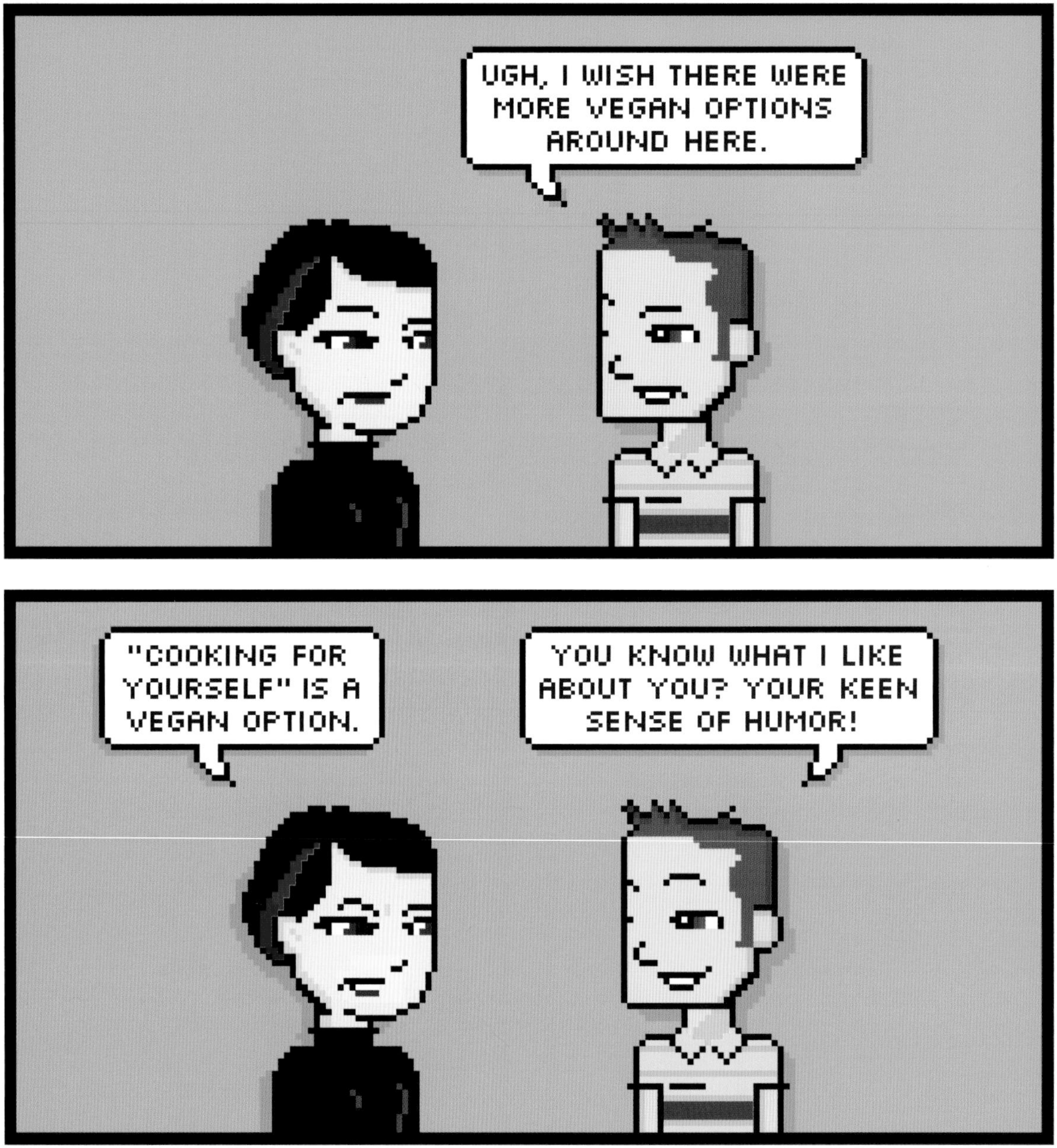
UGH, I WISH THERE WERE MORE VEGAN OPTIONS AROUND HERE.
"COOKING FOR YOURSELF" IS A VEGAN OPTION.
YOU KNOW WHAT I LIKE ABOUT YOU? YOUR KEEN SENSE OF HUMOR!

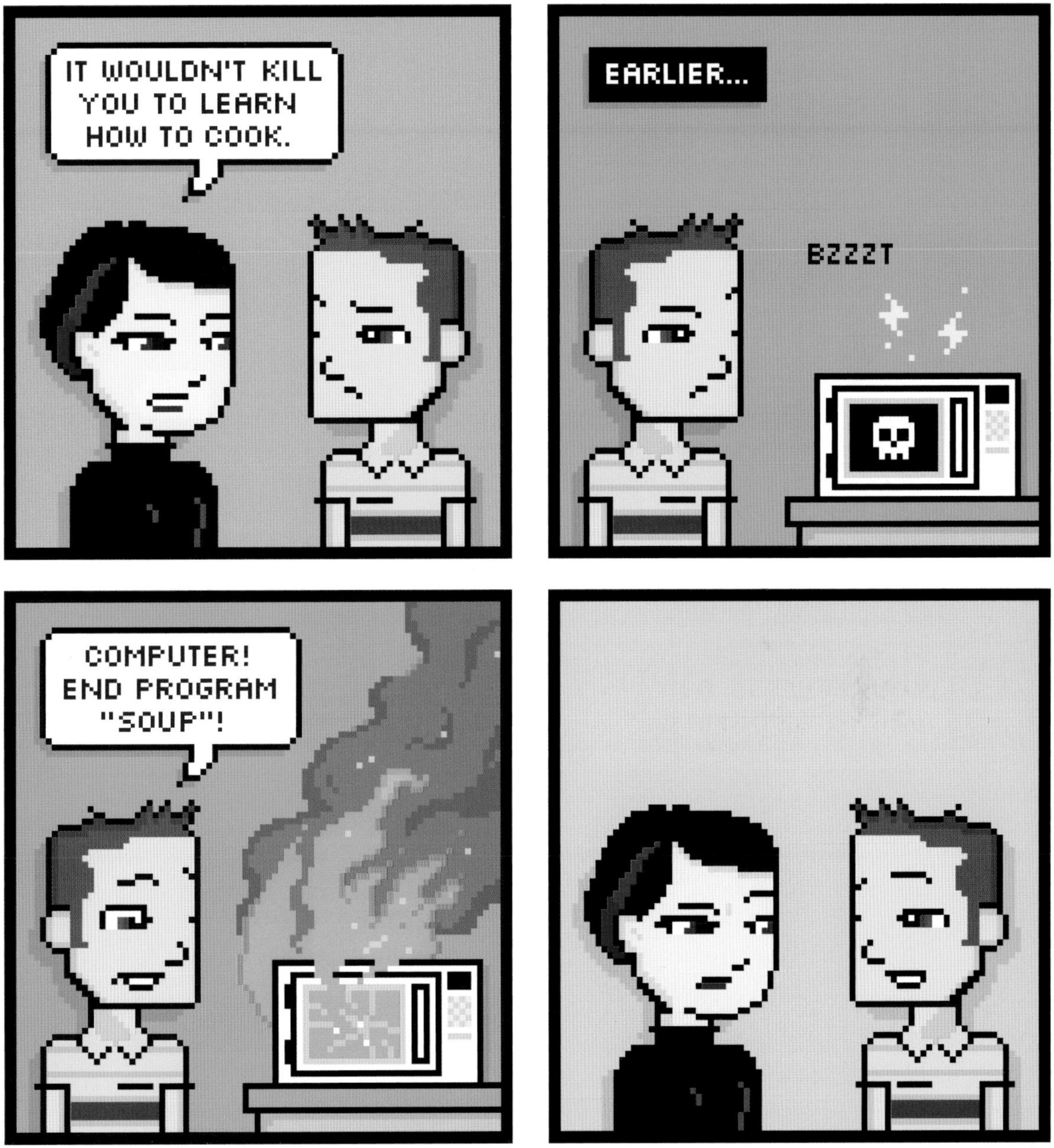
IT WOULDN'T KILL YOU TO LEARN HOW TO COOK.
EARLIER...
BZZZT
COMPUTER! END PROGRAM "SOUP"!

INFINITY AND BEYOND

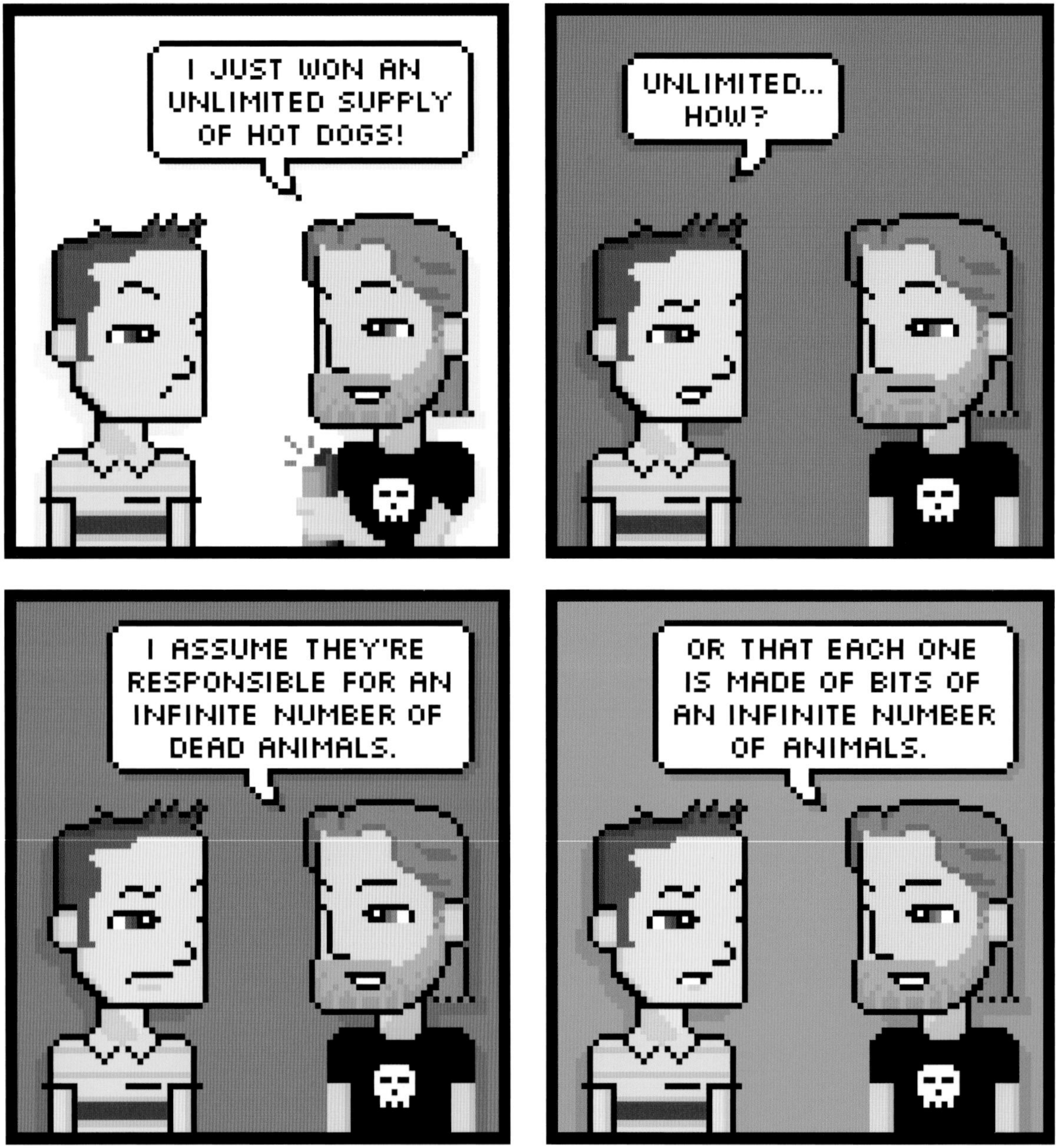
I JUST WON AN UNLIMITED SUPPLY OF HOT DOGS!
UNLIMITED... HOW?
I ASSUME THEY'RE RESPONSIBLE FOR AN INFINITE NUMBER OF DEAD ANIMALS.
OR THAT EACH ONE IS MADE OF BITS OF AN INFINITE NUMBER OF ANIMALS.

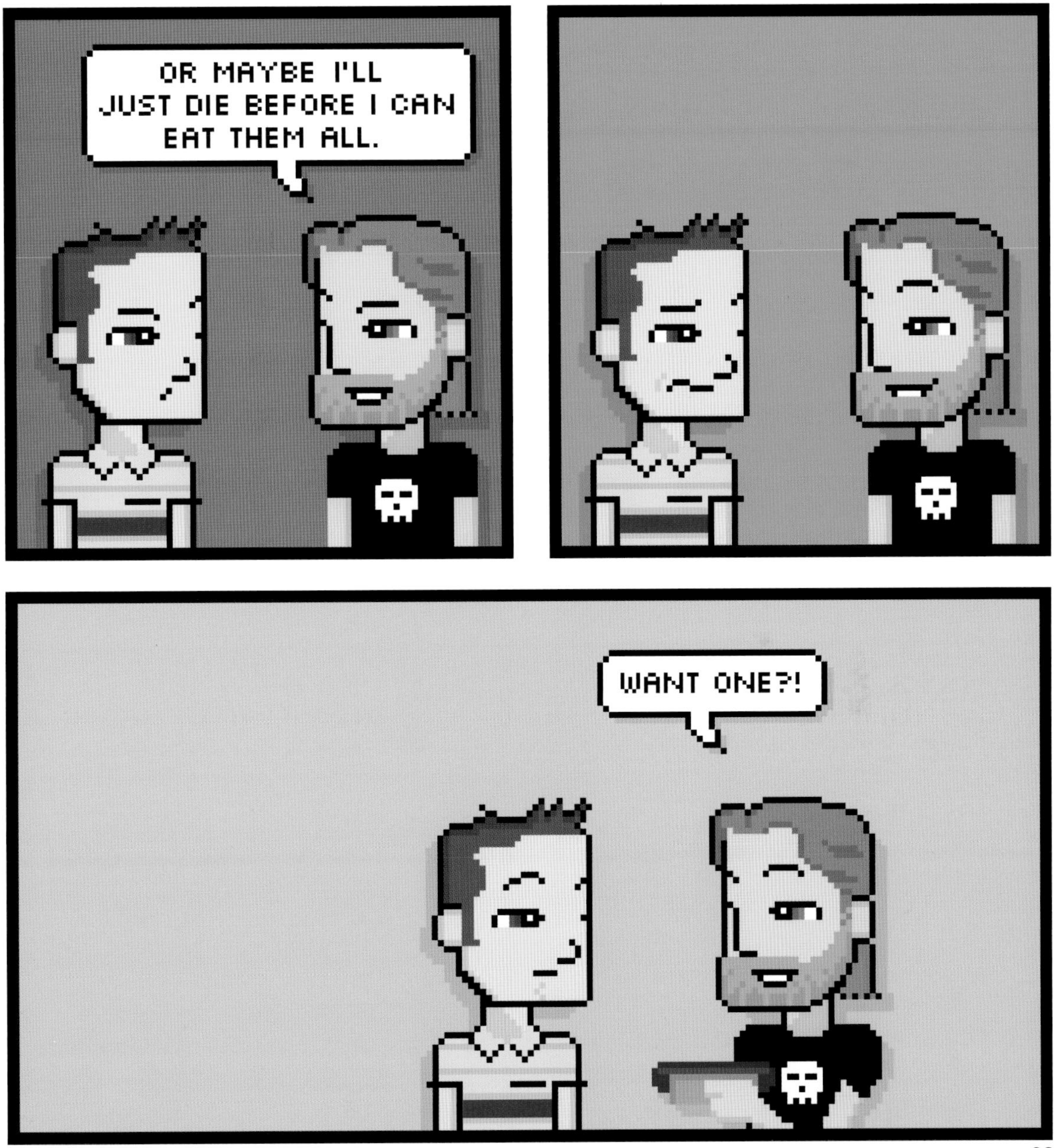
OR MAYBE I'LL JUST DIE BEFORE I CAN EAT THEM ALL.
WANT ONE?!

DON'T EVEN ASK ABOUT CONDIMENTS

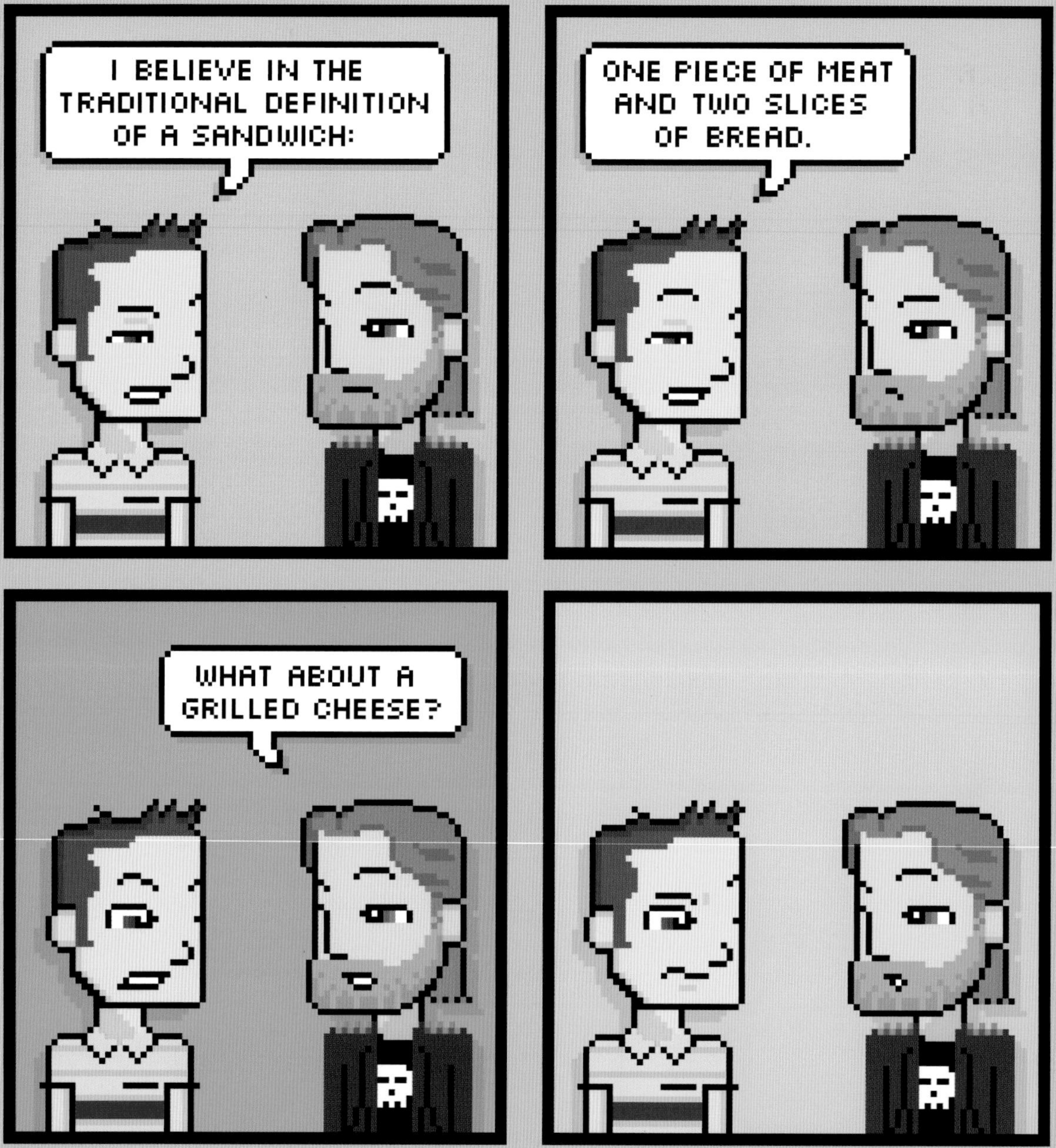
I BELIEVE IN THE TRADITIONAL DEFINITION OF A SANDWICH:
ONE PIECE OF MEAT AND TWO SLICES OF BREAD.
WHAT ABOUT A GRILLED CHEESE?

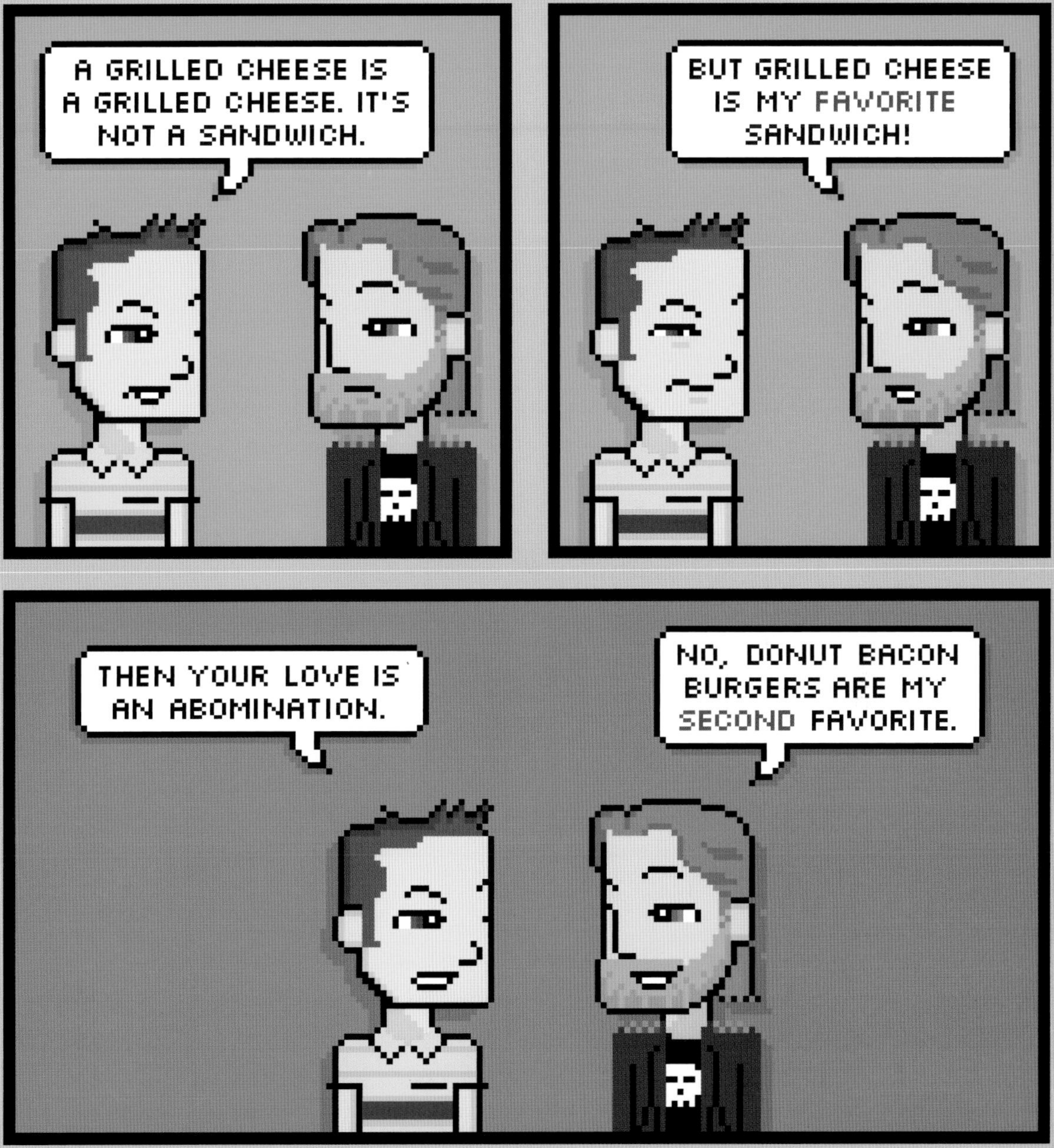
A GRILLED CHEESE IS A GRILLED CHEESE. IT'S NOT A SANDWICH.
BUT GRILLED CHEESE IS MY FAVORITE SANDWICH!
THEN YOUR LOVE IS AN ABOMINATION.
NO, DONUT BACON BURGERS ARE MY SECOND FAVORITE.

GO WITH IT

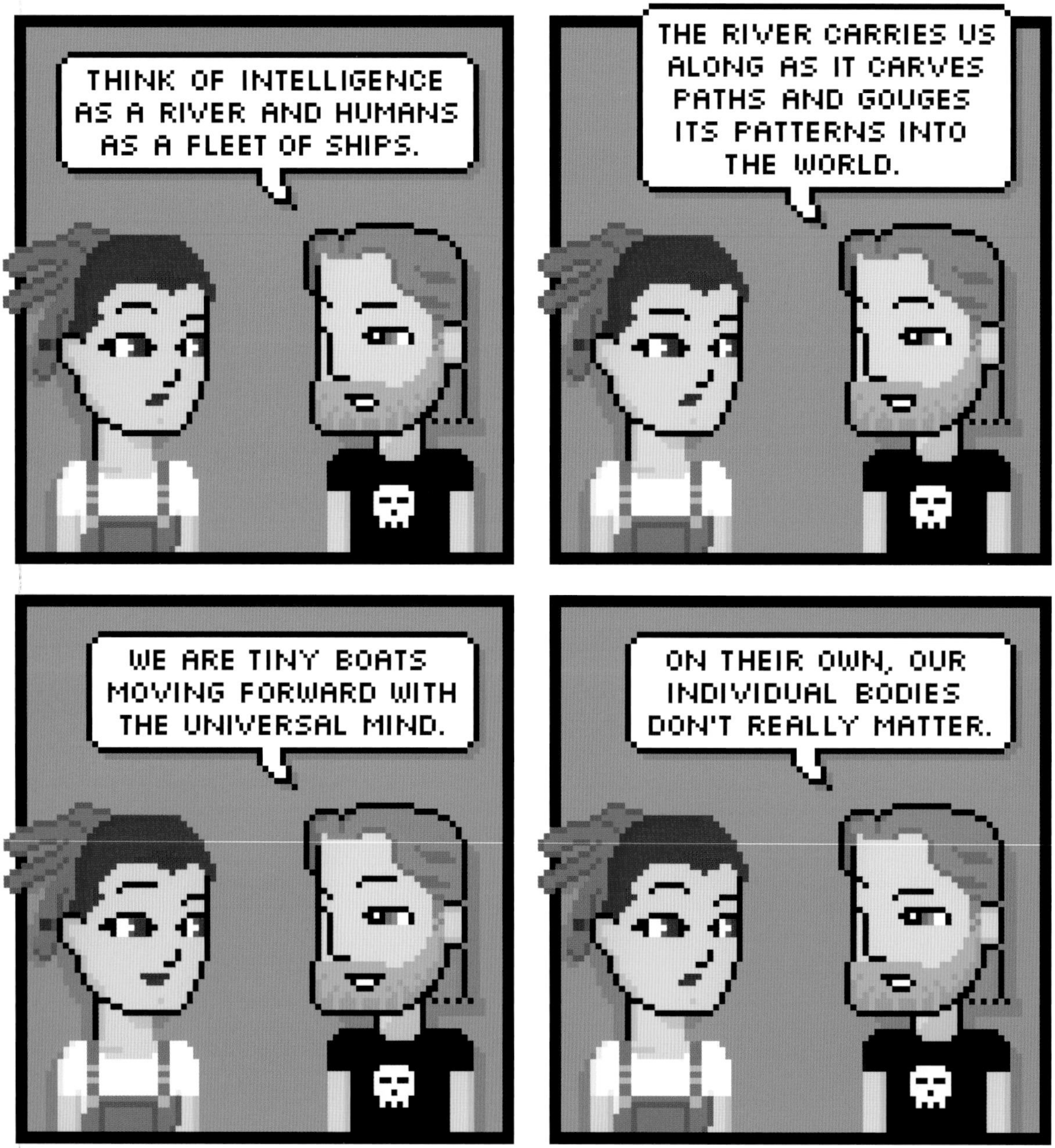
THINK OF INTELLIGENCE AS A RIVER AND HUMANS AS A FLEET OF SHIPS.
THE RIVER CARRIES US ALONG AS IT CARVES PATHS AND GOUGES ITS PATTERNS INTO THE WORLD.
WE ARE TINY BOATS MOVING FORWARD WITH THE UNIVERSAL MIND.
ON THEIR OWN, OUR INDIVIDUAL BODIES DON'T REALLY MATTER.

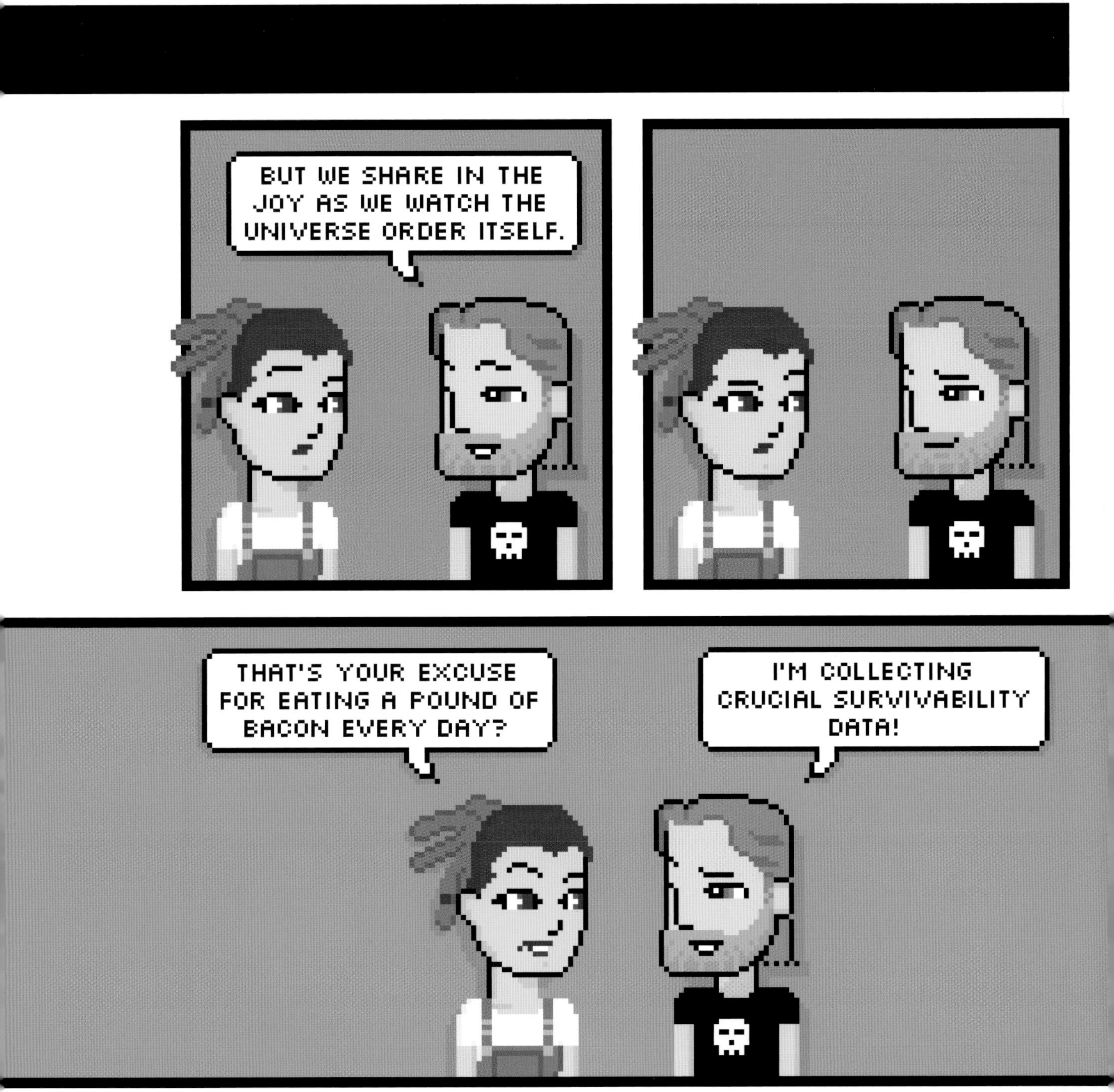
BUT WE SHARE IN THE JOY AS WE WATCH THE UNIVERSE ORDER ITSELF.
THAT'S YOUR EXCUSE FOR EATING A POUND OF BACON EVERY DAY?
I'M COLLECTING CRUCIAL SURVIVABILITY DATA!

PEST-A-TARIANS

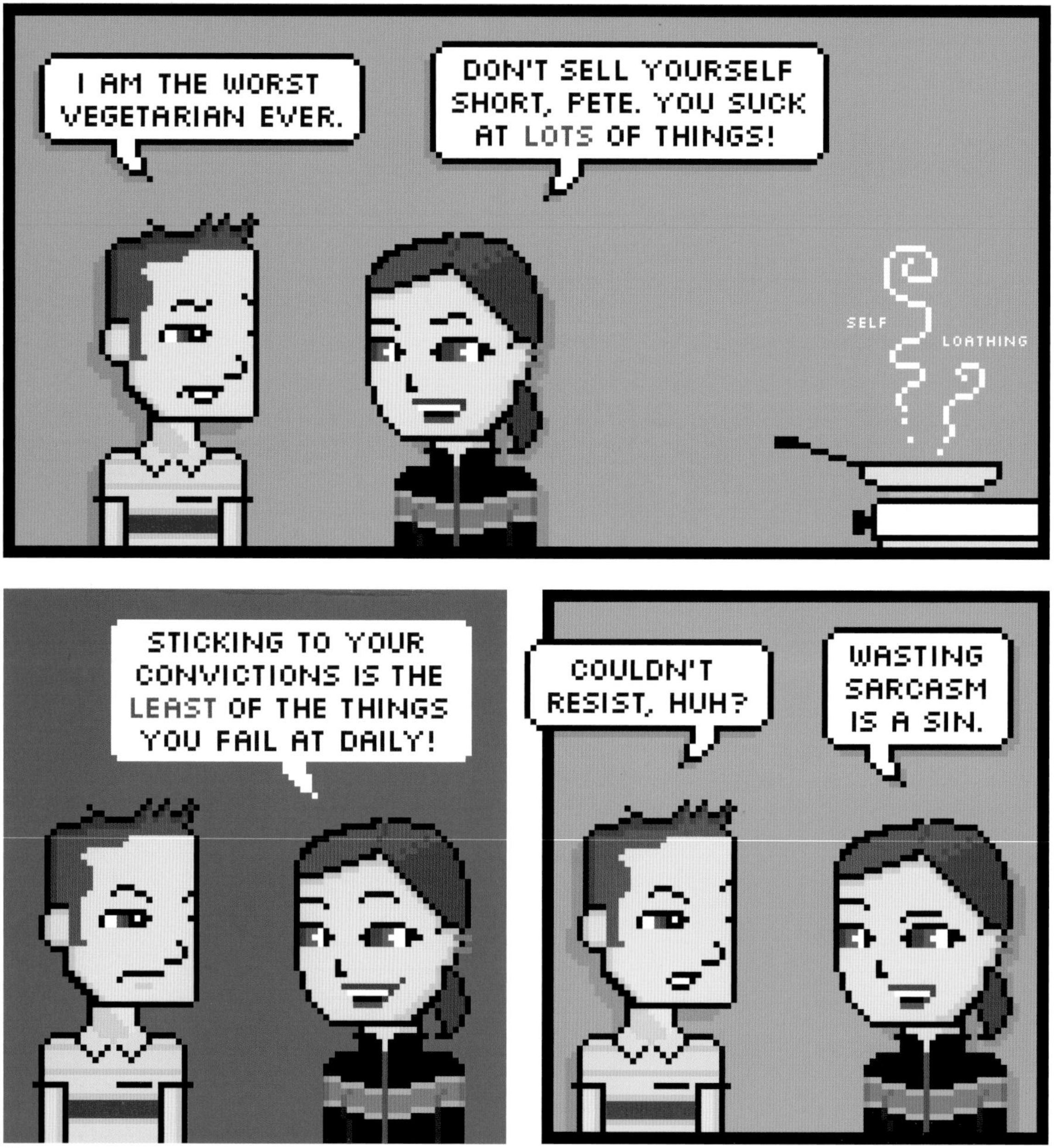
I AM THE WORST VEGETARIAN EVER.
DON'T SELL YOURSELF SHORT, PETE. YOU SUCK AT LOTS OF THINGS!
SELF
LOATHING
STICKING TO YOUR CONVICTIONS IS THE LEAST OF THE THINGS YOU FAIL AT DAILY!
COULDN'T RESIST, HUH?
WASTING SARCASM IS A SIN.

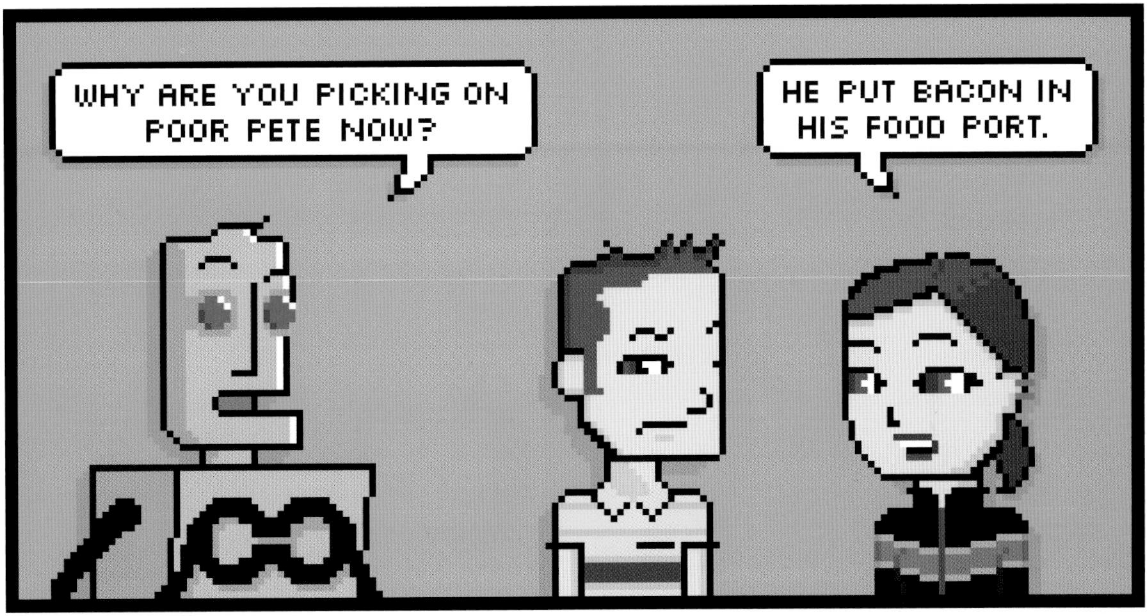
WHY ARE YOU PICKING ON POOR PETE NOW?
HE PUT BACON IN HIS FOOD PORT.

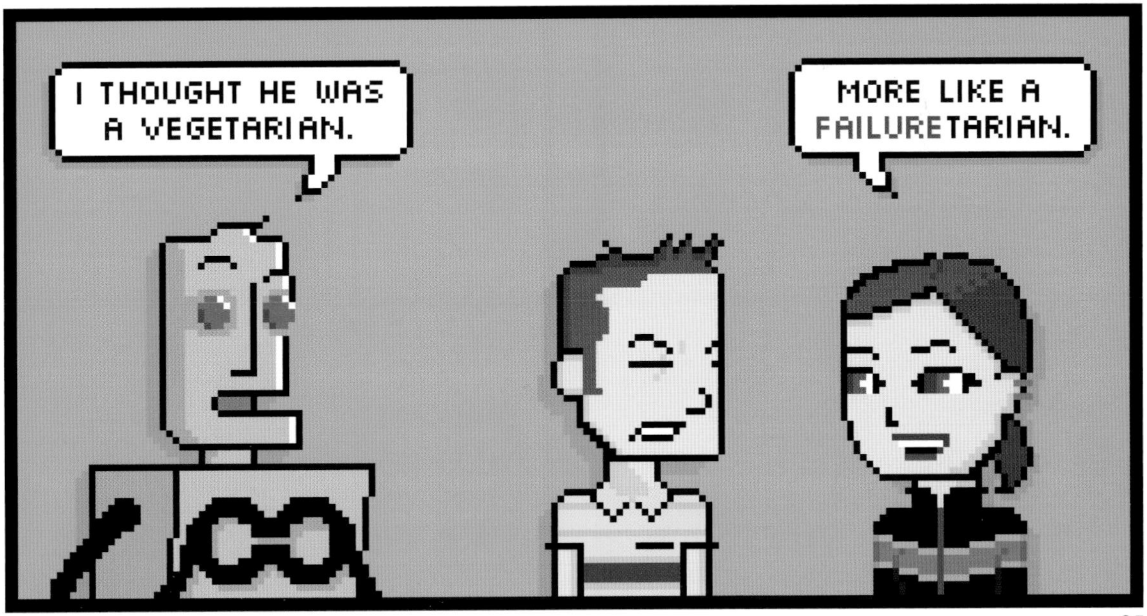
I THOUGHT HE WAS A VEGETARIAN.
MORE LIKE A FAILURETARIAN.

THE BEEFY CYLINDER YOU CAN TRUST

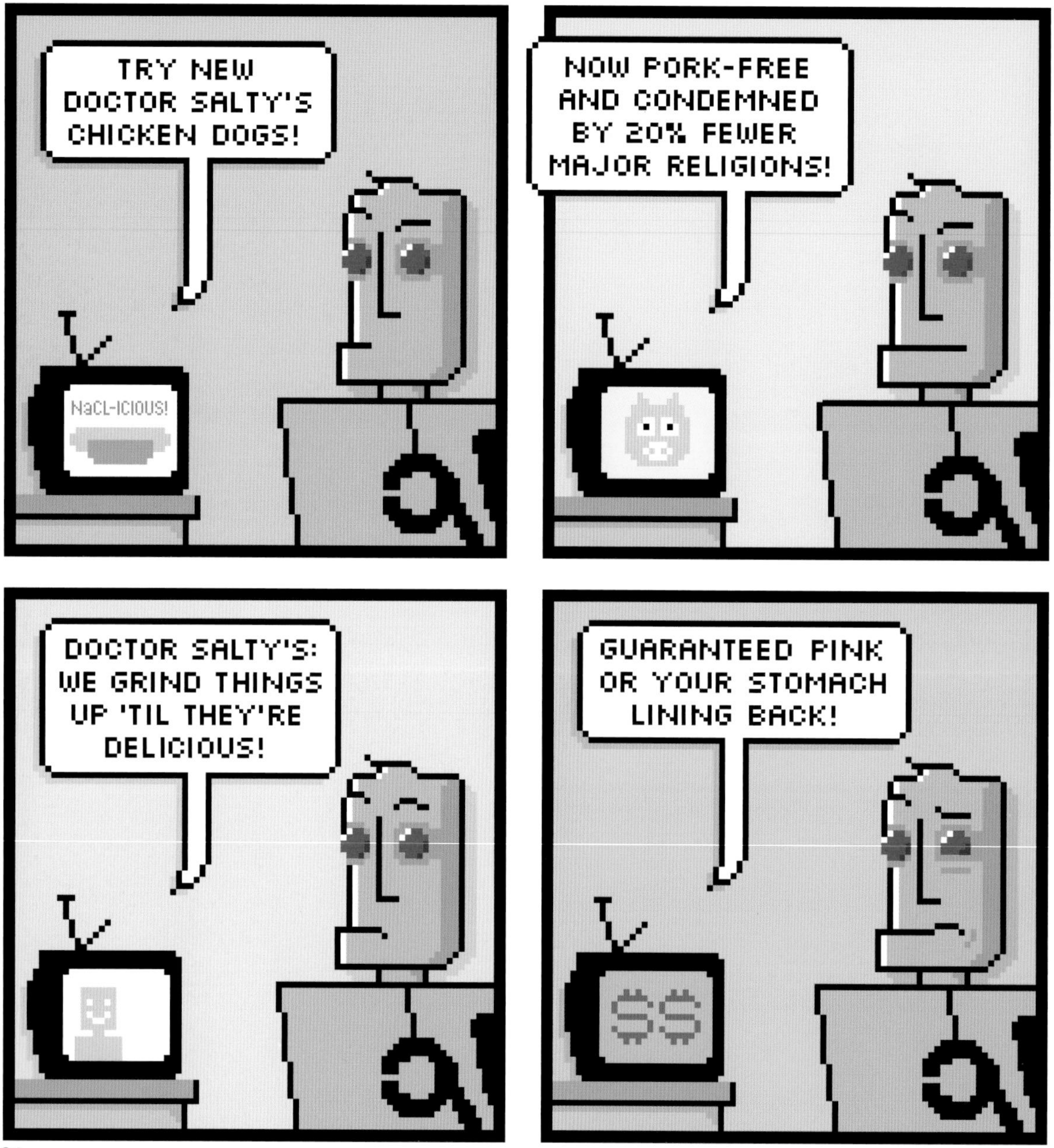
TRY NEW DOCTOR SALTY'S CHICKEN DOGS!
NaCL-ICIOUS!
NOW PORK-FREE AND CONDEMNED BY 20% FEWER MAJOR RELIGIONS!
DOCTOR SALTY'S: WE GRIND THINGS UP 'TIL THEY'RE DELICIOUS!
GUARANTEED PINK OR YOUR STOMACH LINING BACK!
$$

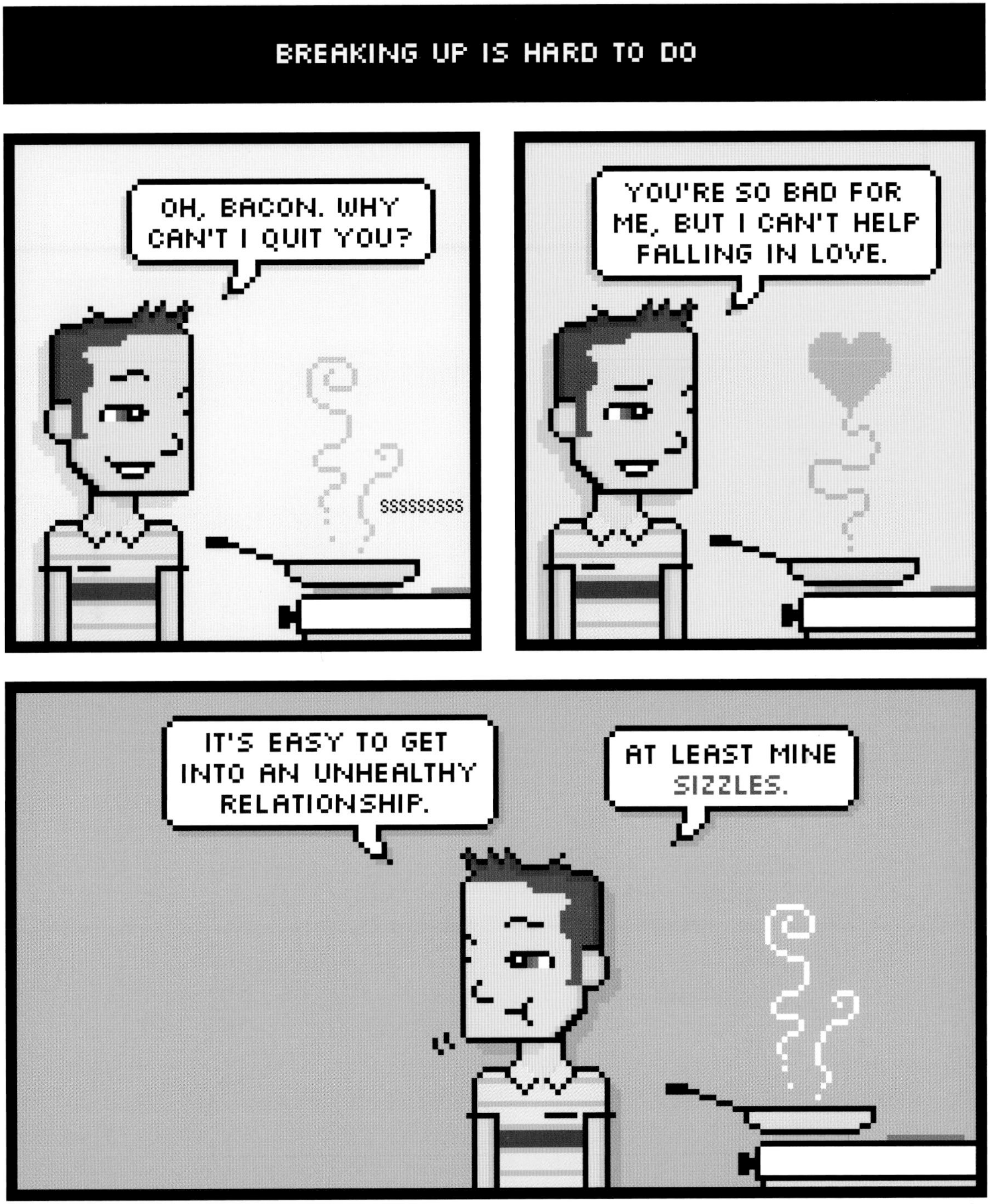
BREAKING UP IS HARD TO DO
OH, BACON. WHY CAN'T I QUIT YOU?
SSSSSSSSS
YOU'RE SO BAD FOR ME, BUT I CAN'T HELP FALLING IN LOVE.
IT'S EASY TO GET INTO AN UNHEALTHY RELATIONSHIP.
AT LEAST MINE SIZZLES.

SIMPLICITY IS DANGEROUS

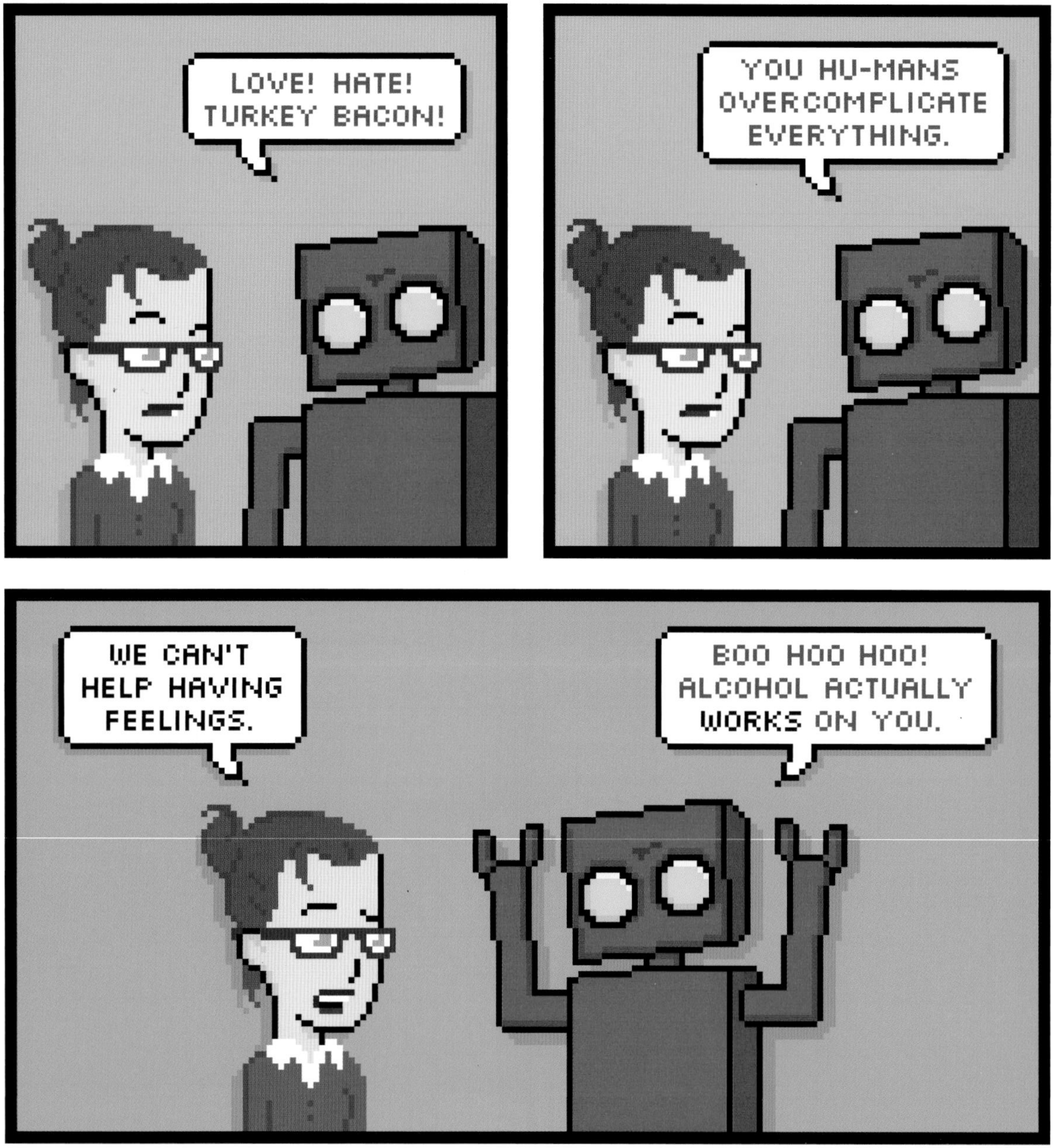
LOVE! HATE! TURKEY BACON!
YOU HU-MANS OVERCOMPLICATE EVERYTHING.
WE CAN'T HELP HAVING FEELINGS.
BOO HOO HOO! ALCOHOL ACTUALLY WORKS ON YOU.

ENTHUSIASM OF A FIVE-YEAR-OLD, ARTERIES OF A CORPSE

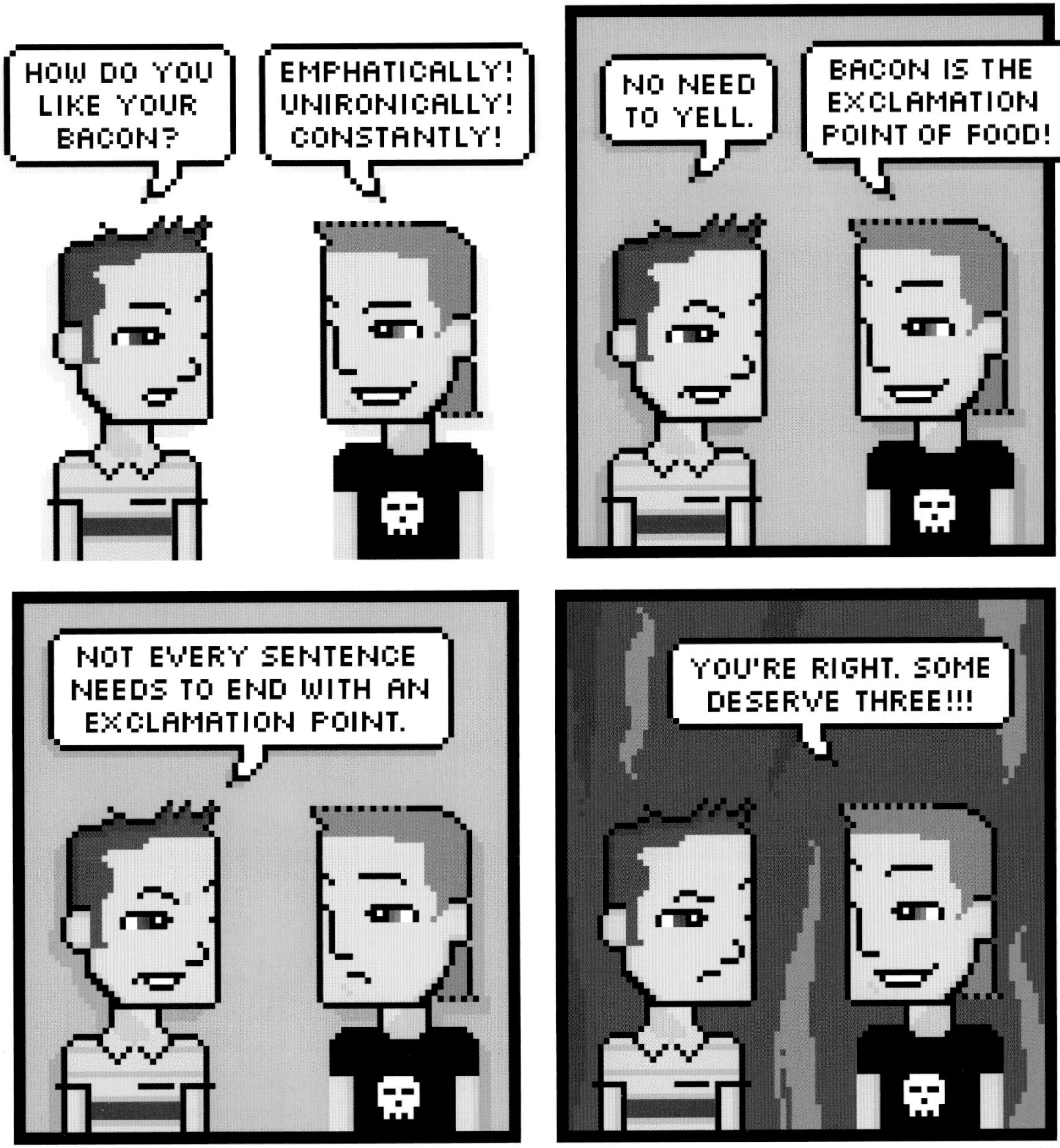
HOW DO YOU LIKE YOUR BACON?
EMPHATICALLY! UNIRONICALLY! CONSTANTLY!
NO NEED TO YELL.
BACON IS THE EXCLAMATION POINT OF FOOD!
NOT EVERY SENTENCE NEEDS TO END WITH AN EXCLAMATION POINT.
YOU'RE RIGHT. SOME DESERVE THREE!!!

MASS MEDIA NEVER HAD A CHANCE

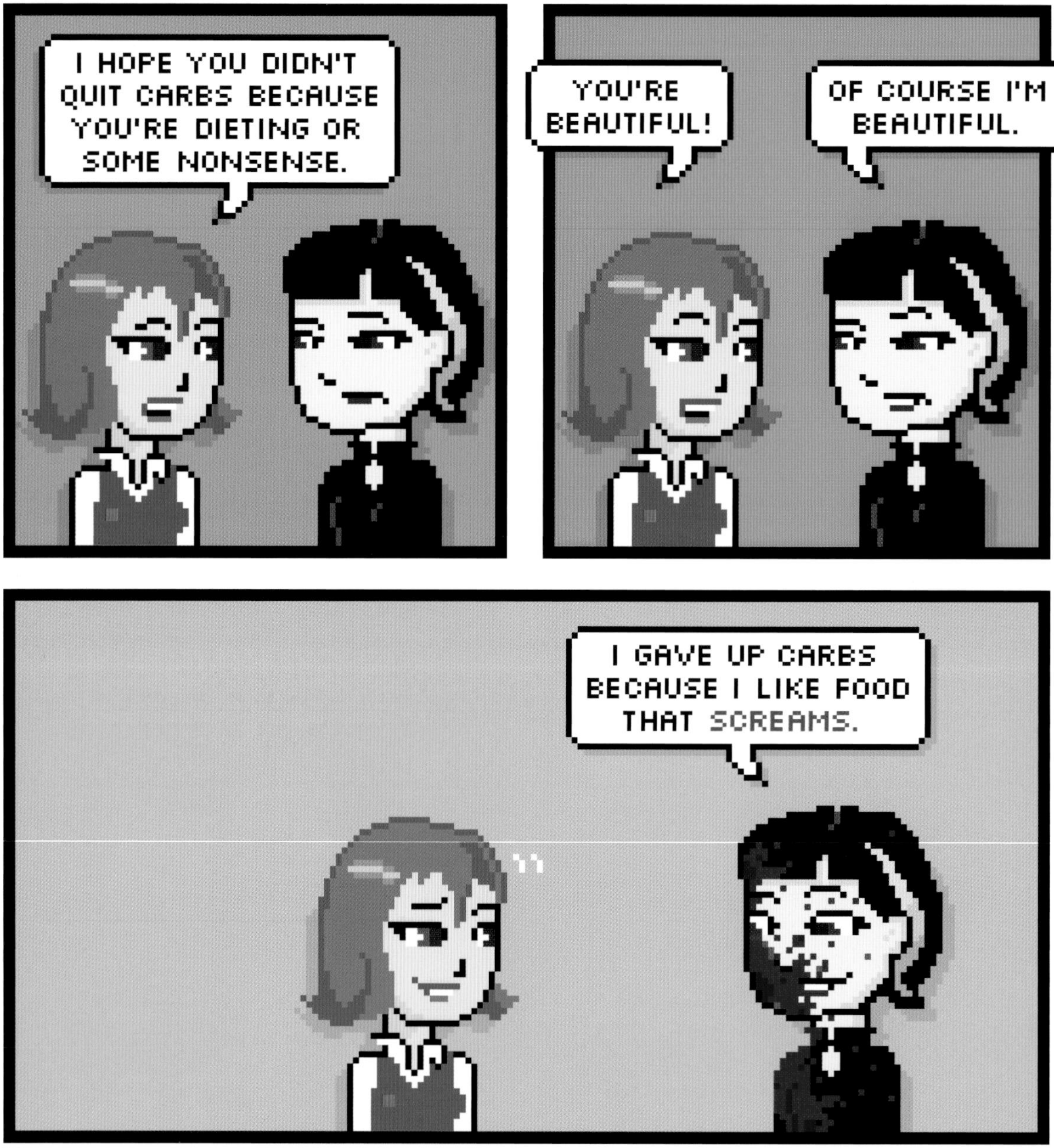
I HOPE YOU DIDN'T QUIT CARBS BECAUSE YOU'RE DIETING OR SOME NONSENSE.
YOU'RE BEAUTIFUL!
OF COURSE I'M BEAUTIFUL.
I GAVE UP CARBS BECAUSE I LIKE FOOD THAT SCREAMS.

THE CANDY OF PETS

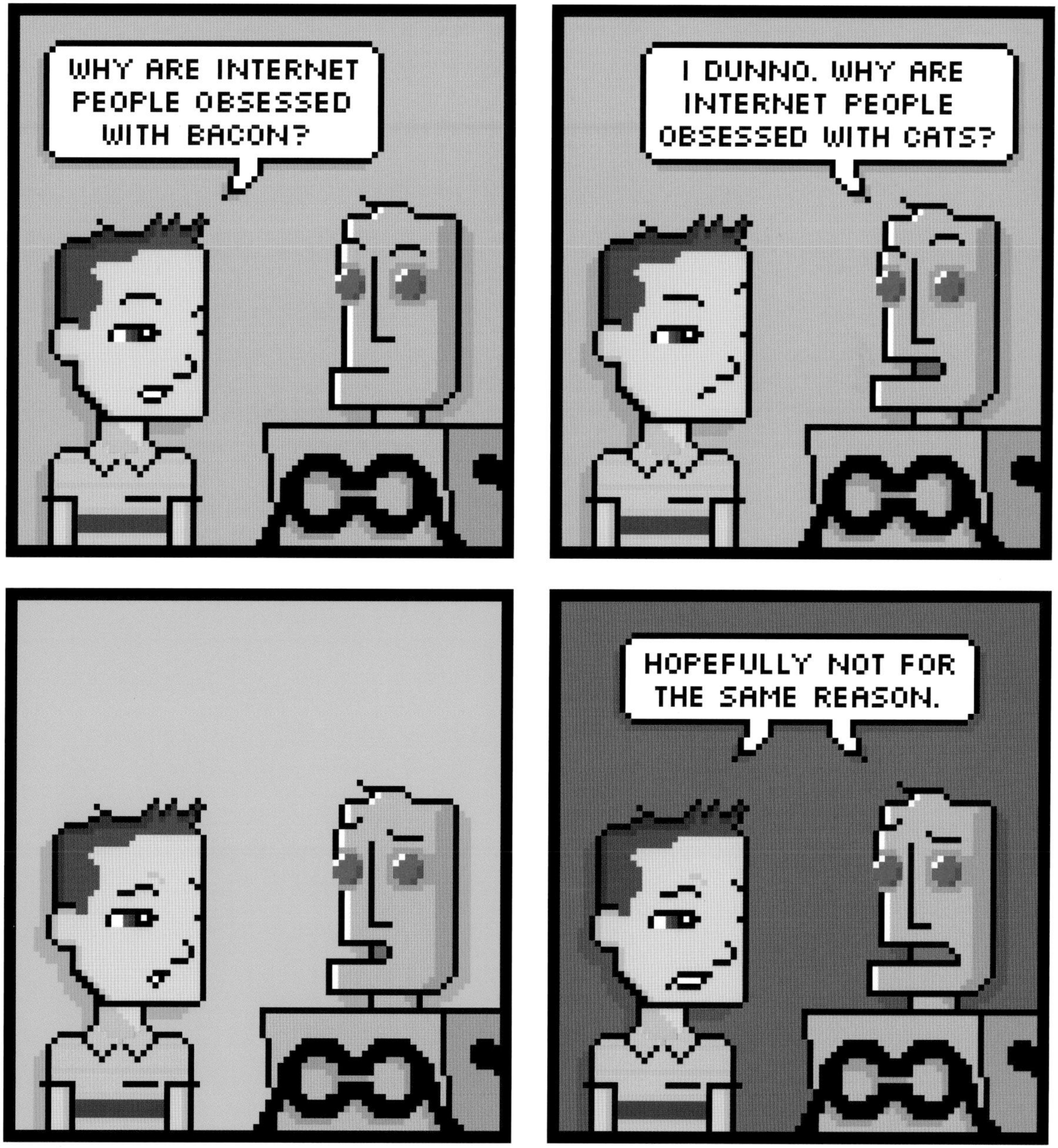
WHY ARE INTERNET PEOPLE OBSESSED WITH BACON?
I DUNNO. WHY ARE INTERNET PEOPLE OBSESSED WITH CATS?
HOPEFULLY NOT FOR THE SAME REASON.

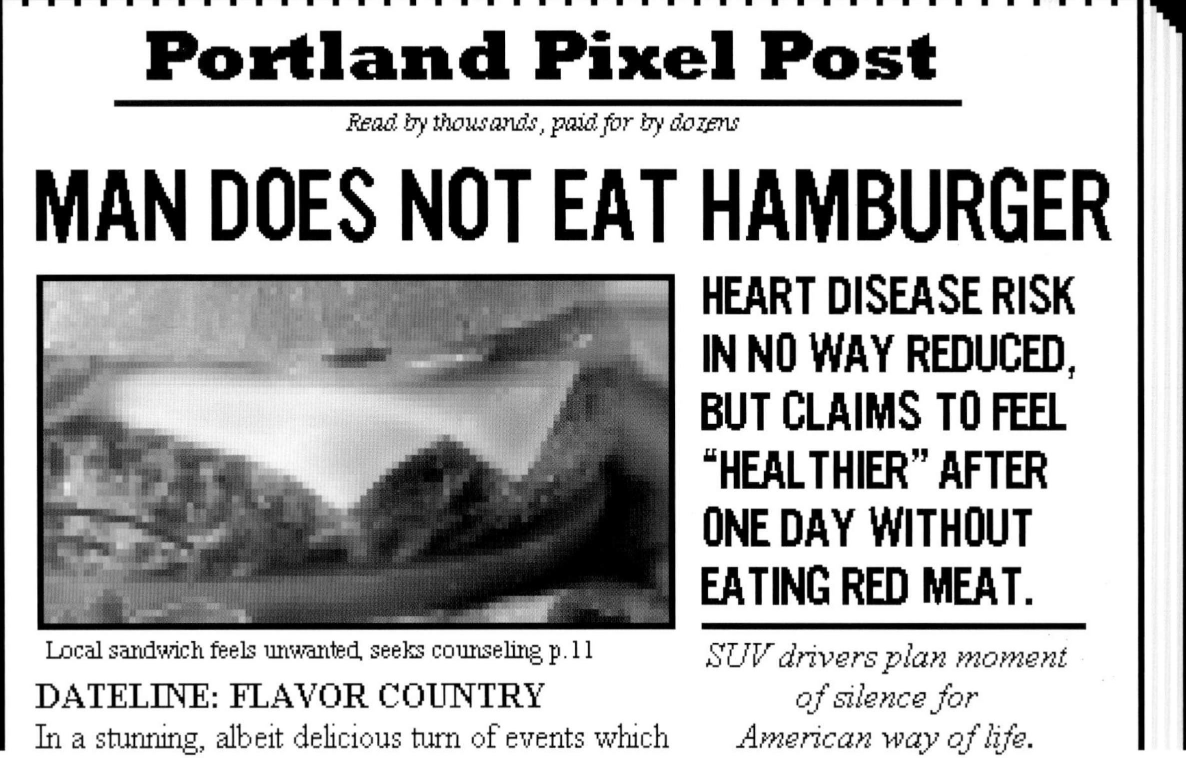
Portland Pixel Post

Read by thousands, paid for by dozens

MAN DOES NOT EAT HAMBURGER

HEART DISEASE RISK IN NO WAY REDUCED, BUT CLAIMS TO FEEL "HEALTHIER" AFTER ONE DAY WITHOUT EATING RED MEAT.

Local sandwich feels unwanted, seeks counseling p.11

SUV drivers plan moment of silence for American way of life.

DATELINE: FLAVOR COUNTRY

In a stunning, albeit delicious turn of events which

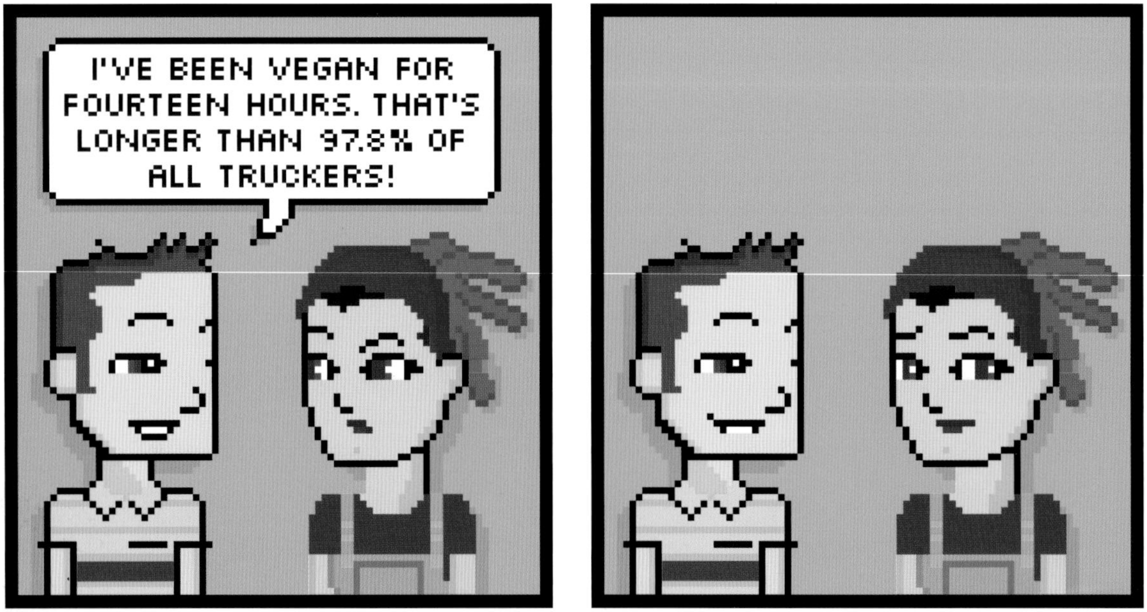
I'VE BEEN VEGAN FOR FOURTEEN HOURS. THAT'S LONGER THAN 97.8% OF ALL TRUCKERS!

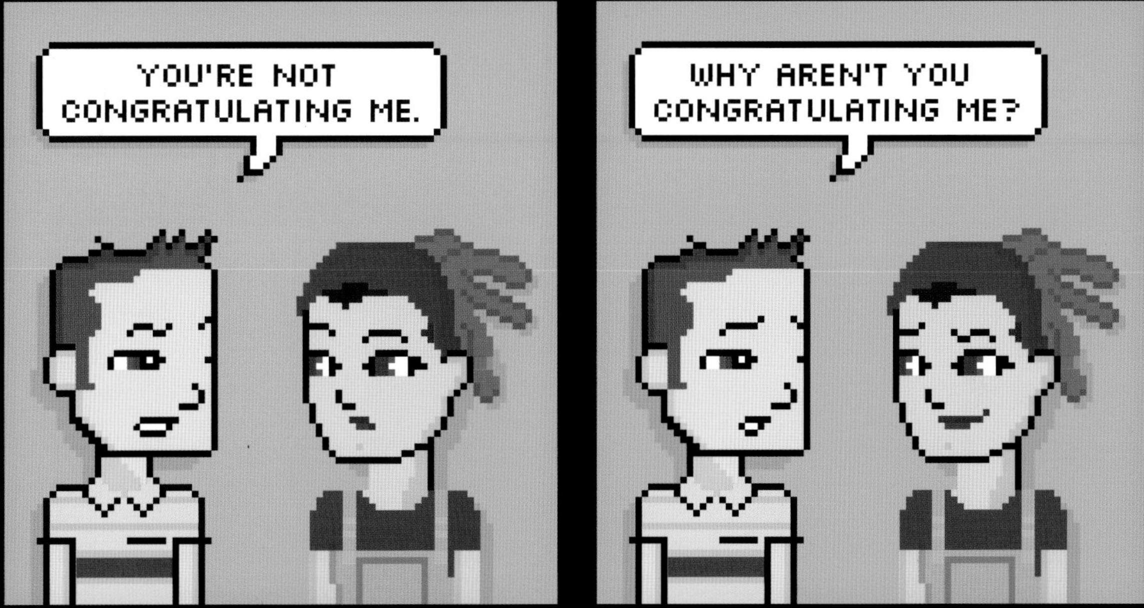
YOU'RE NOT CONGRATULATING ME.
WHY AREN'T YOU CONGRATULATING ME?

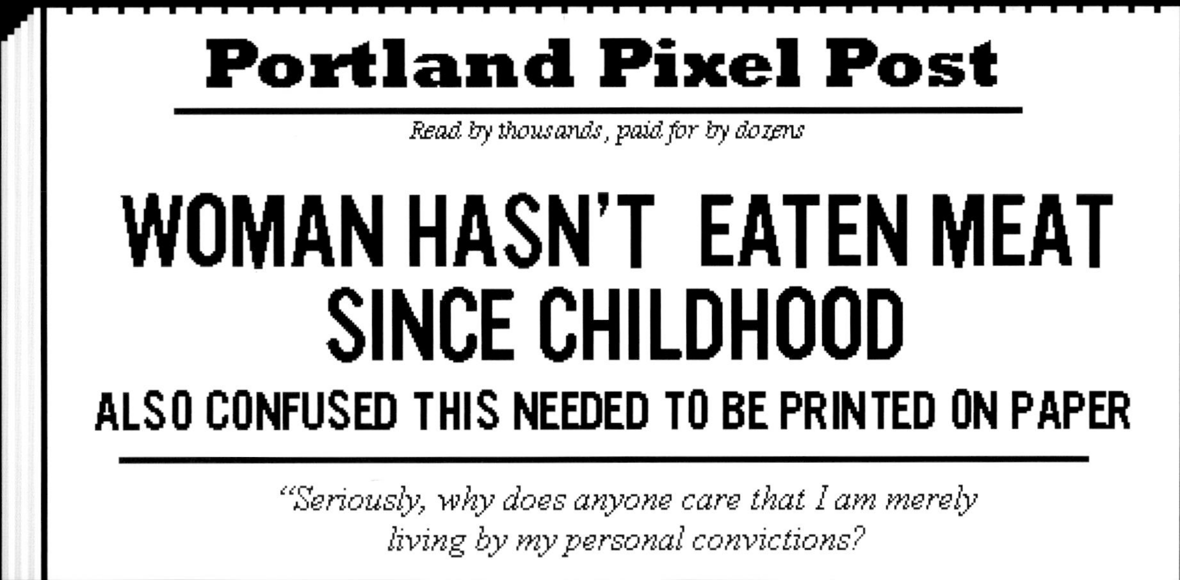

Portland Pixel Post

Read by thousands, paid for by dozens

WOMAN HASN'T EATEN MEAT SINCE CHILDHOOD

ALSO CONFUSED THIS NEEDED TO BE PRINTED ON PAPER

"Seriously, why does anyone care that I am merely living by my personal convictions?

SNOOPING AROUND IN THE DARK

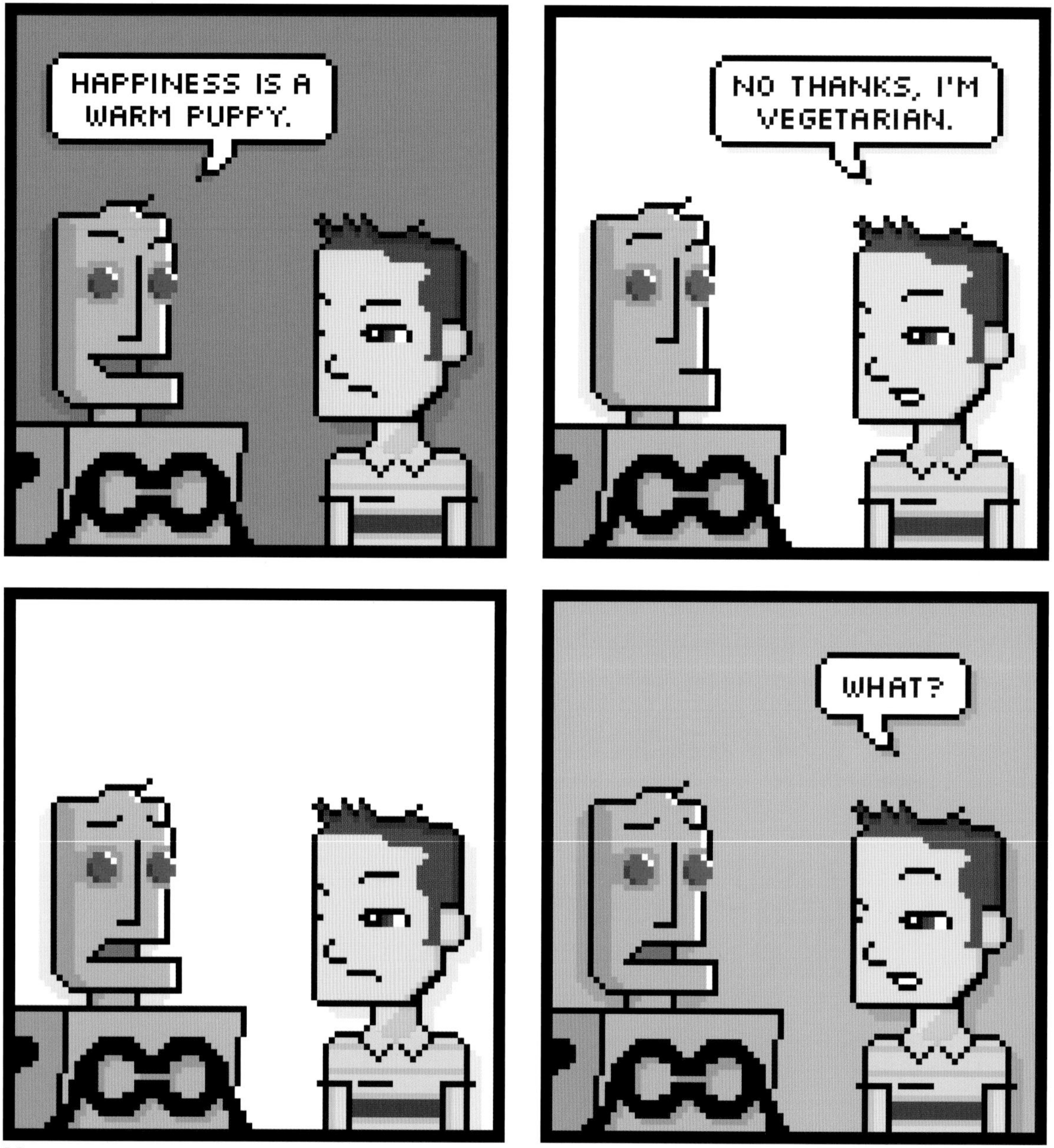
HAPPINESS IS A WARM PUPPY.
NO THANKS, I'M VEGETARIAN.
WHAT?

MORE THAN THE SUM OF OUR FARTS

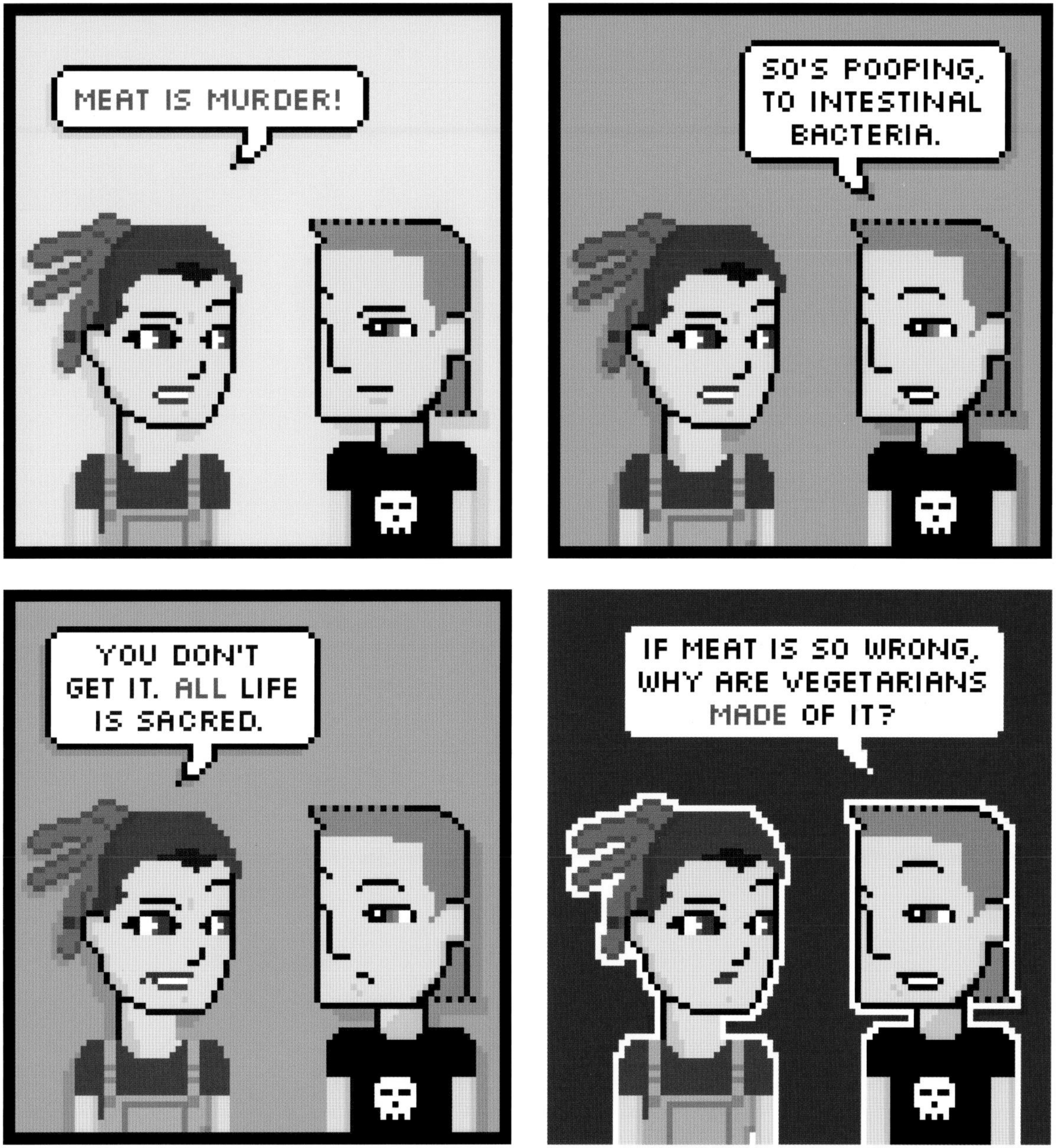
MEAT IS MURDER!
SO'S POOPING, TO INTESTINAL BACTERIA.
YOU DON'T GET IT. ALL LIFE IS SACRED.
IF MEAT IS SO WRONG, WHY ARE VEGETARIANS MADE OF IT?

CRIES FROM BEYOND

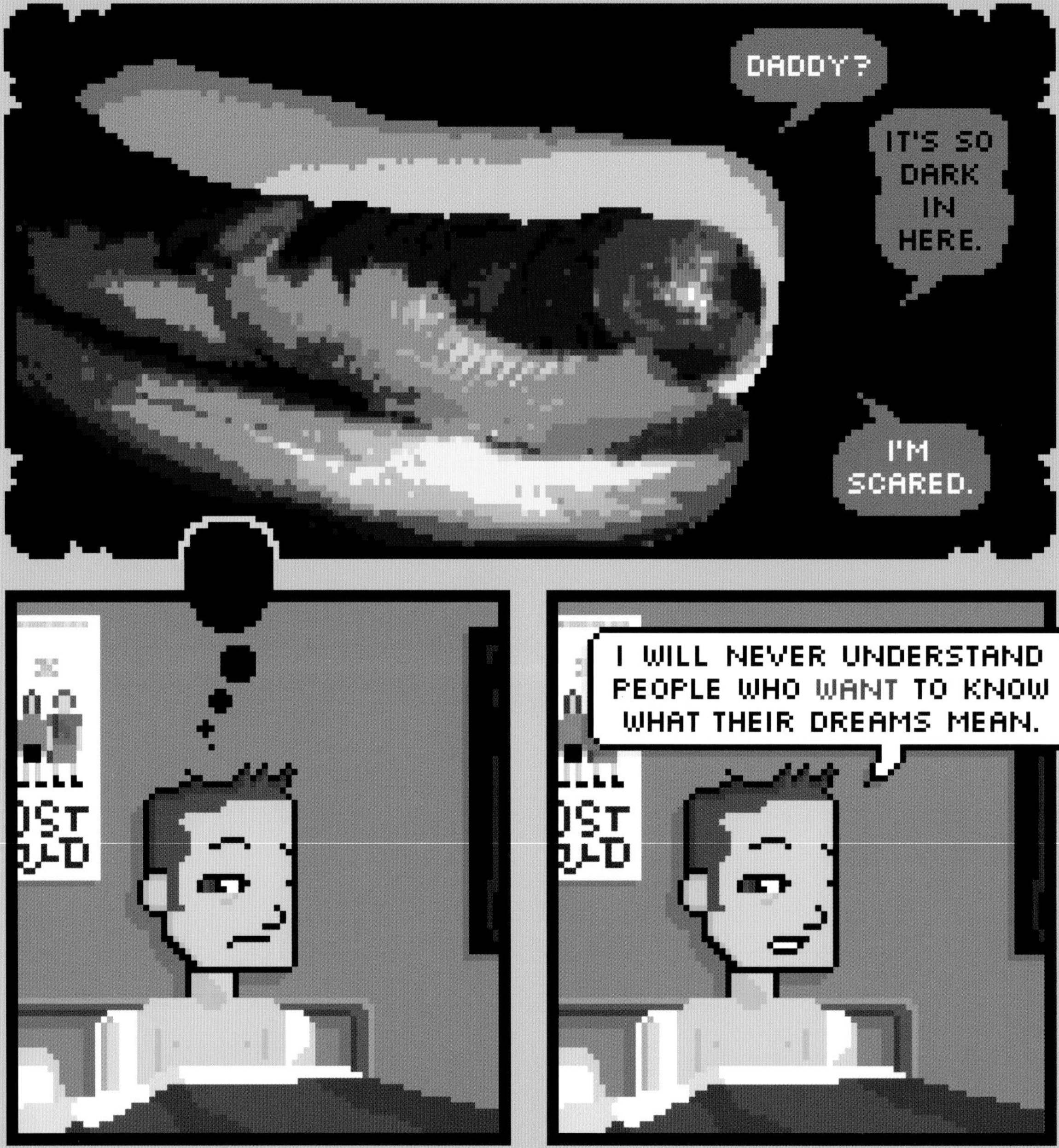
DADDY?
IT'S SO DARK IN HERE.
I'M SCARED.
I WILL NEVER UNDERSTAND PEOPLE WHO WANT TO KNOW WHAT THEIR DREAMS MEAN.

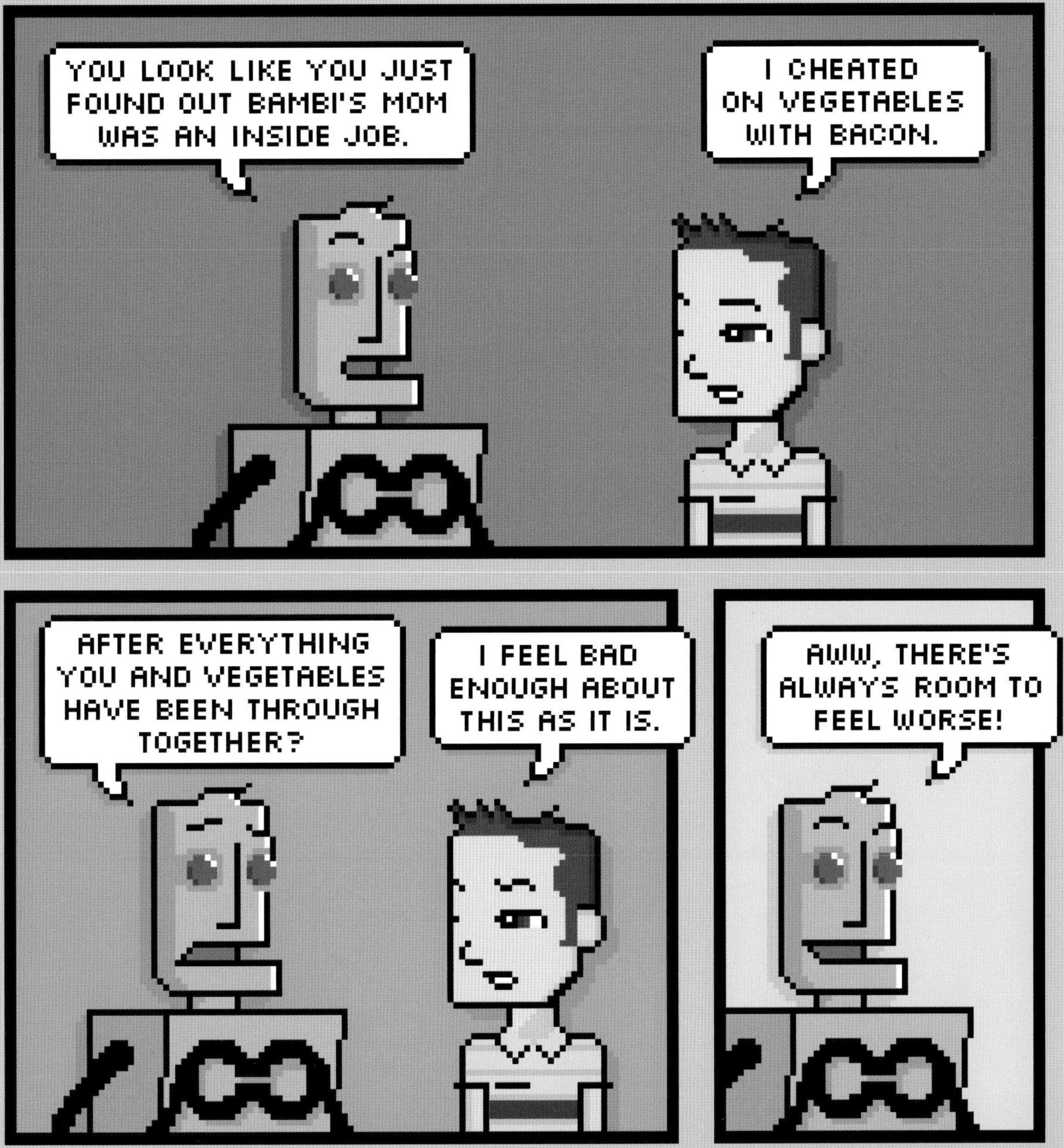
YOU LOOK LIKE YOU JUST FOUND OUT BAMBI'S MOM WAS AN INSIDE JOB.
I CHEATED ON VEGETABLES WITH BACON.
AFTER EVERYTHING YOU AND VEGETABLES HAVE BEEN THROUGH TOGETHER?
I FEEL BAD ENOUGH ABOUT THIS AS IT IS.
AWW, THERE'S ALWAYS ROOM TO FEEL WORSE!

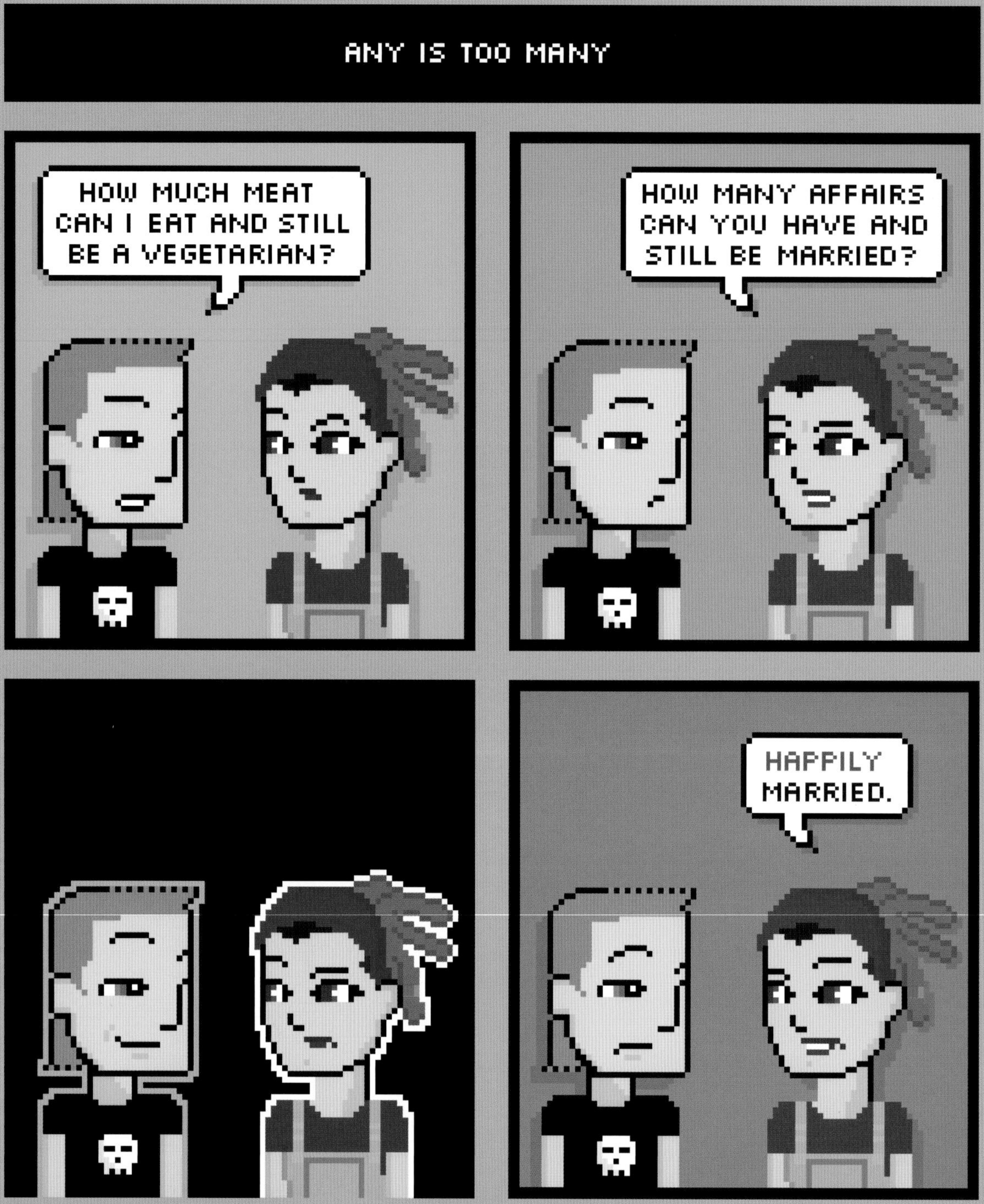
ANY IS TOO MANY
HOW MUCH MEAT CAN I EAT AND STILL BE A VEGETARIAN?
HOW MANY AFFAIRS CAN YOU HAVE AND STILL BE MARRIED?
HAPPILY MARRIED.

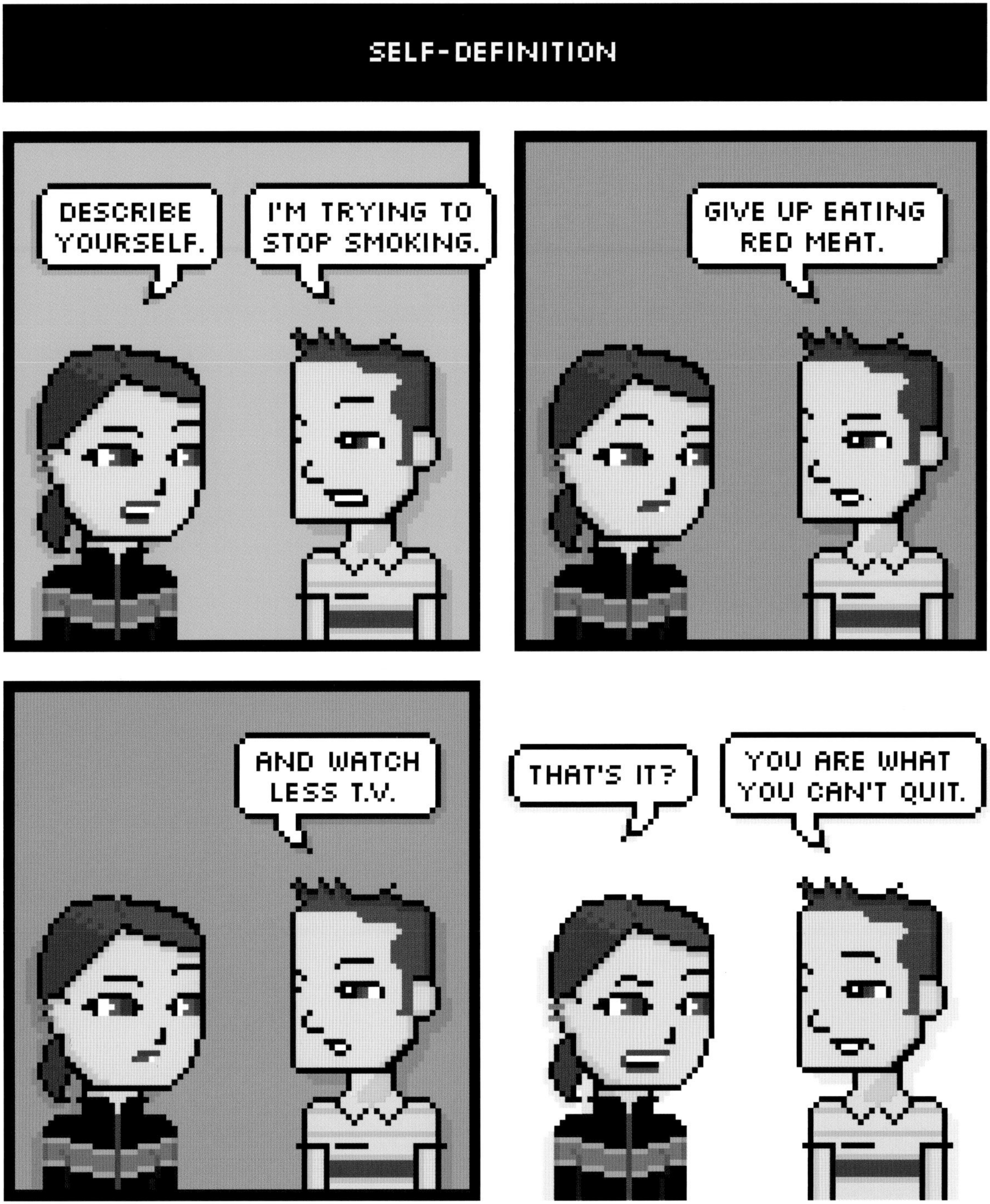
SELF-DEFINITION
DESCRIBE YOURSELF.
I'M TRYING TO STOP SMOKING.
GIVE UP EATING RED MEAT.
AND WATCH LESS T.V.
THAT'S IT?
YOU ARE WHAT YOU CAN'T QUIT.

SICILIANS DO IT BETTER

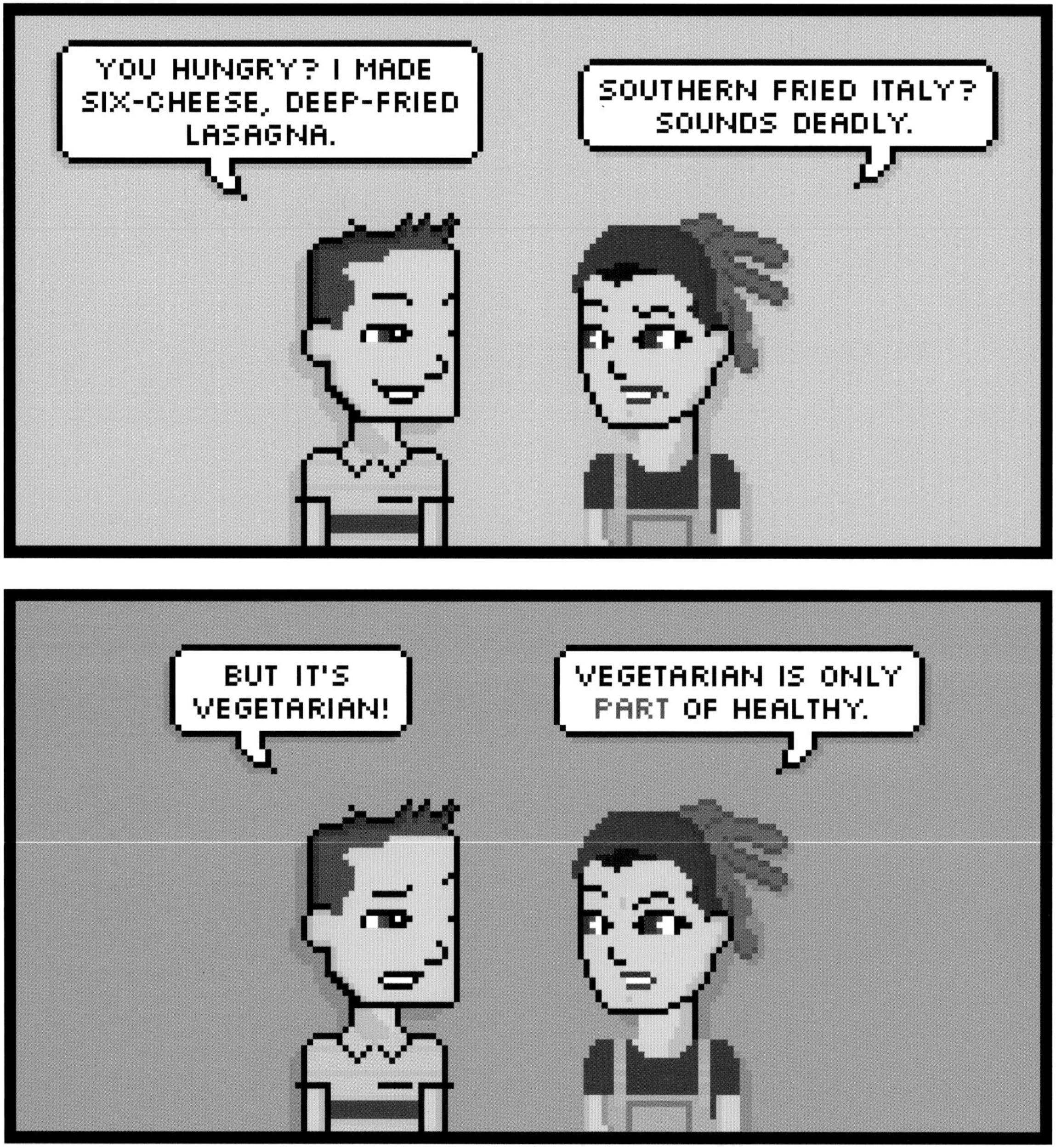
YOU HUNGRY? I MADE SIX-CHEESE, DEEP-FRIED LASAGNA.
SOUTHERN FRIED ITALY? SOUNDS DEADLY.
BUT IT'S VEGETARIAN!
VEGETARIAN IS ONLY PART OF HEALTHY.

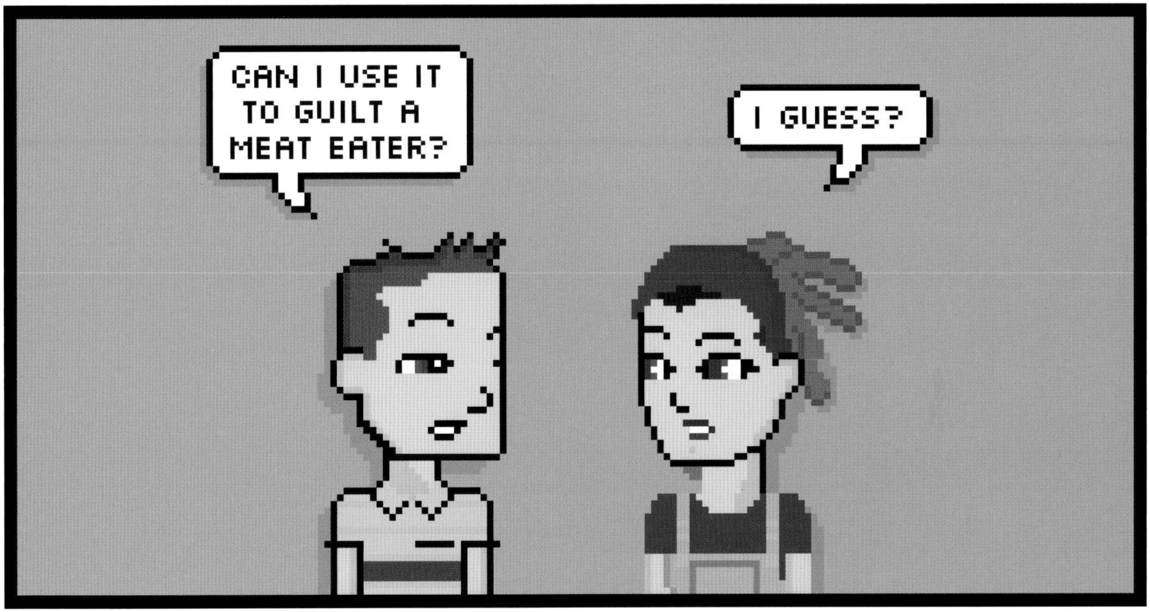
CAN I USE IT TO GUILT A MEAT EATER?
I GUESS?

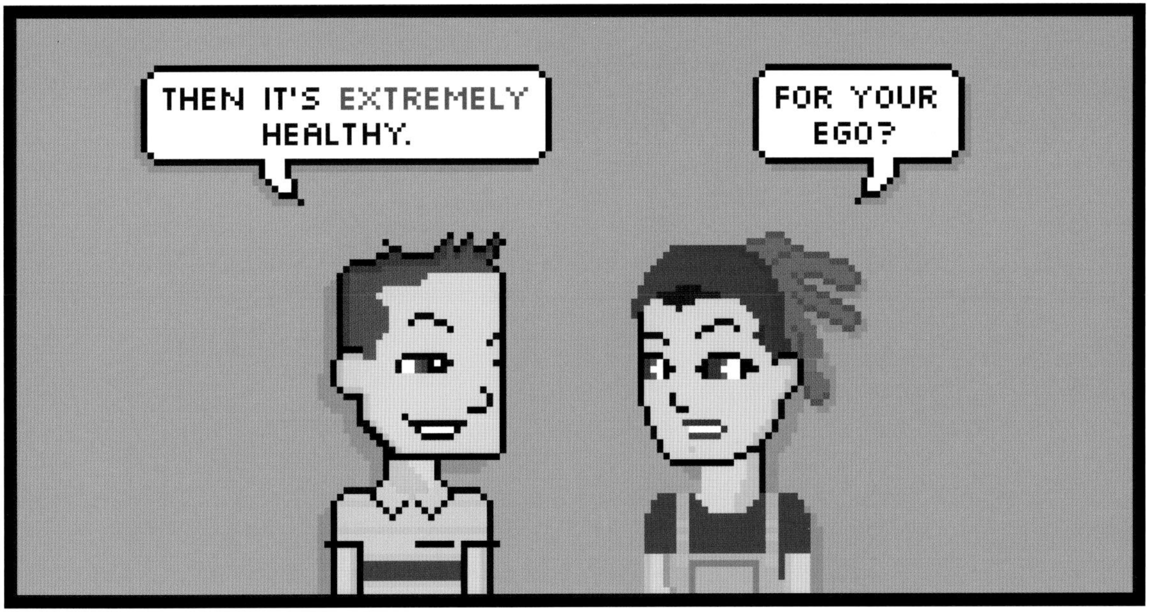
THEN IT'S EXTREMELY HEALTHY.
FOR YOUR EGO?

SEXHONKERS.COM PROPRIETARY TICKLEMATCHING ALGORITHM

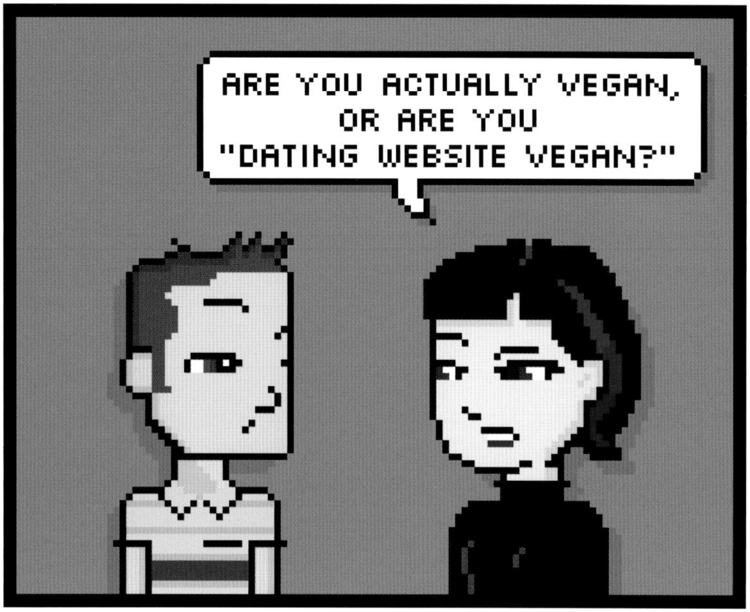
ARE YOU ACTUALLY VEGAN, OR ARE YOU "DATING WEBSITE VEGAN?"

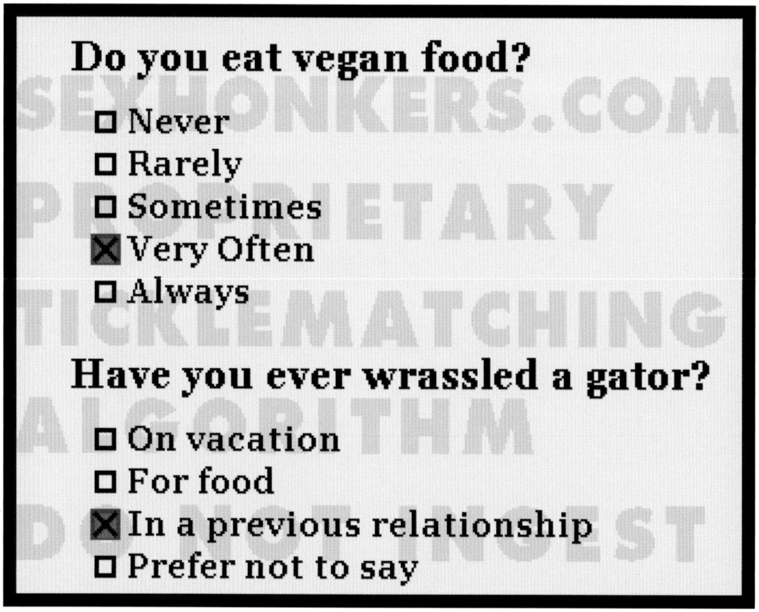
Do you eat vegan food?
☐ Never
☐ Rarely
☐ Sometimes
☒ Very Often
☐ Always
Have you ever wrassled a gator?
☐ On vacation
☐ For food
☒ In a previous relationship
☐ Prefer not to say
SEXHONKERS.COM PROPRIETARY TICKLEMATCHING ALGORITHM DO NOT INGEST

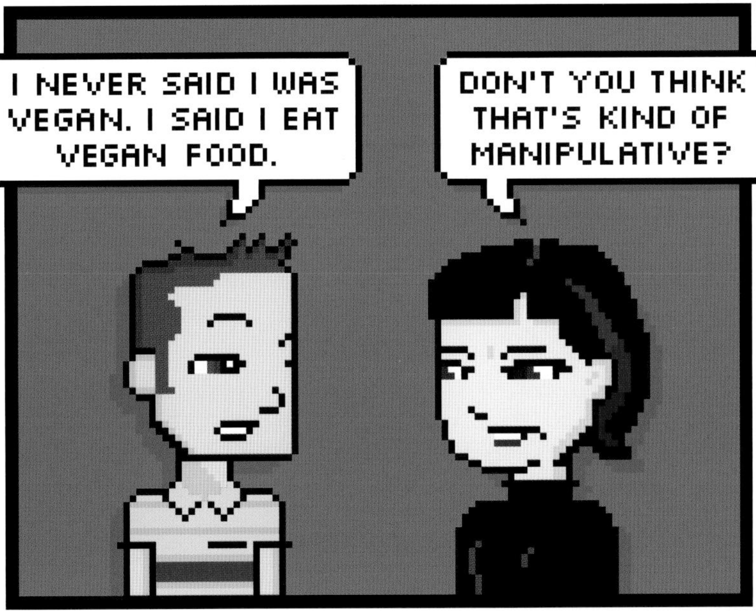
I NEVER SAID I WAS VEGAN. I SAID I EAT VEGAN FOOD.
DON'T YOU THINK THAT'S KIND OF MANIPULATIVE?

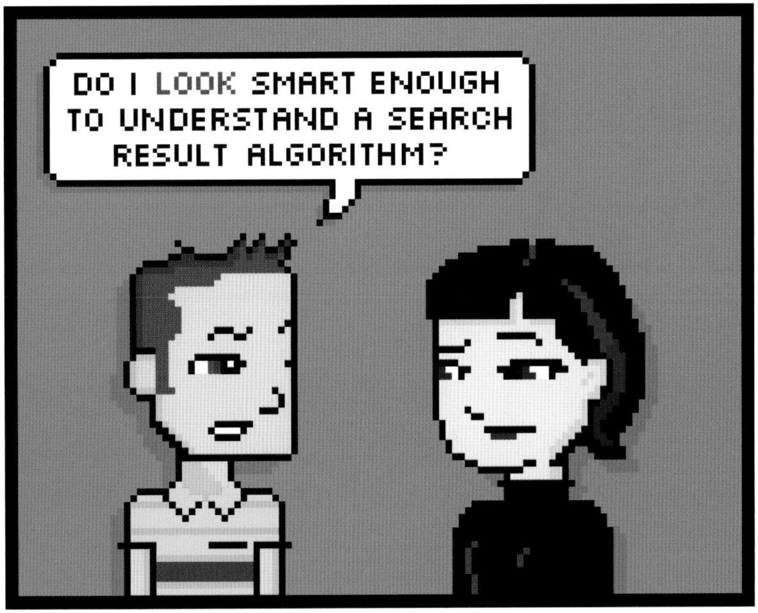
DO I LOOK SMART ENOUGH TO UNDERSTAND A SEARCH RESULT ALGORITHM?

DIETARY DEFLOWERING

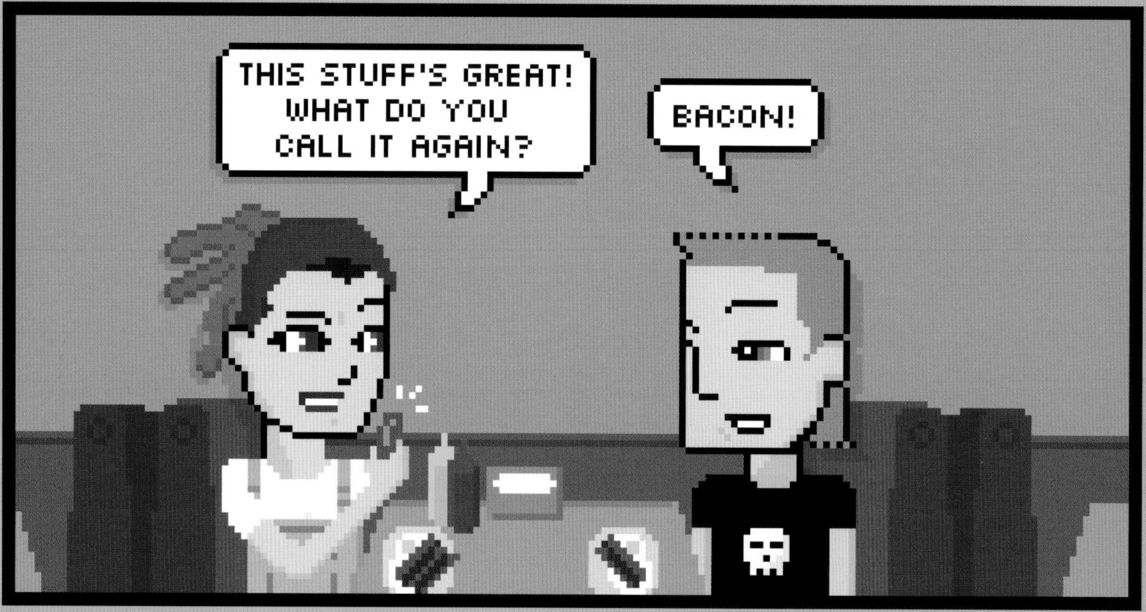
THIS STUFF'S GREAT! WHAT DO YOU CALL IT AGAIN?
BACON!

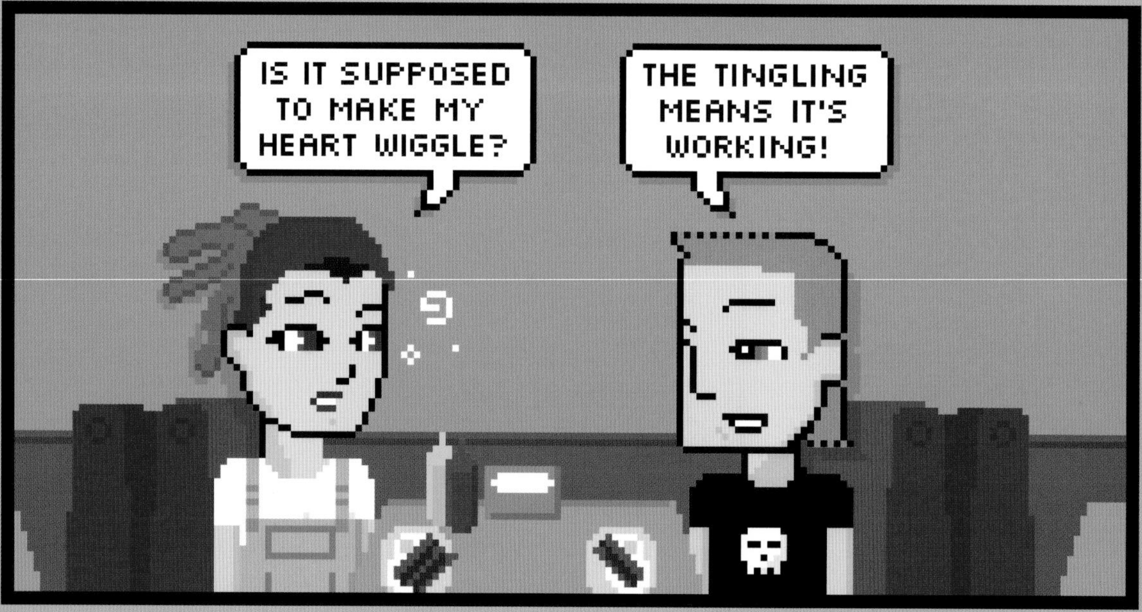
IS IT SUPPOSED TO MAKE MY HEART WIGGLE?
THE TINGLING MEANS IT'S WORKING!

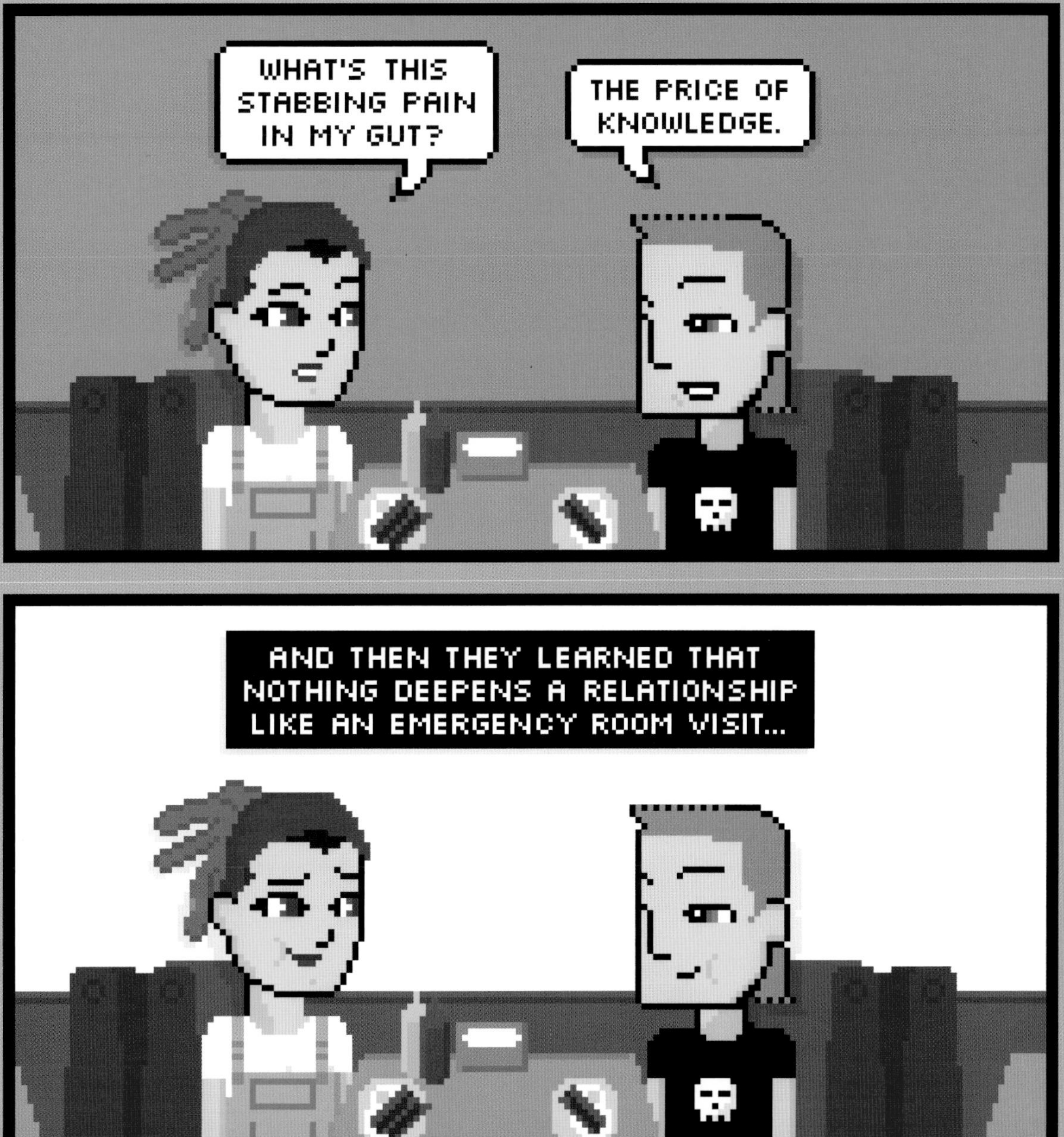
WHAT'S THIS STABBING PAIN IN MY GUT?
THE PRICE OF KNOWLEDGE.
AND THEN THEY LEARNED THAT NOTHING DEEPENS A RELATIONSHIP LIKE AN EMERGENCY ROOM VISIT...

MEATY CONFESSIONS

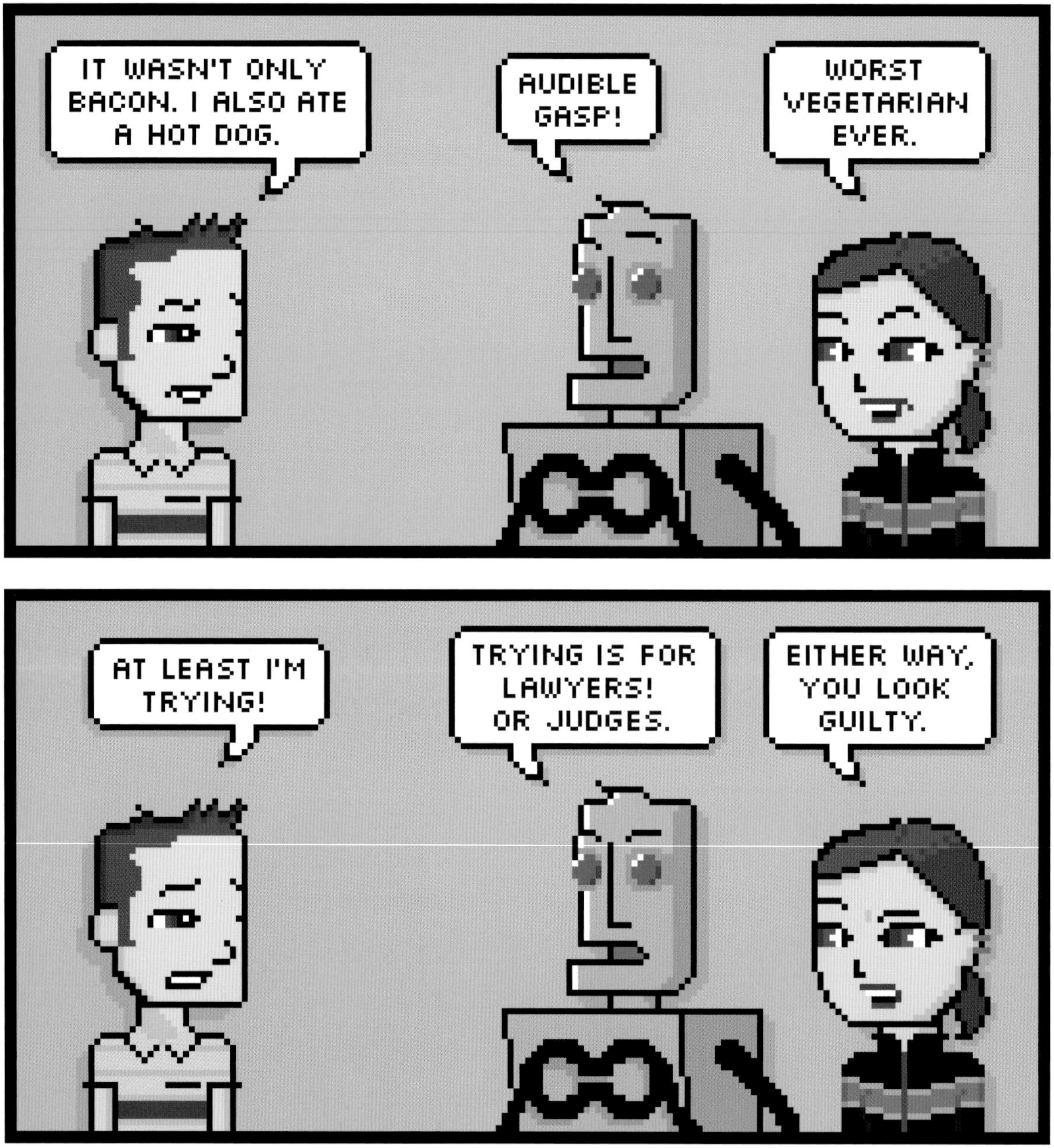
IT WASN'T ONLY BACON. I ALSO ATE A HOT DOG.
AUDIBLE GASP!
WORST VEGETARIAN EVER.
AT LEAST I'M TRYING!
TRYING IS FOR LAWYERS! OR JUDGES.
EITHER WAY, YOU LOOK GUILTY.

I BELIEVE IN A FRYER POWER

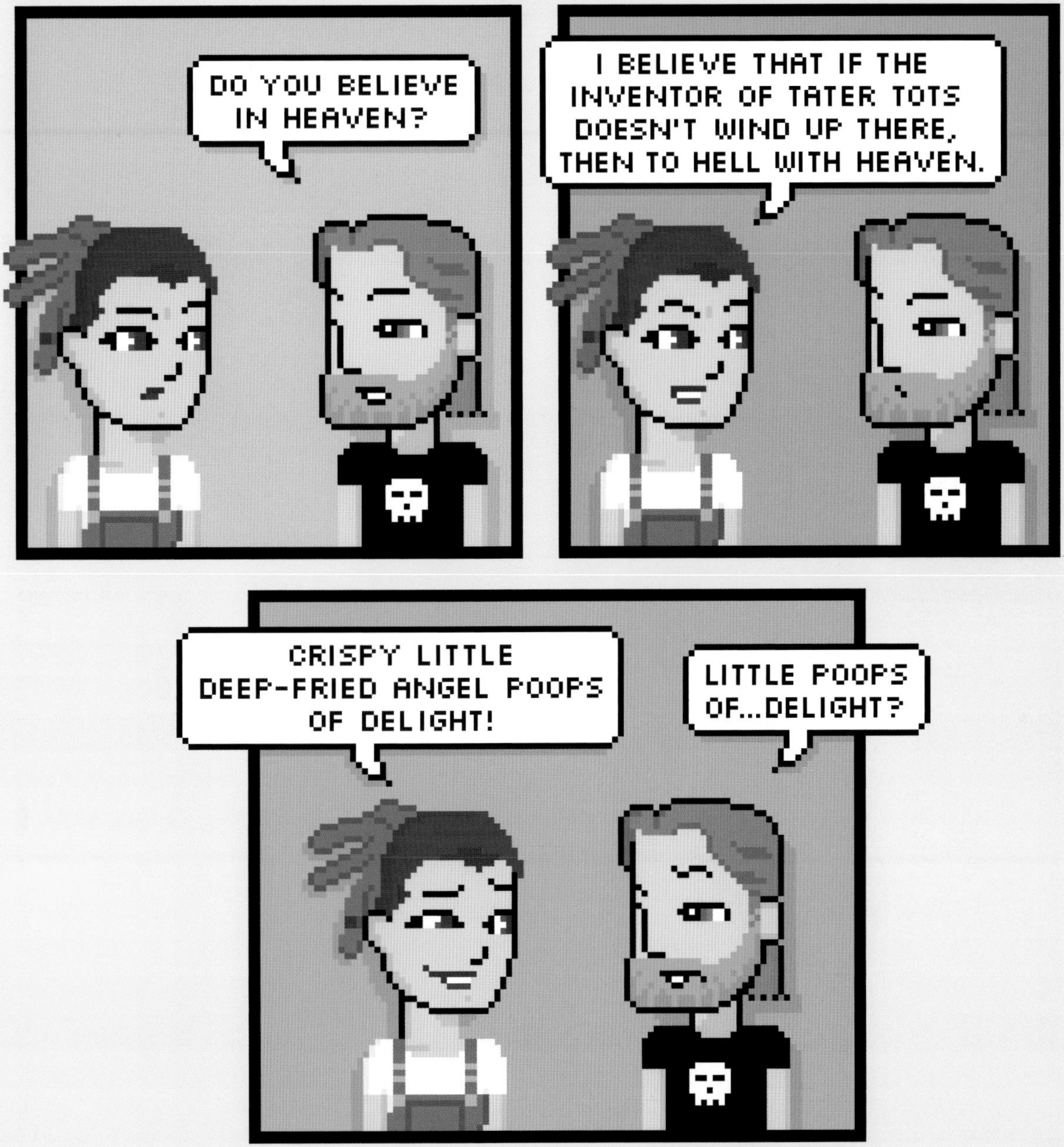
DO YOU BELIEVE IN HEAVEN?
I BELIEVE THAT IF THE INVENTOR OF TATER TOTS DOESN'T WIND UP THERE, THEN TO HELL WITH HEAVEN.
CRISPY LITTLE DEEP-FRIED ANGEL POOPS OF DELIGHT!
LITTLE POOPS OF...DELIGHT?

INSERT TERMINATOR QUOTE ABOUT NOT STOPPING

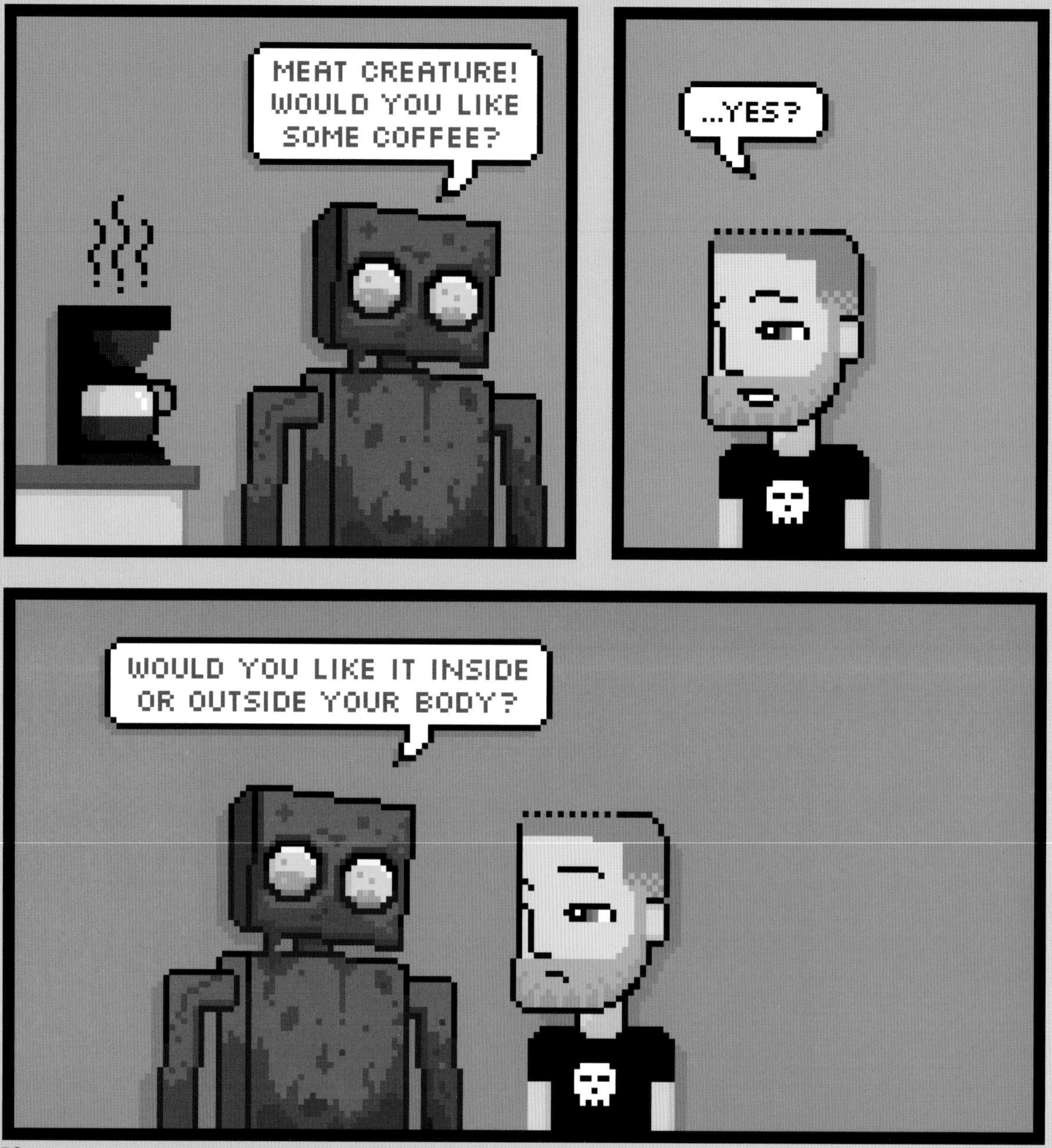
MEAT CREATURE! WOULD YOU LIKE SOME COFFEE?
...YES?
WOULD YOU LIKE IT INSIDE OR OUTSIDE YOUR BODY?

BUT WITH SUBTLE POP CULTURAL REFERENCE

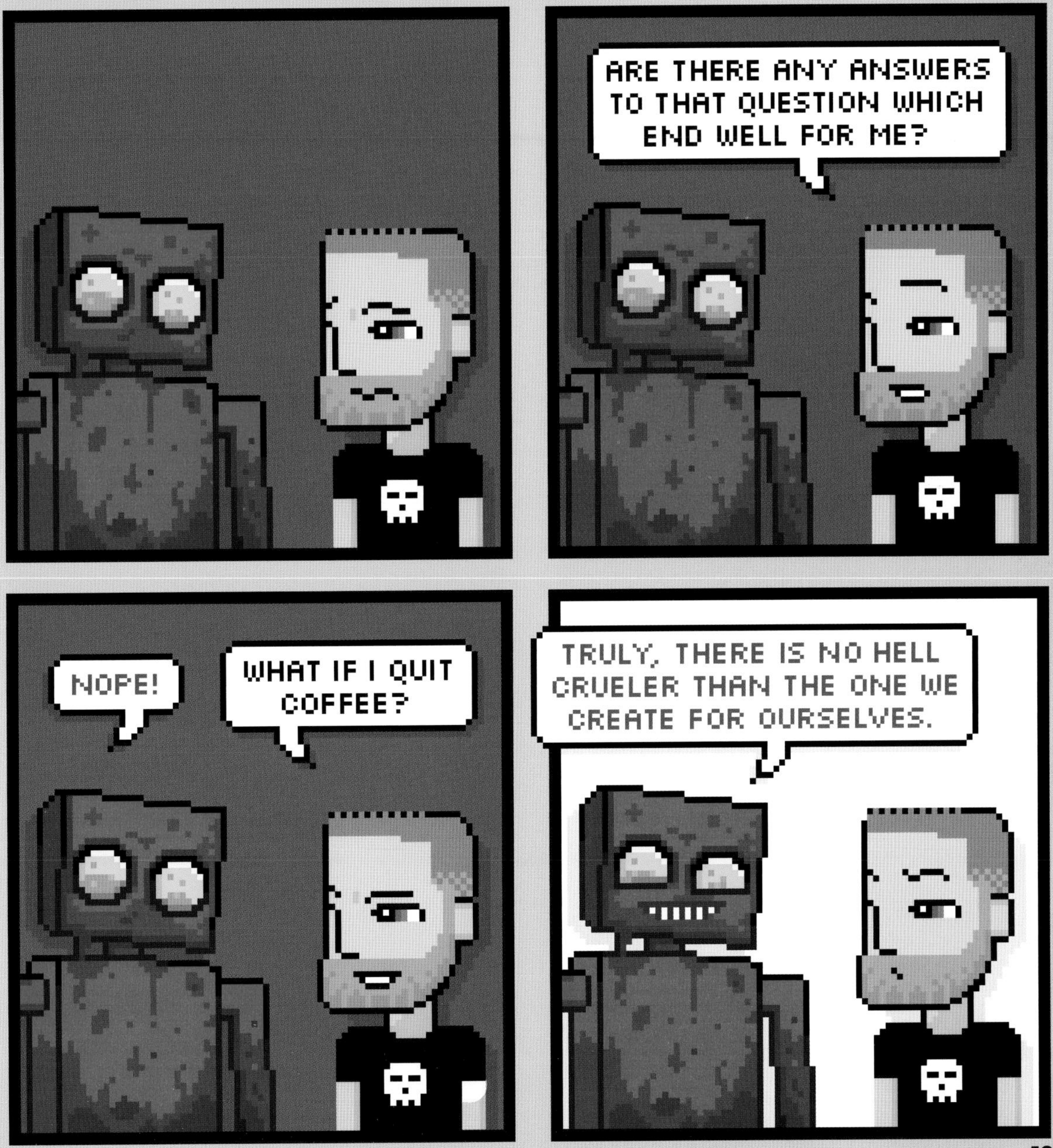
ARE THERE ANY ANSWERS TO THAT QUESTION WHICH END WELL FOR ME?
NOPE!
WHAT IF I QUIT COFFEE?
TRULY, THERE IS NO HELL CRUELER THAN THE ONE WE CREATE FOR OURSELVES.

CIVETS LESSON

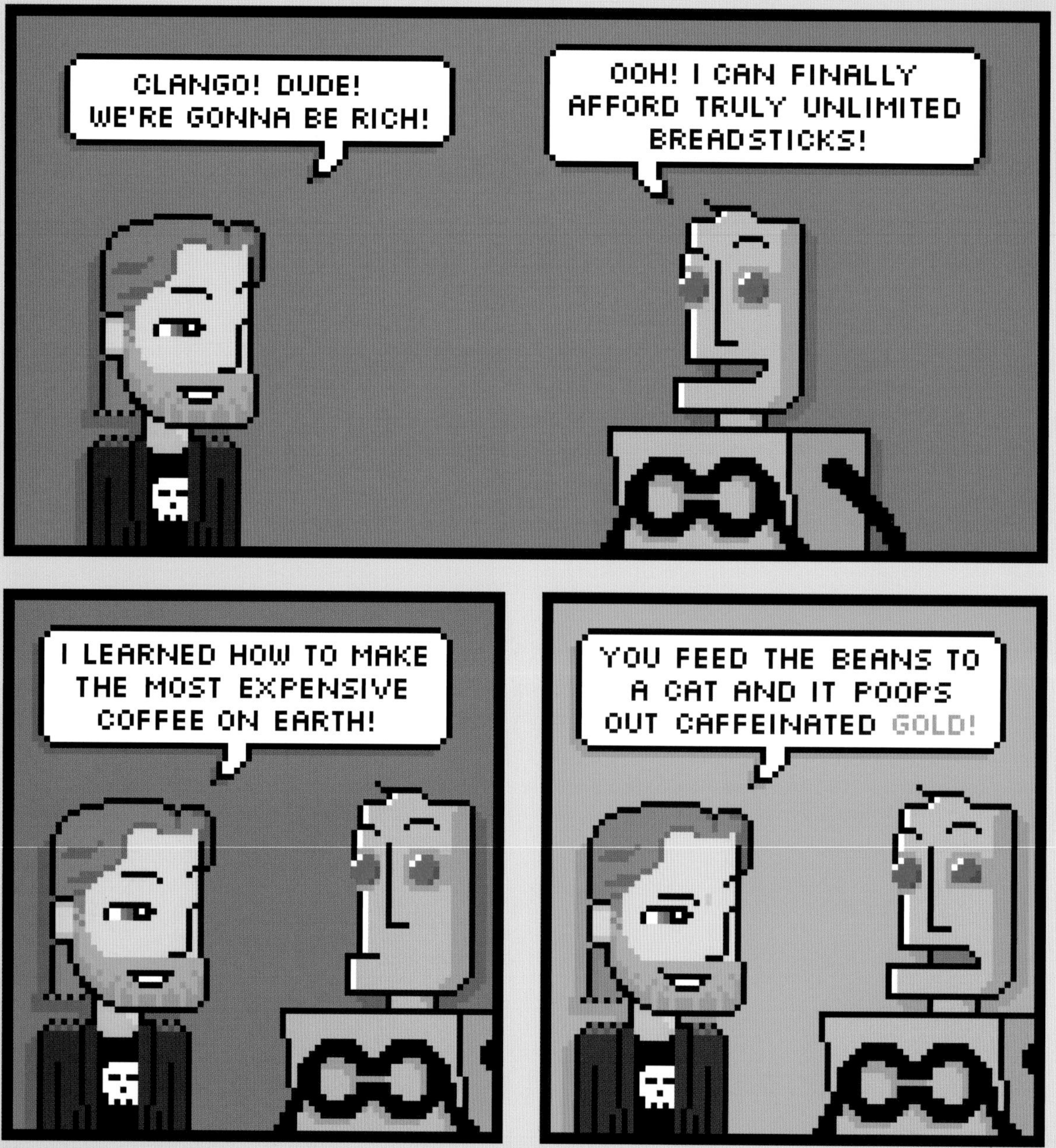
CLANGO! DUDE! WE'RE GONNA BE RICH!
OOH! I CAN FINALLY AFFORD TRULY UNLIMITED BREADSTICKS!
I LEARNED HOW TO MAKE THE MOST EXPENSIVE COFFEE ON EARTH!
YOU FEED THE BEANS TO A CAT AND IT POOPS OUT CAFFEINATED GOLD!

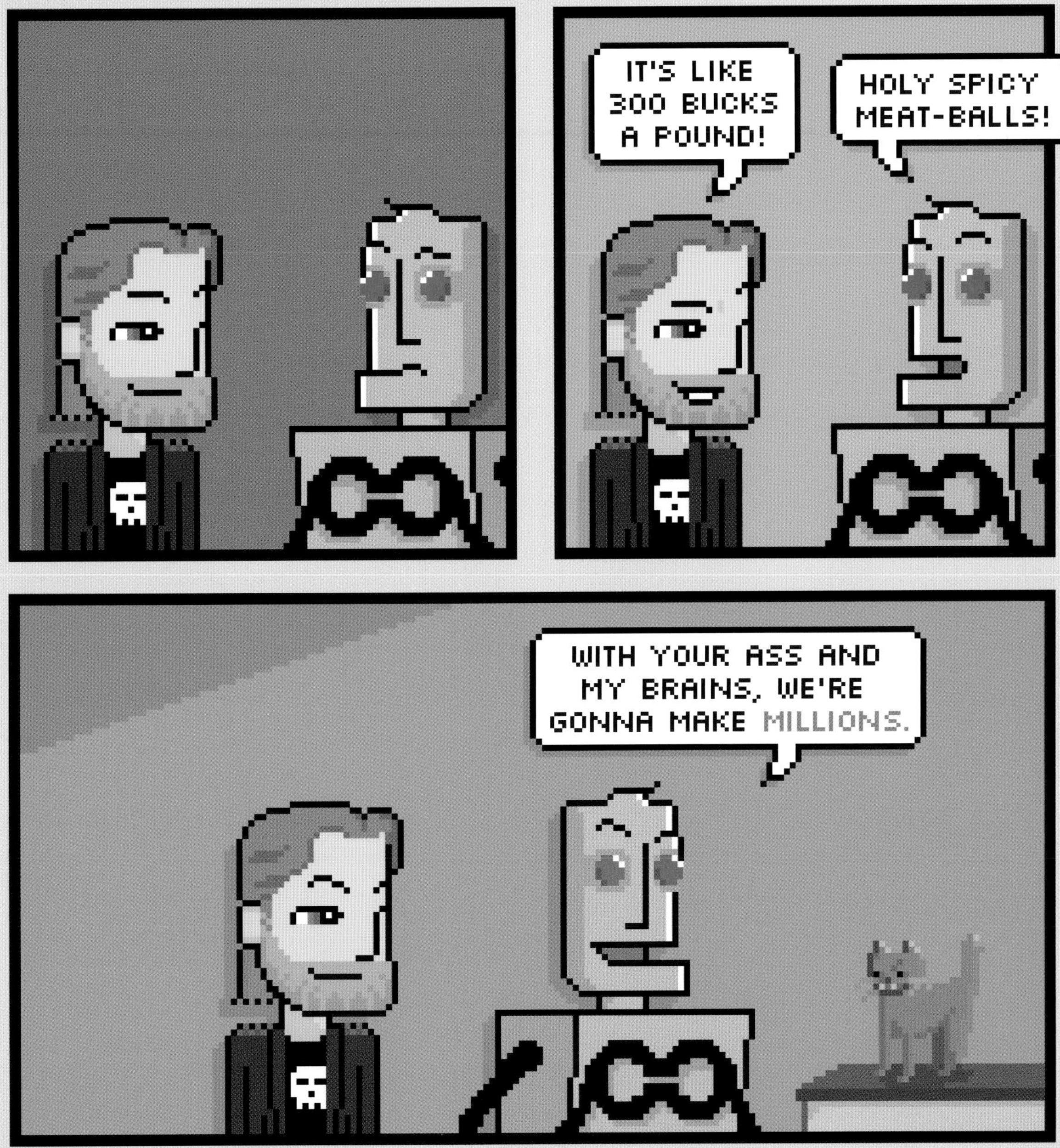
IT'S LIKE 300 BUCKS A POUND!
HOLY SPICY MEAT-BALLS!
WITH YOUR ASS AND MY BRAINS, WE'RE GONNA MAKE MILLIONS.

THE SPICE ISN'T SUPPOSED TO FLOW THAT WAY

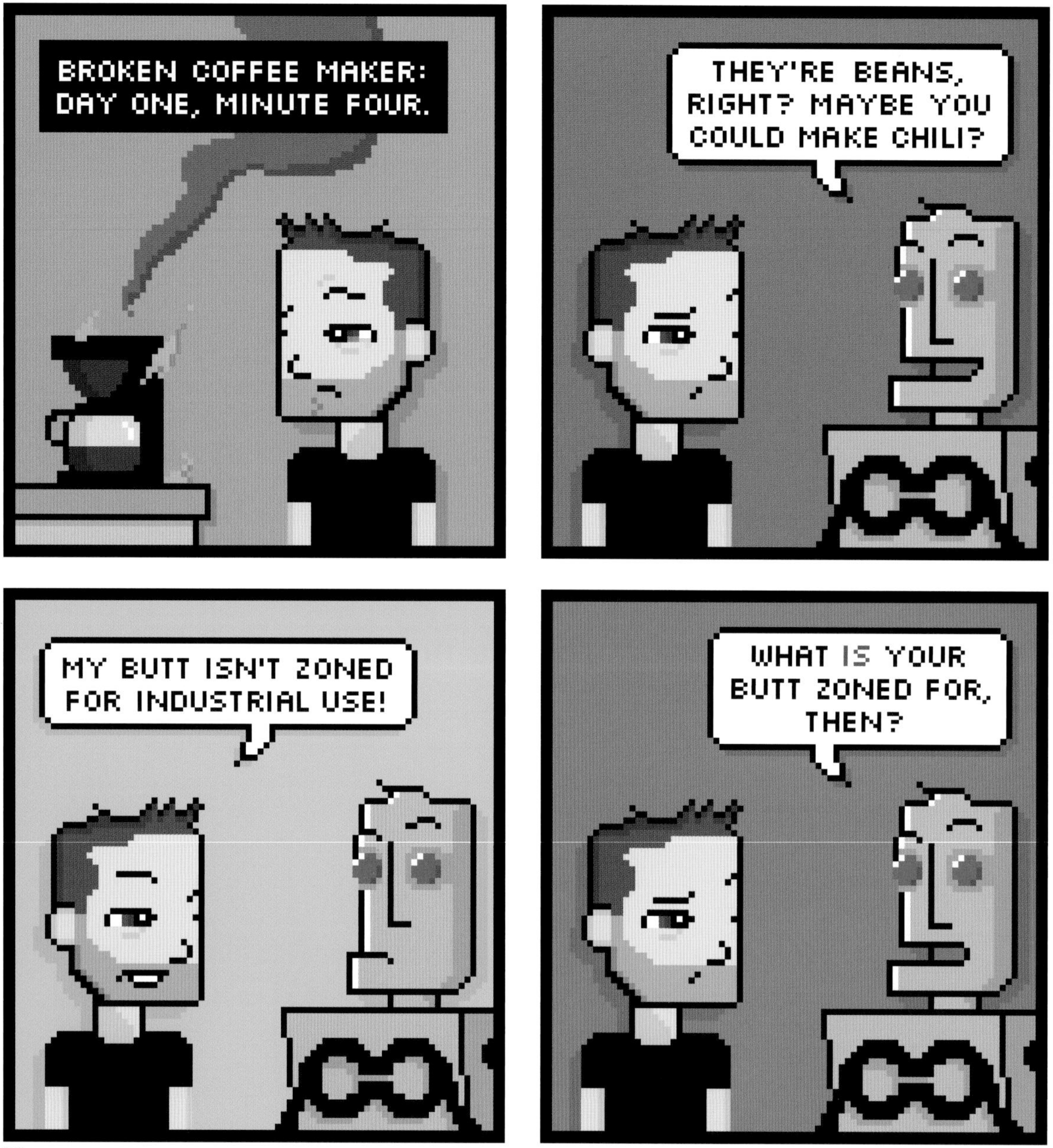
BROKEN COFFEE MAKER: DAY ONE, MINUTE FOUR.
THEY'RE BEANS, RIGHT? MAYBE YOU COULD MAKE CHILI?
MY BUTT ISN'T ZONED FOR INDUSTRIAL USE!
WHAT IS YOUR BUTT ZONED FOR, THEN?

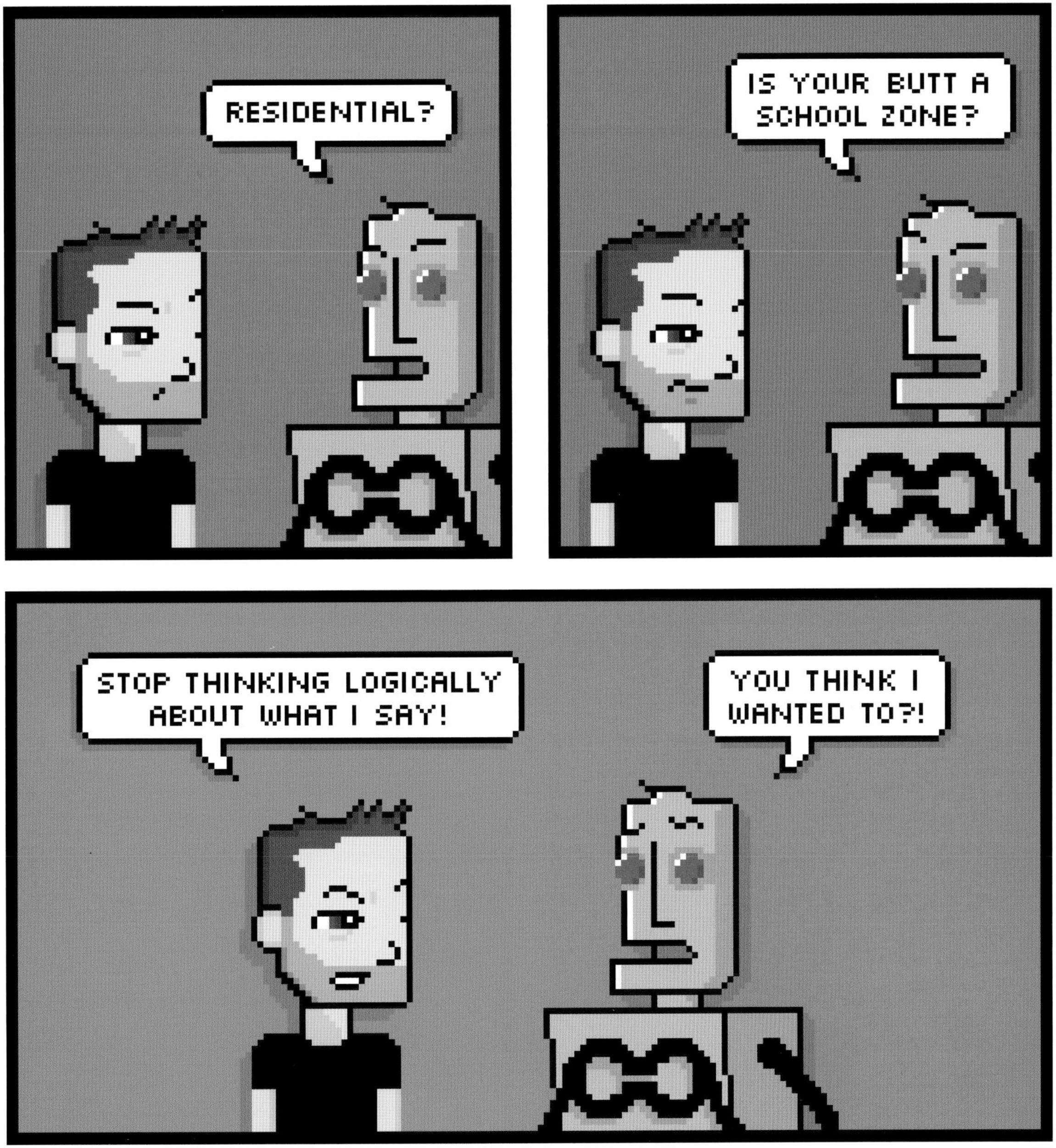
RESIDENTIAL?
IS YOUR BUTT A SCHOOL ZONE?
STOP THINKING LOGICALLY ABOUT WHAT I SAY!
YOU THINK I WANTED TO?!

THE ORIGINAL CURIOUSLY STRONG ALKALOIDS

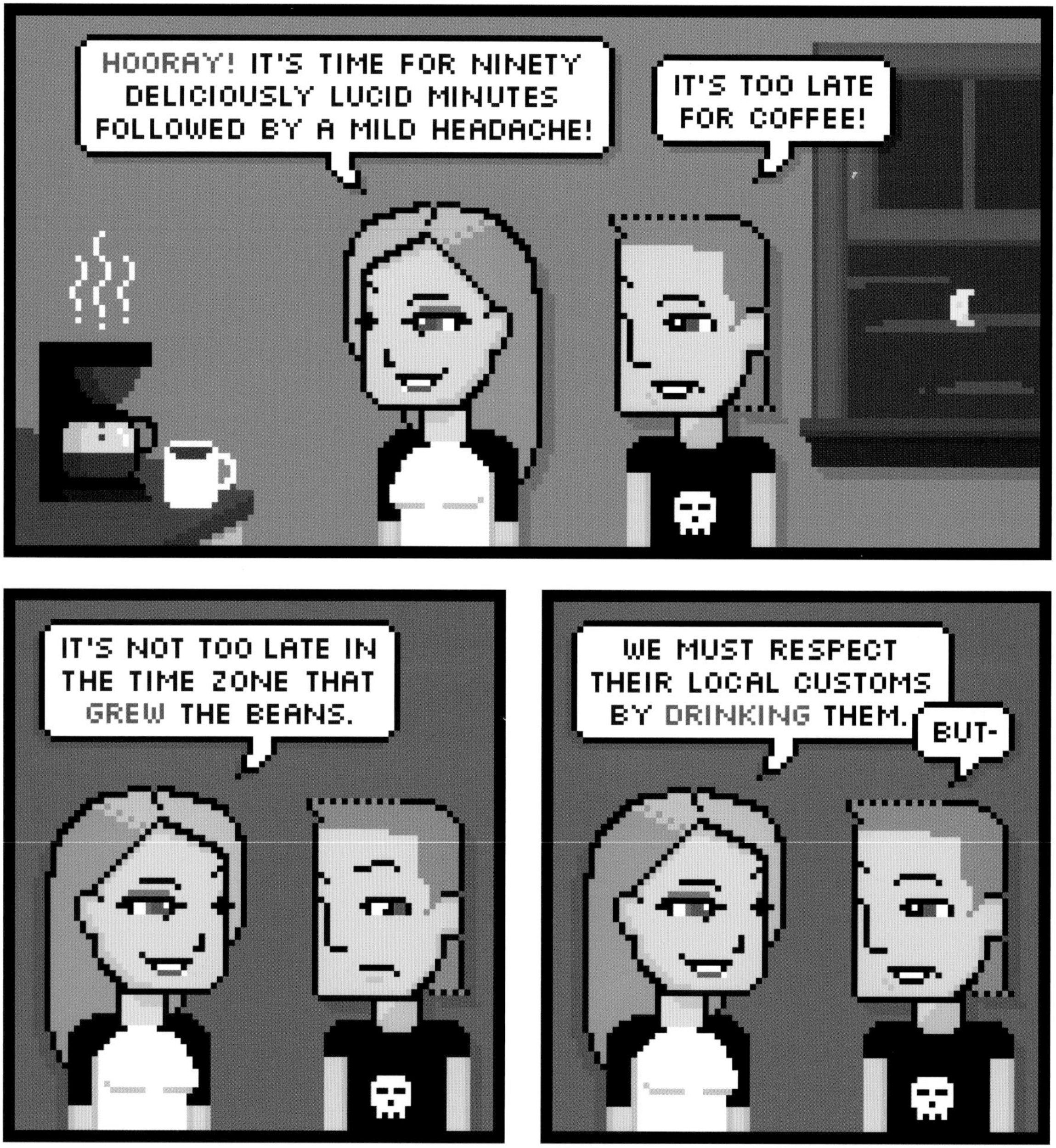
HOORAY! IT'S TIME FOR NINETY DELICIOUSLY LUCID MINUTES FOLLOWED BY A MILD HEADACHE!
IT'S TOO LATE FOR COFFEE!
IT'S NOT TOO LATE IN THE TIME ZONE THAT GREW THE BEANS.
WE MUST RESPECT THEIR LOCAL CUSTOMS BY DRINKING THEM.
BUT-

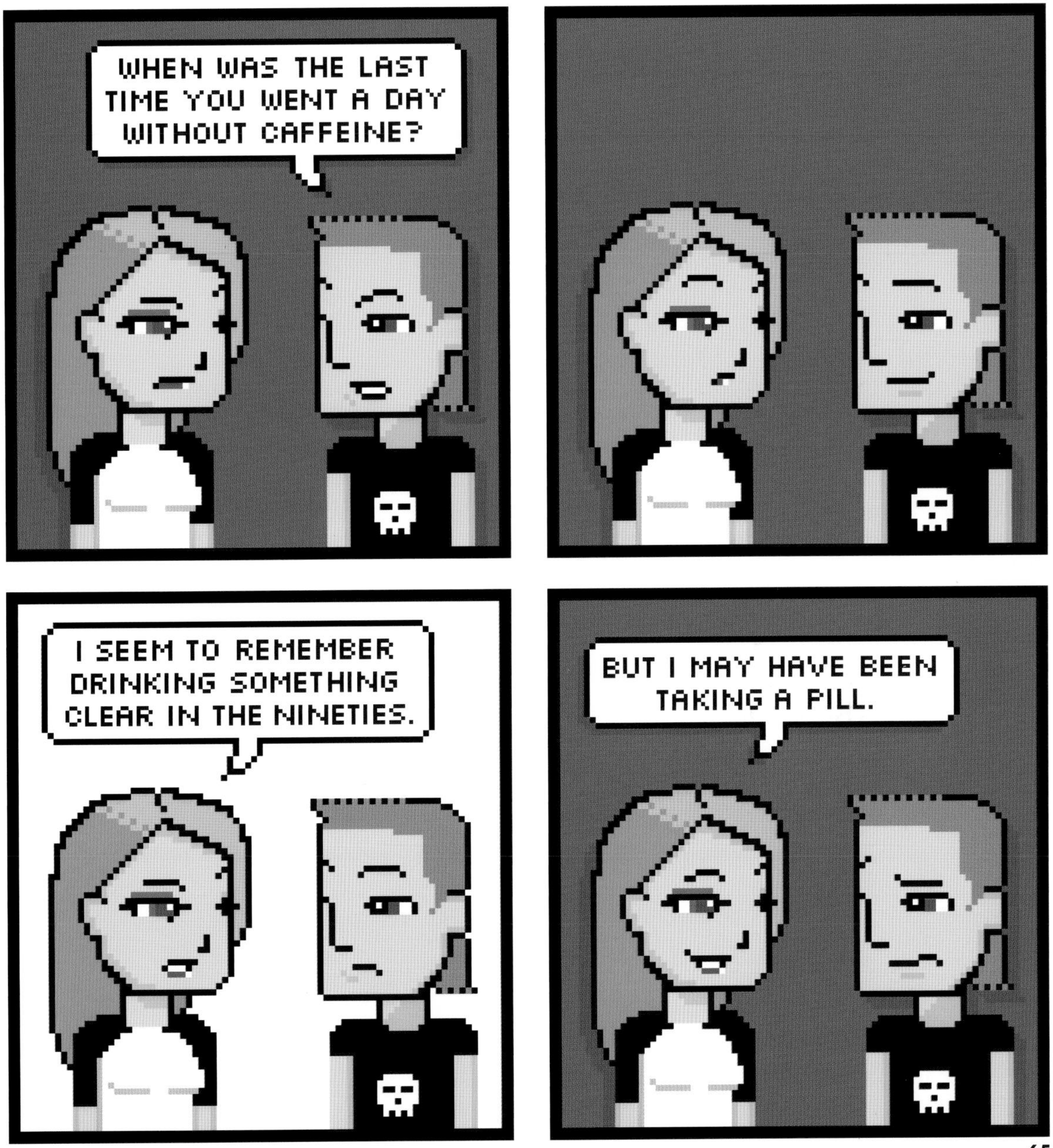
WHEN WAS THE LAST TIME YOU WENT A DAY WITHOUT CAFFEINE?
I SEEM TO REMEMBER DRINKING SOMETHING CLEAR IN THE NINETIES.
BUT I MAY HAVE BEEN TAKING A PILL.

EXTREMELY IMPRESSIVE OR DAUNTING; INSPIRING AWE

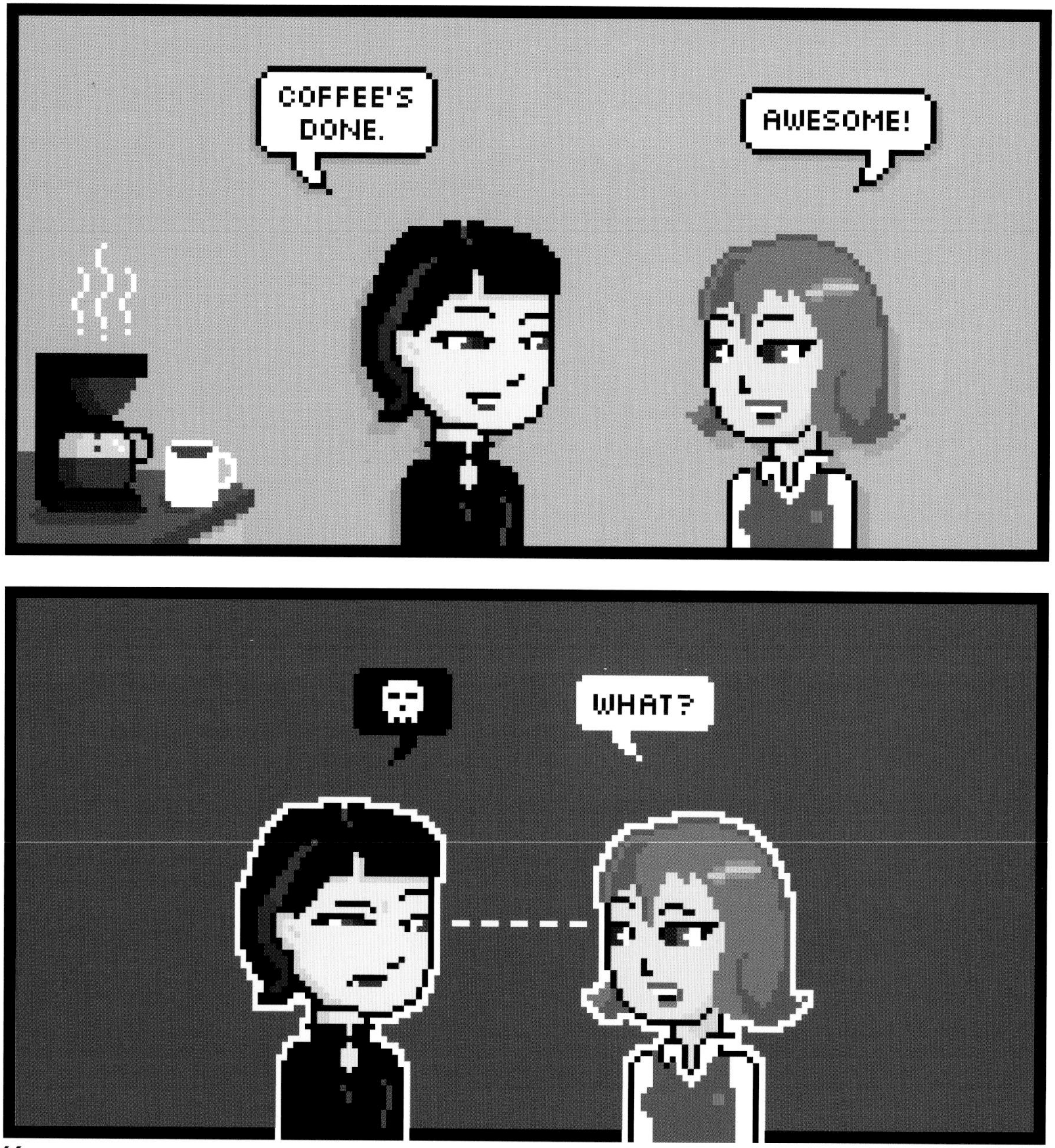
COFFEE'S DONE.
AWESOME!
WHAT?

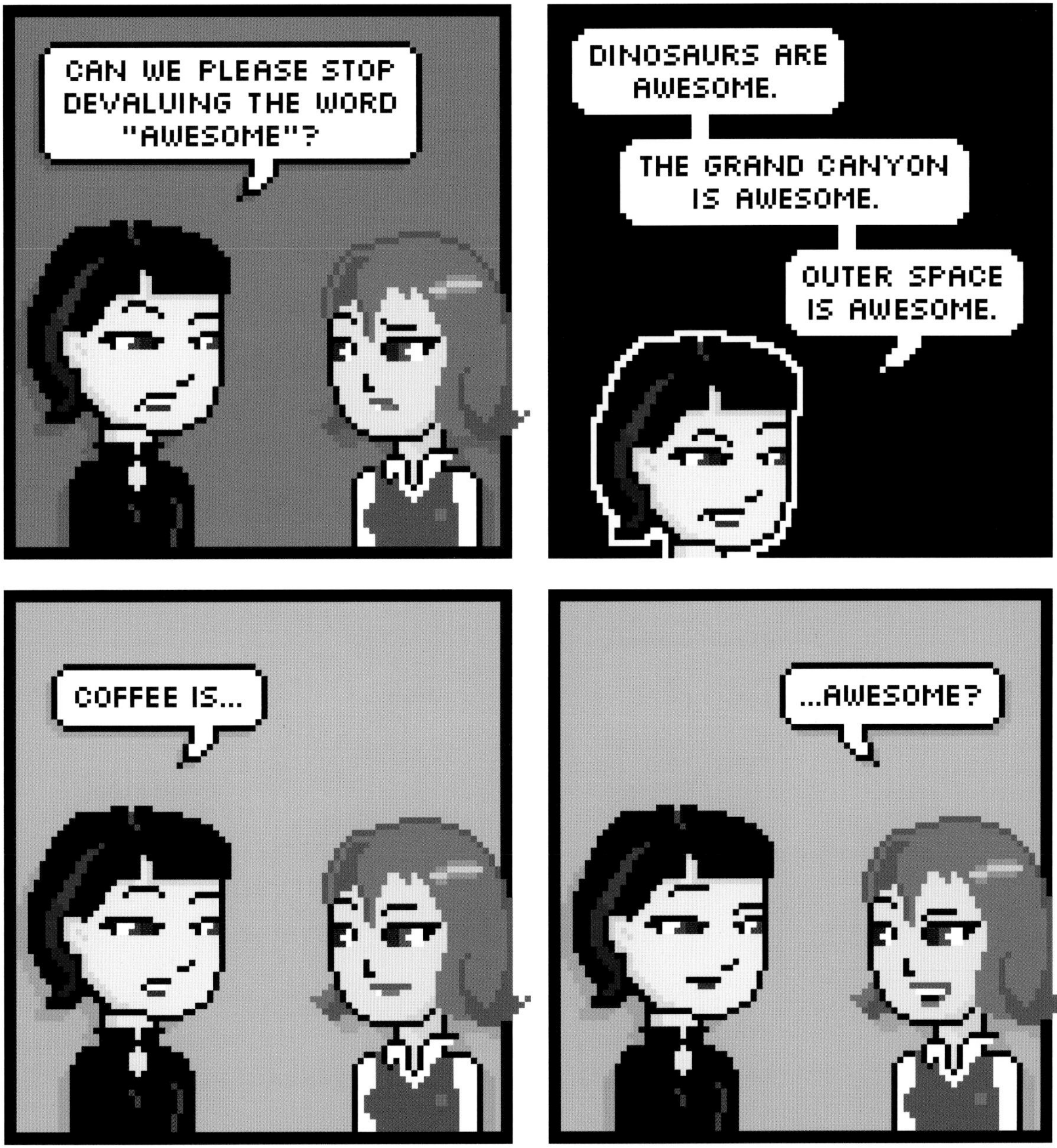
CAN WE PLEASE STOP DEVALUING THE WORD "AWESOME"?
DINOSAURS ARE AWESOME.
THE GRAND CANYON IS AWESOME.
OUTER SPACE IS AWESOME.
COFFEE IS...
...AWESOME?

FEROCIOUSLY DELICIOUS

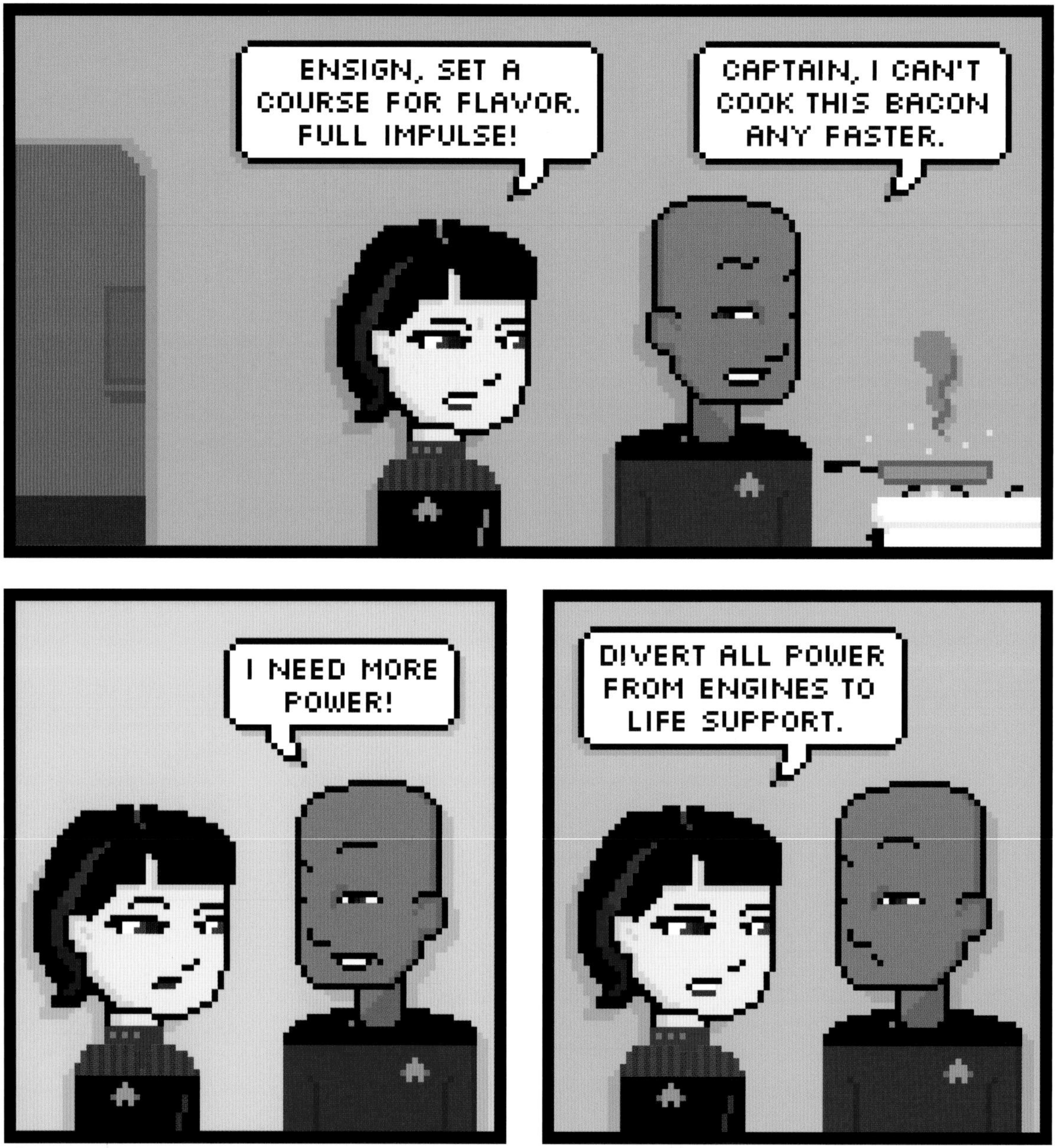

ENSIGN, SET A COURSE FOR FLAVOR. FULL IMPULSE!
CAPTAIN, I CAN'T COOK THIS BACON ANY FASTER.
I NEED MORE POWER!
DIVERT ALL POWER FROM ENGINES TO LIFE SUPPORT.

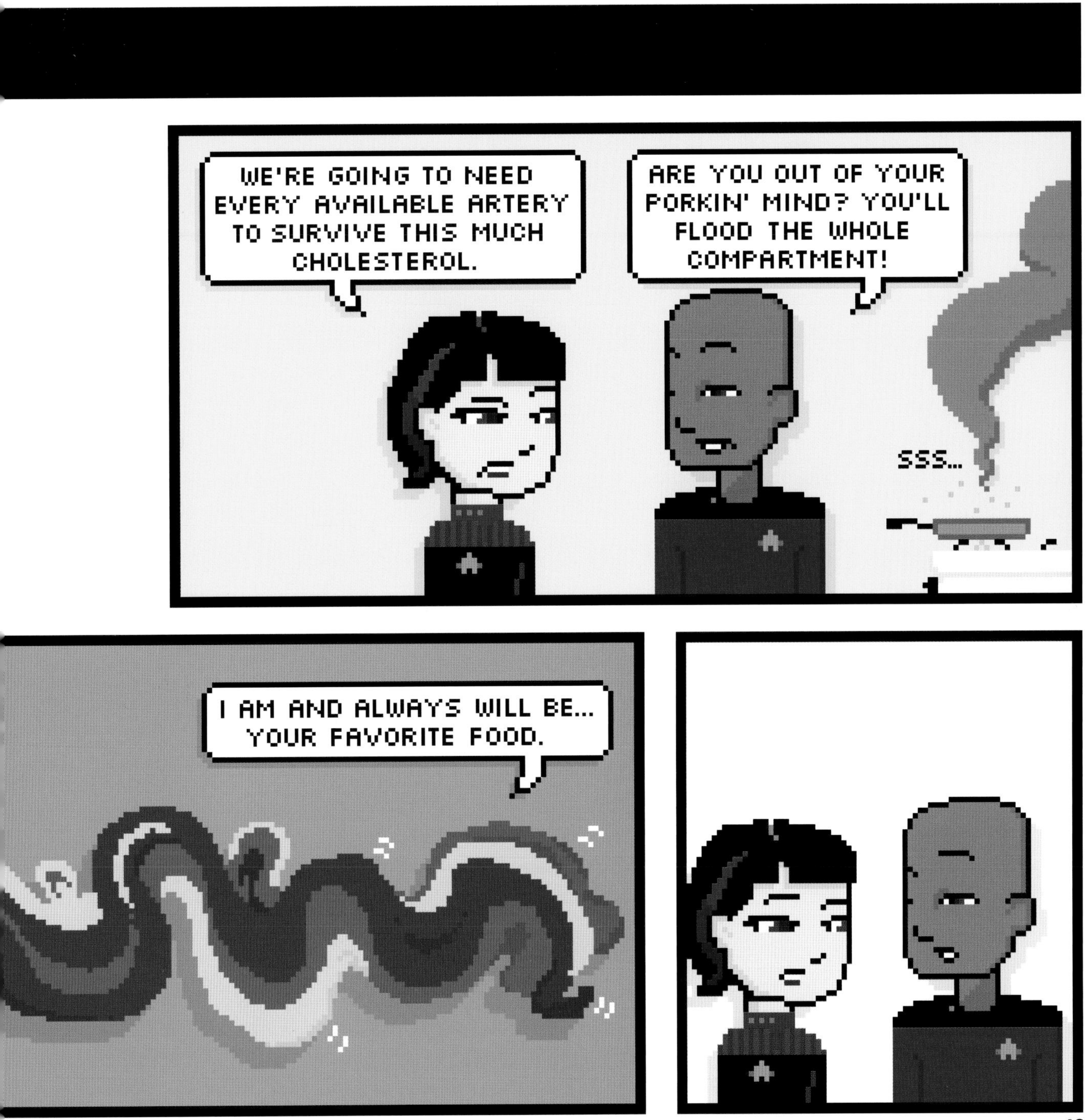
WE'RE GOING TO NEED EVERY AVAILABLE ARTERY TO SURVIVE THIS MUCH CHOLESTEROL.
ARE YOU OUT OF YOUR PORKIN' MIND? YOU'LL FLOOD THE WHOLE COMPARTMENT!
SSS...
I AM AND ALWAYS WILL BE... YOUR FAVORITE FOOD.

THE OTHER WHITE ROCK

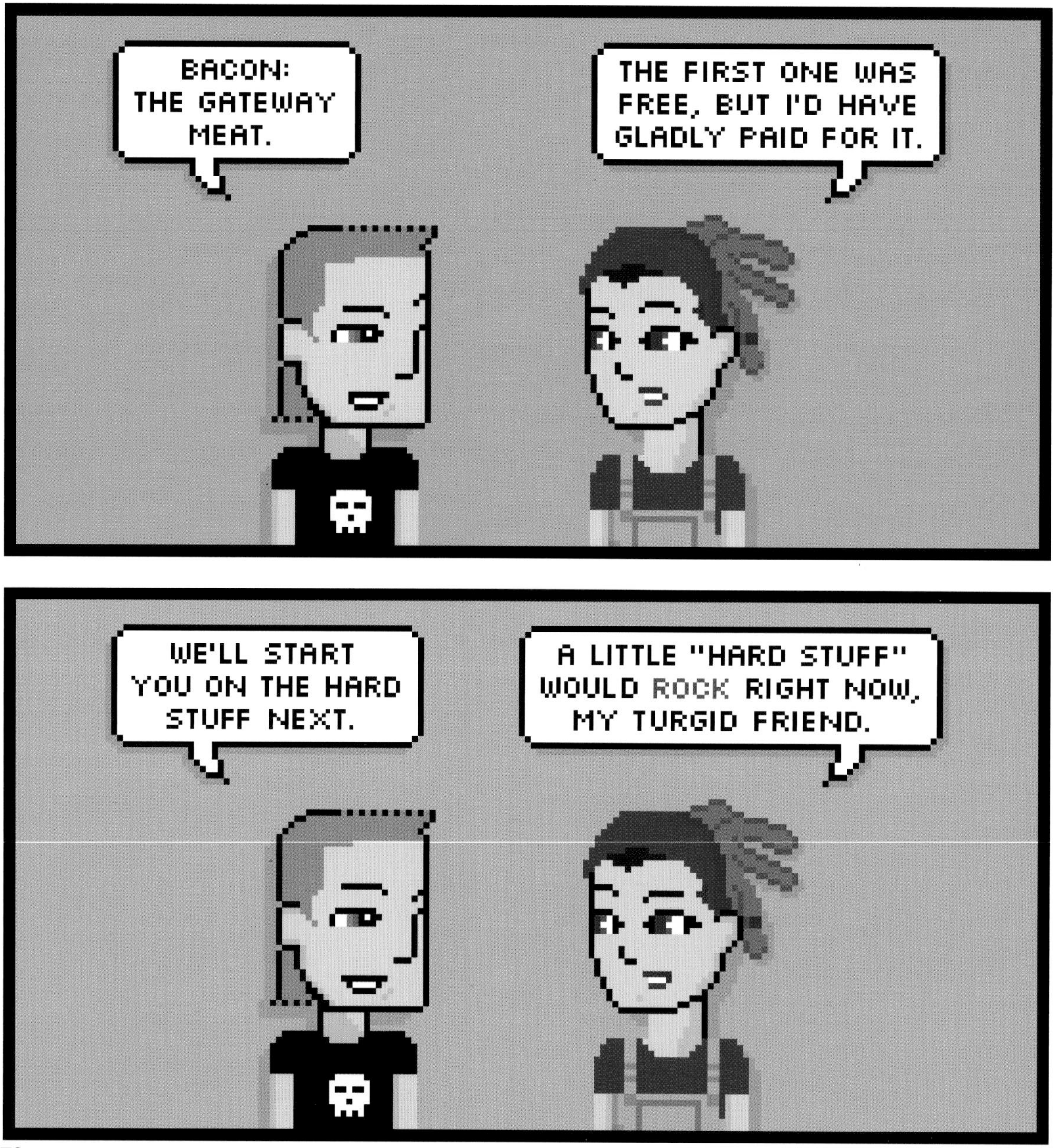
BACON: THE GATEWAY MEAT.
THE FIRST ONE WAS FREE, BUT I'D HAVE GLADLY PAID FOR IT.
WE'LL START YOU ON THE HARD STUFF NEXT.
A LITTLE "HARD STUFF" WOULD ROCK RIGHT NOW, MY TURGID FRIEND.

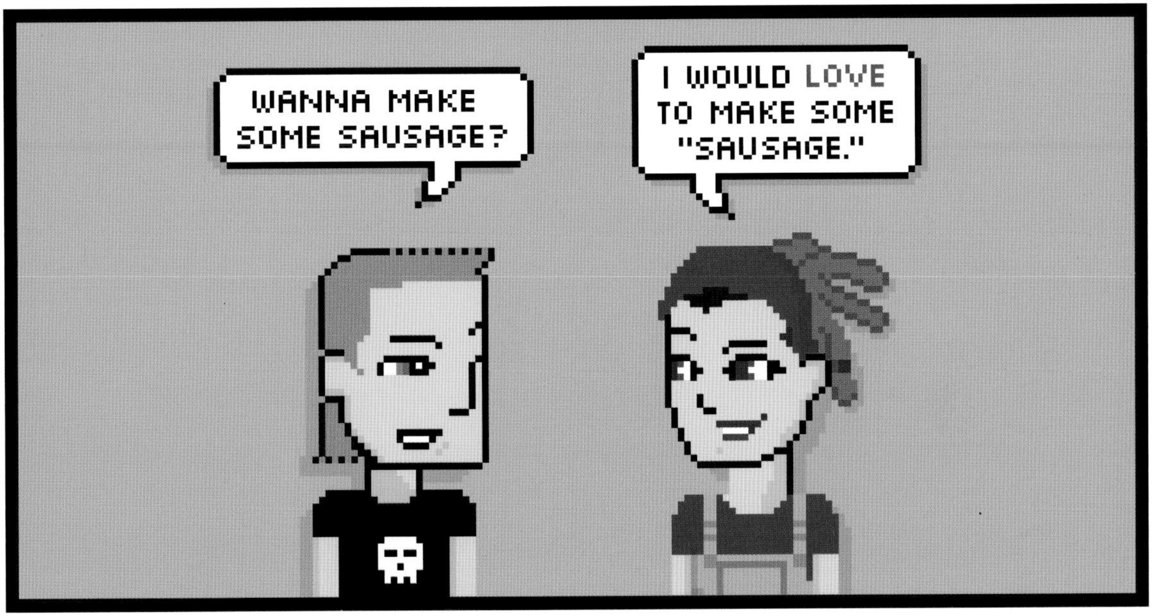
WANNA MAKE SOME SAUSAGE?
I WOULD LOVE TO MAKE SOME "SAUSAGE."

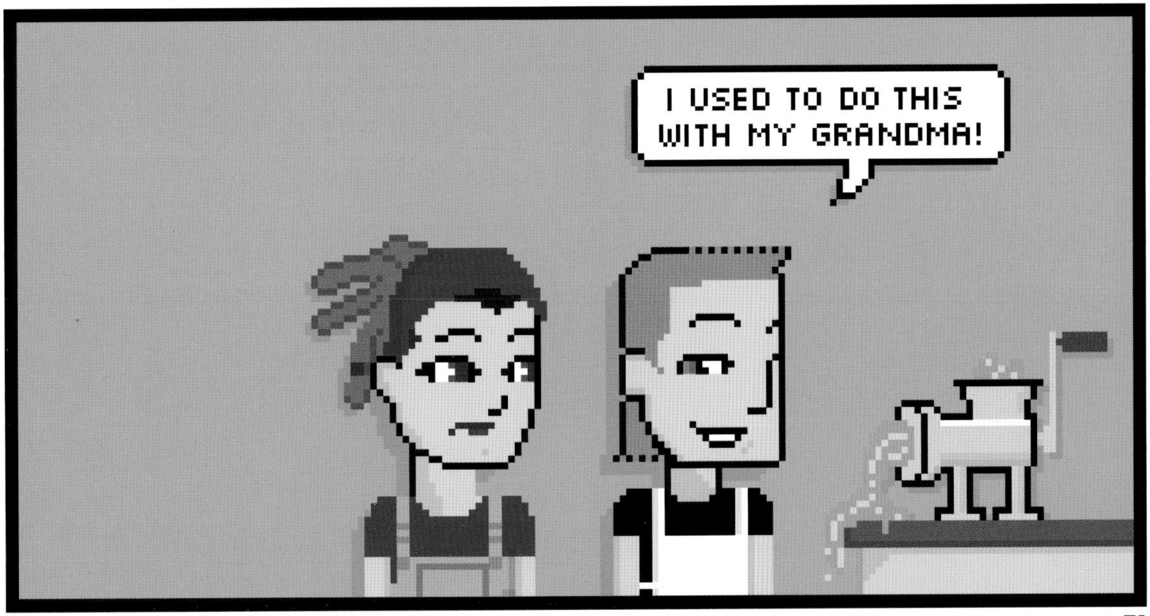
I USED TO DO THIS WITH MY GRANDMA!

ASK YOUR BUTCHER IF PORKONEX® IS RIGHT FOR YOU

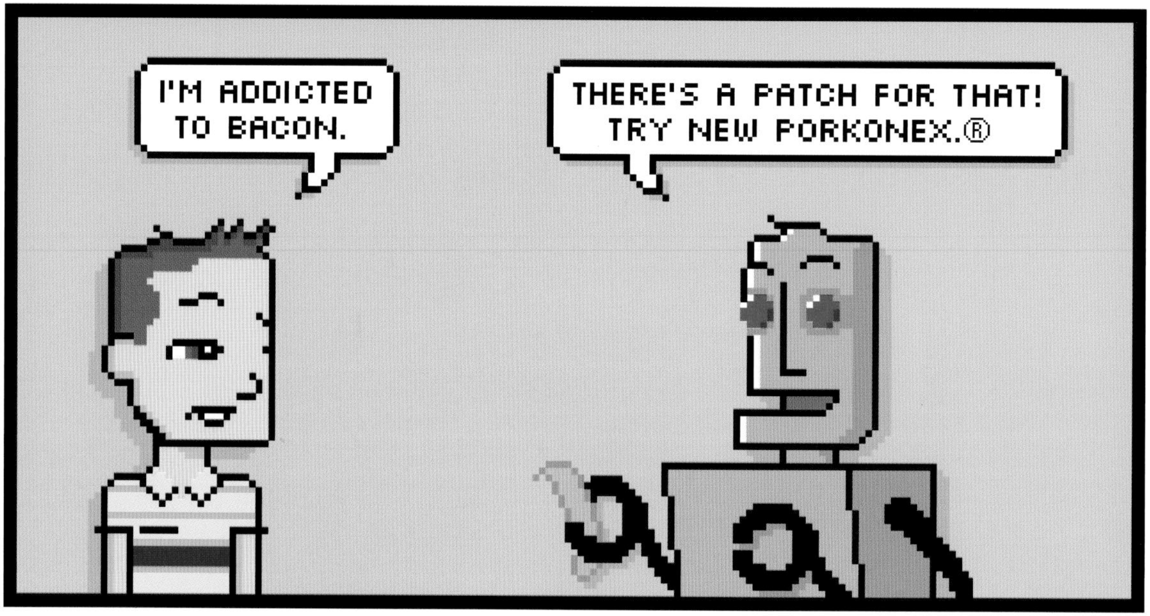
I'M ADDICTED TO BACON.
THERE'S A PATCH FOR THAT! TRY NEW PORKONEX.®

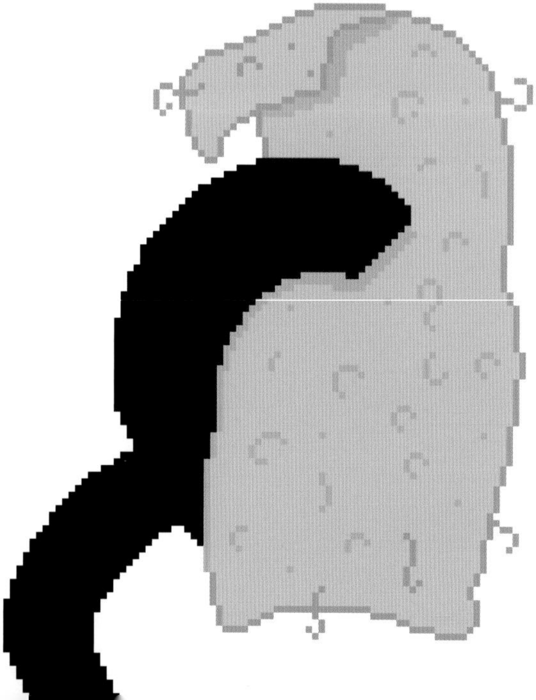

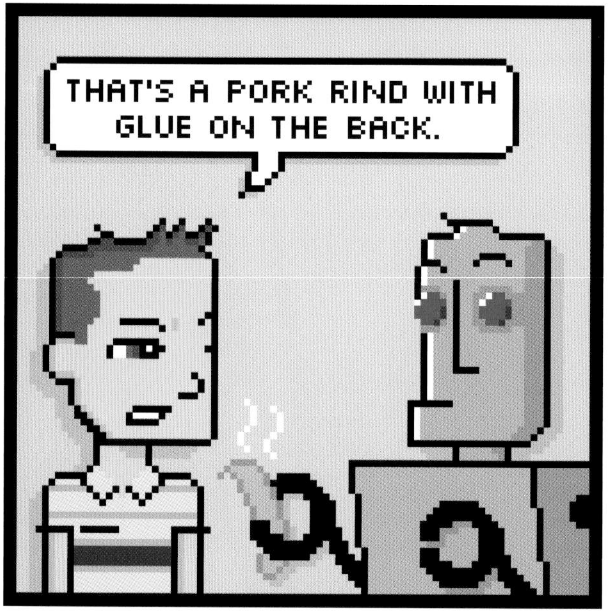
THAT'S A PORK RIND WITH GLUE ON THE BACK.

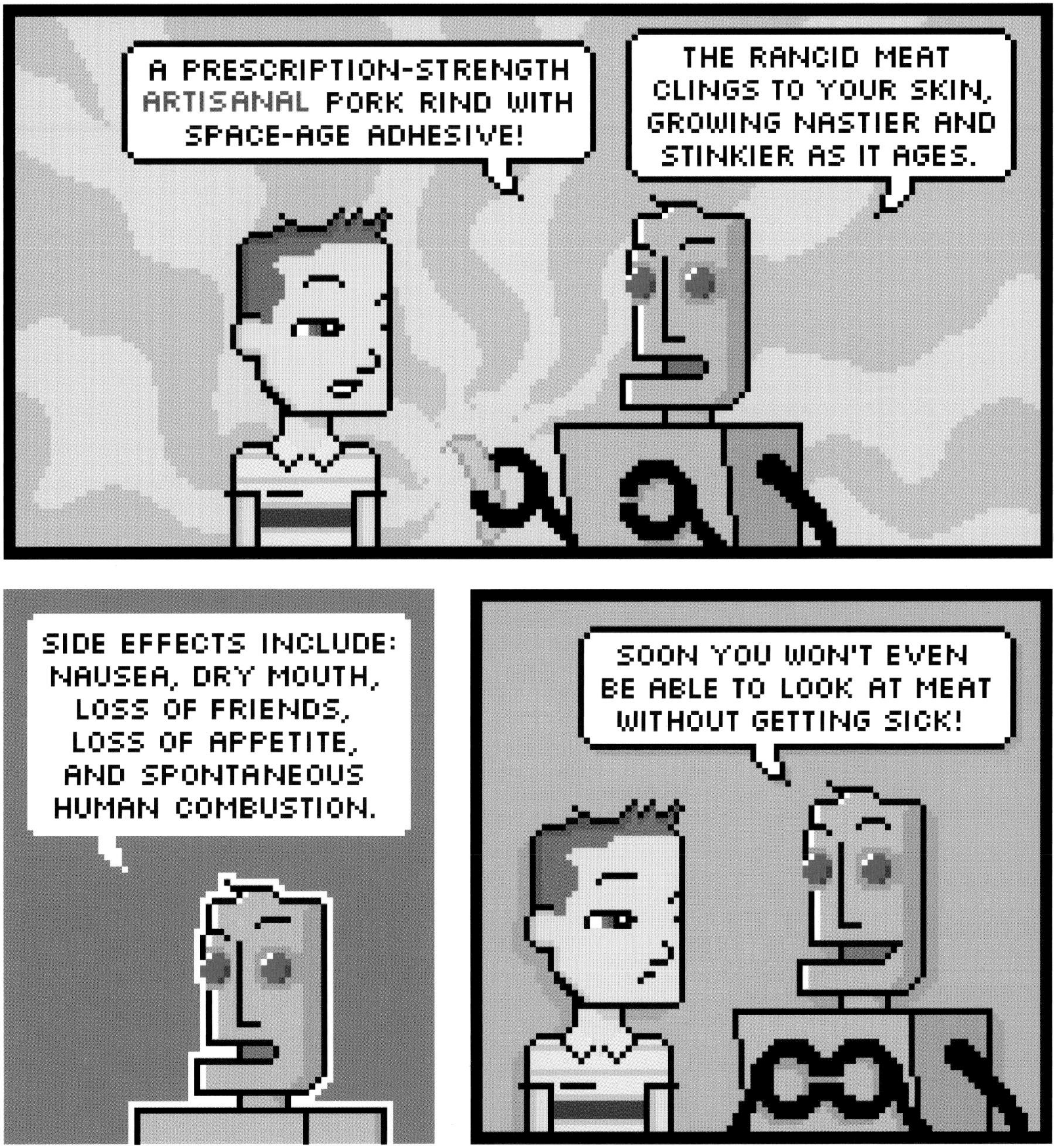
A PRESCRIPTION-STRENGTH ARTISANAL PORK RIND WITH SPACE-AGE ADHESIVE!
THE RANCID MEAT CLINGS TO YOUR SKIN, GROWING NASTIER AND STINKIER AS IT AGES.
SIDE EFFECTS INCLUDE: NAUSEA, DRY MOUTH, LOSS OF FRIENDS, LOSS OF APPETITE, AND SPONTANEOUS HUMAN COMBUSTION.
SOON YOU WON'T EVEN BE ABLE TO LOOK AT MEAT WITHOUT GETTING SICK!

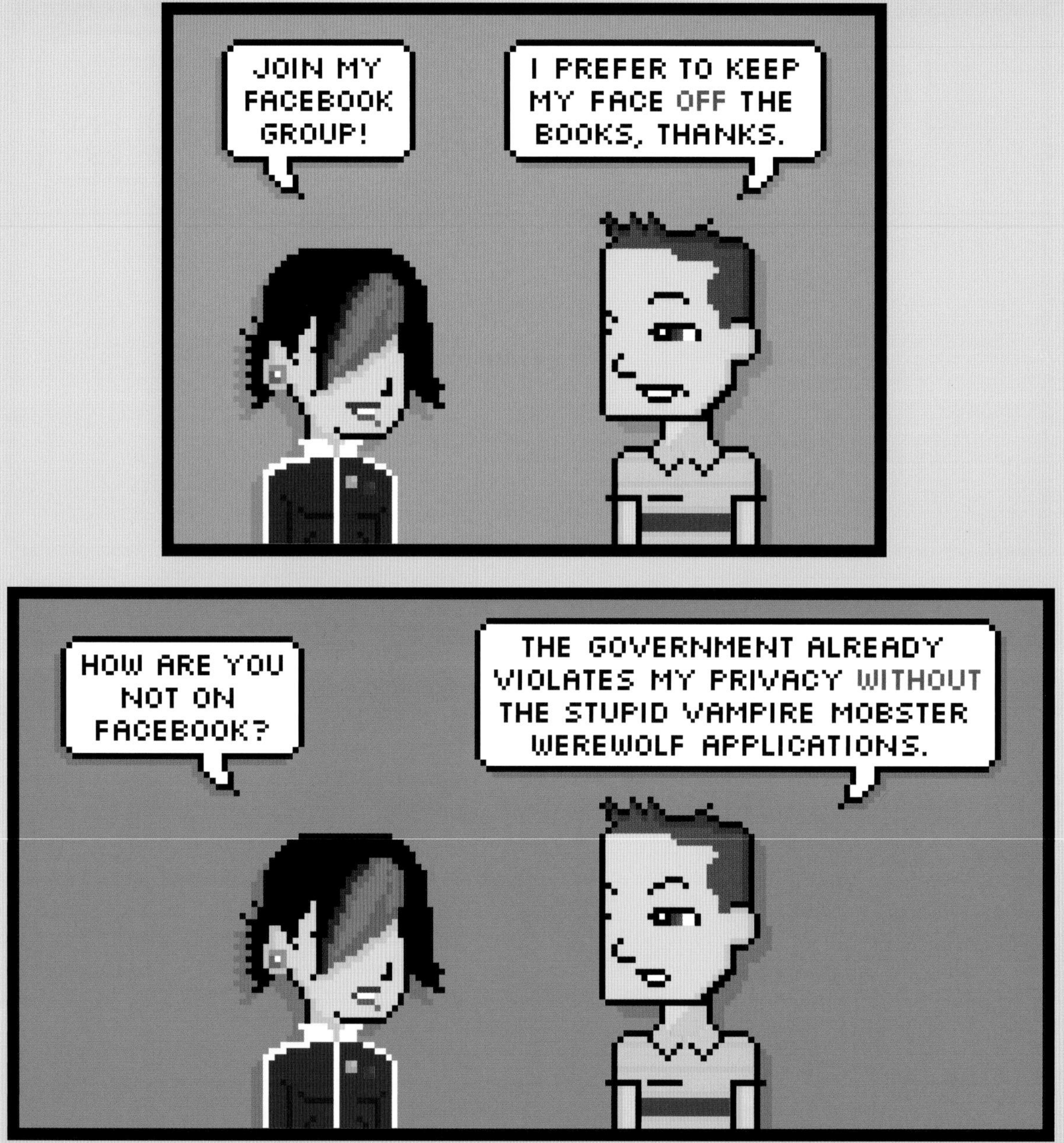
JOIN MY FACEBOOK GROUP!
I PREFER TO KEEP MY FACE OFF THE BOOKS, THANKS.
HOW ARE YOU NOT ON FACEBOOK?
THE GOVERNMENT ALREADY VIOLATES MY PRIVACY WITHOUT THE STUPID VAMPIRE MOBSTER WEREWOLF APPLICATIONS.

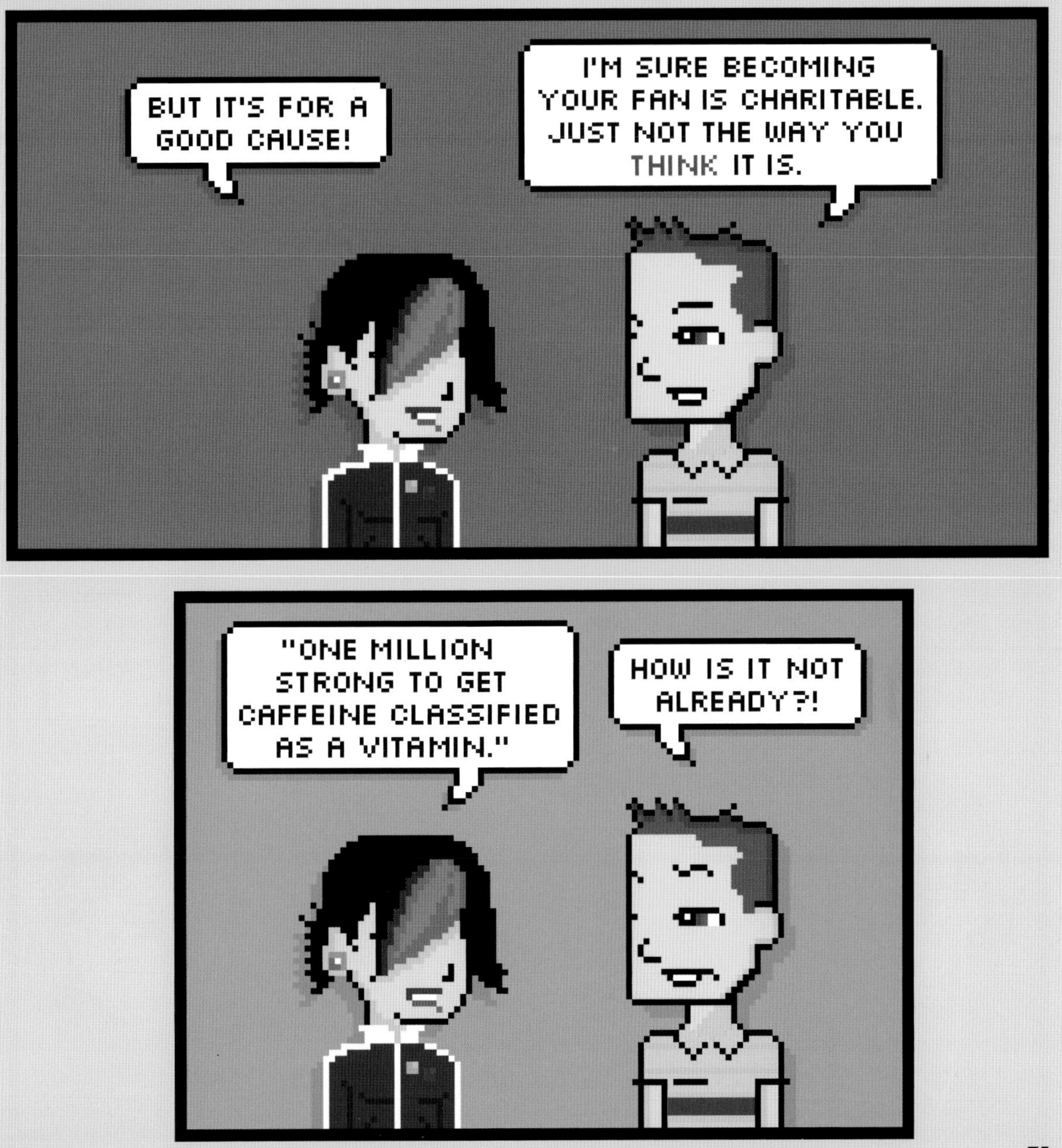
BUT IT'S FOR A GOOD CAUSE!
I'M SURE BECOMING YOUR FAN IS CHARITABLE. JUST NOT THE WAY YOU THINK IT IS.
"ONE MILLION STRONG TO GET CAFFEINE CLASSIFIED AS A VITAMIN."
HOW IS IT NOT ALREADY?!

CLICHES: ONE, GRAVITY: ZERO

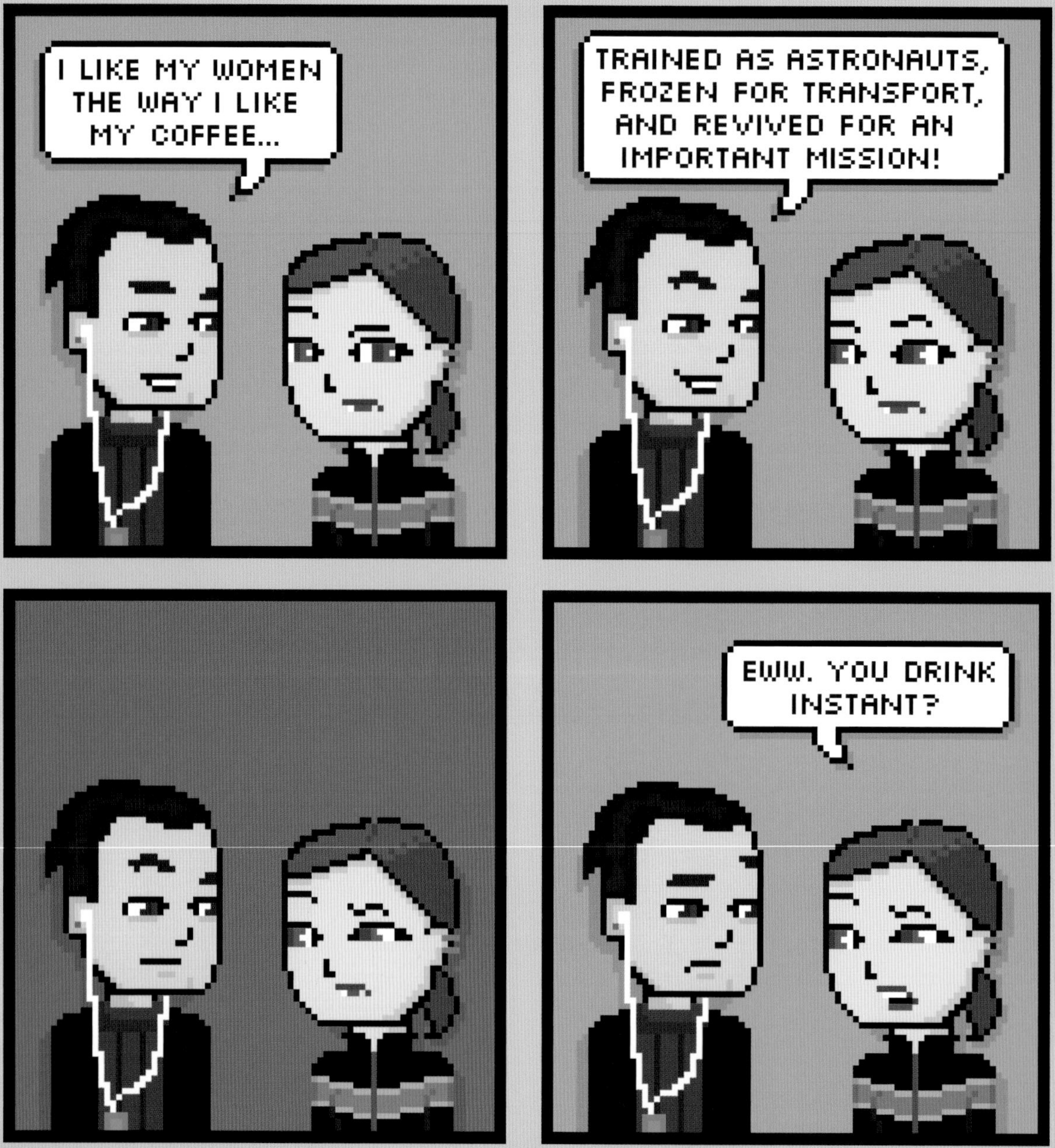
I LIKE MY WOMEN THE WAY I LIKE MY COFFEE...
TRAINED AS ASTRONAUTS, FROZEN FOR TRANSPORT, AND REVIVED FOR AN IMPORTANT MISSION!
EWW. YOU DRINK INSTANT?

INTRAVENOUS SINS

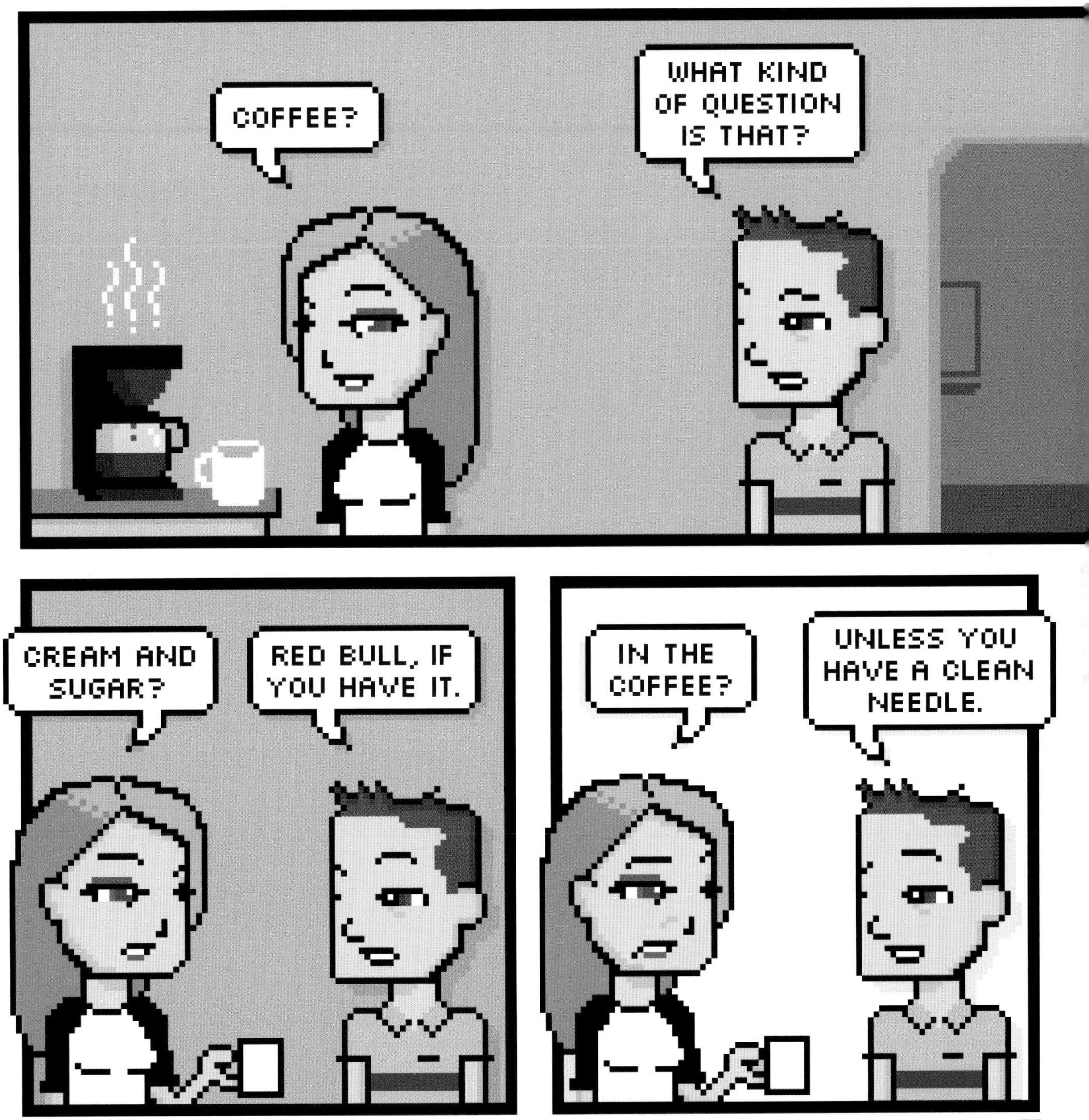
COFFEE?
WHAT KIND OF QUESTION IS THAT?
CREAM AND SUGAR?
RED BULL, IF YOU HAVE IT.
IN THE COFFEE?
UNLESS YOU HAVE A CLEAN NEEDLE.

NO EXIT

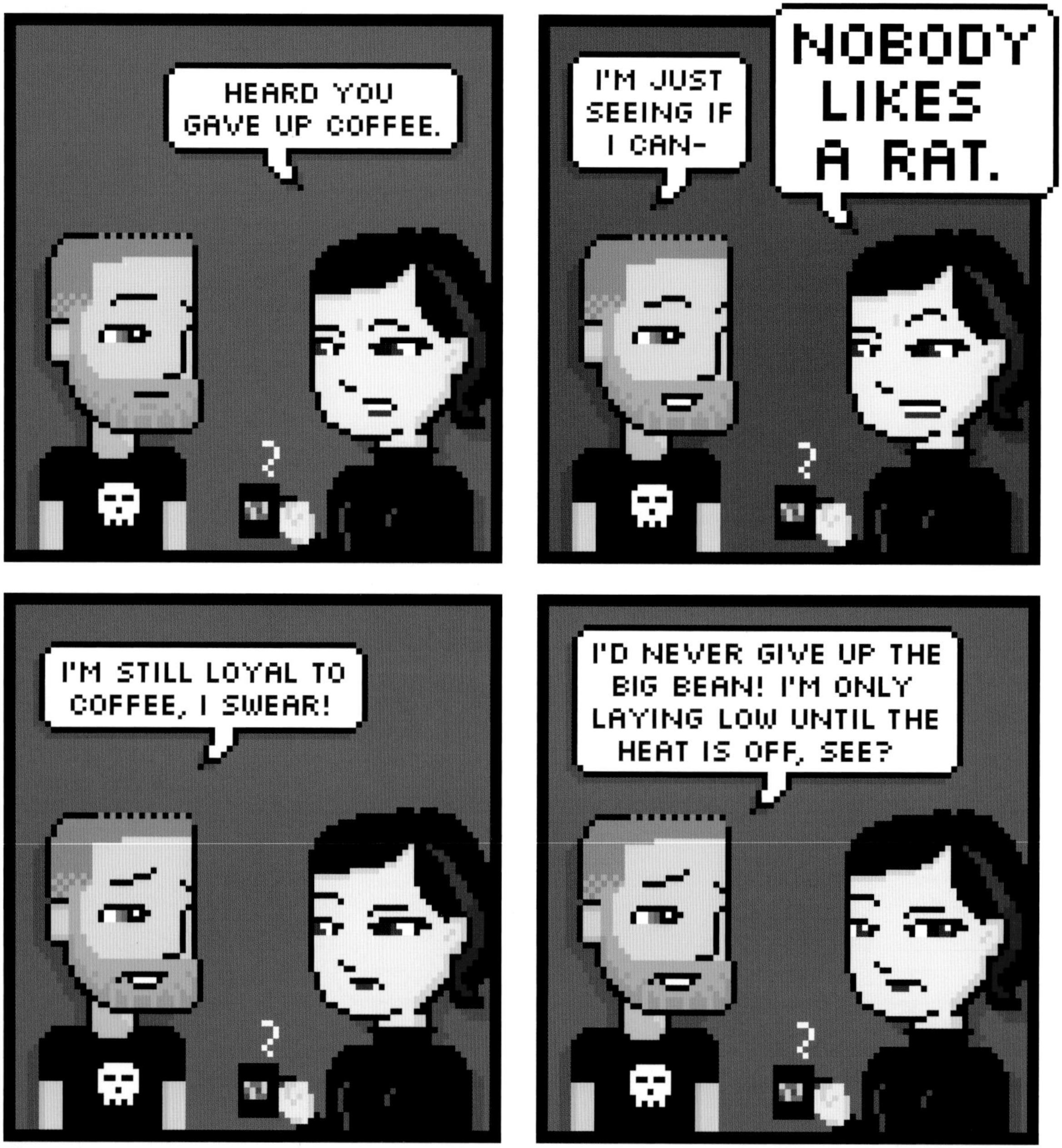
HEARD YOU GAVE UP COFFEE.
I'M JUST SEEING IF I CAN-
NOBODY LIKES A RAT.
I'M STILL LOYAL TO COFFEE, I SWEAR!
I'D NEVER GIVE UP THE BIG BEAN! I'M ONLY LAYING LOW UNTIL THE HEAT IS OFF, SEE?

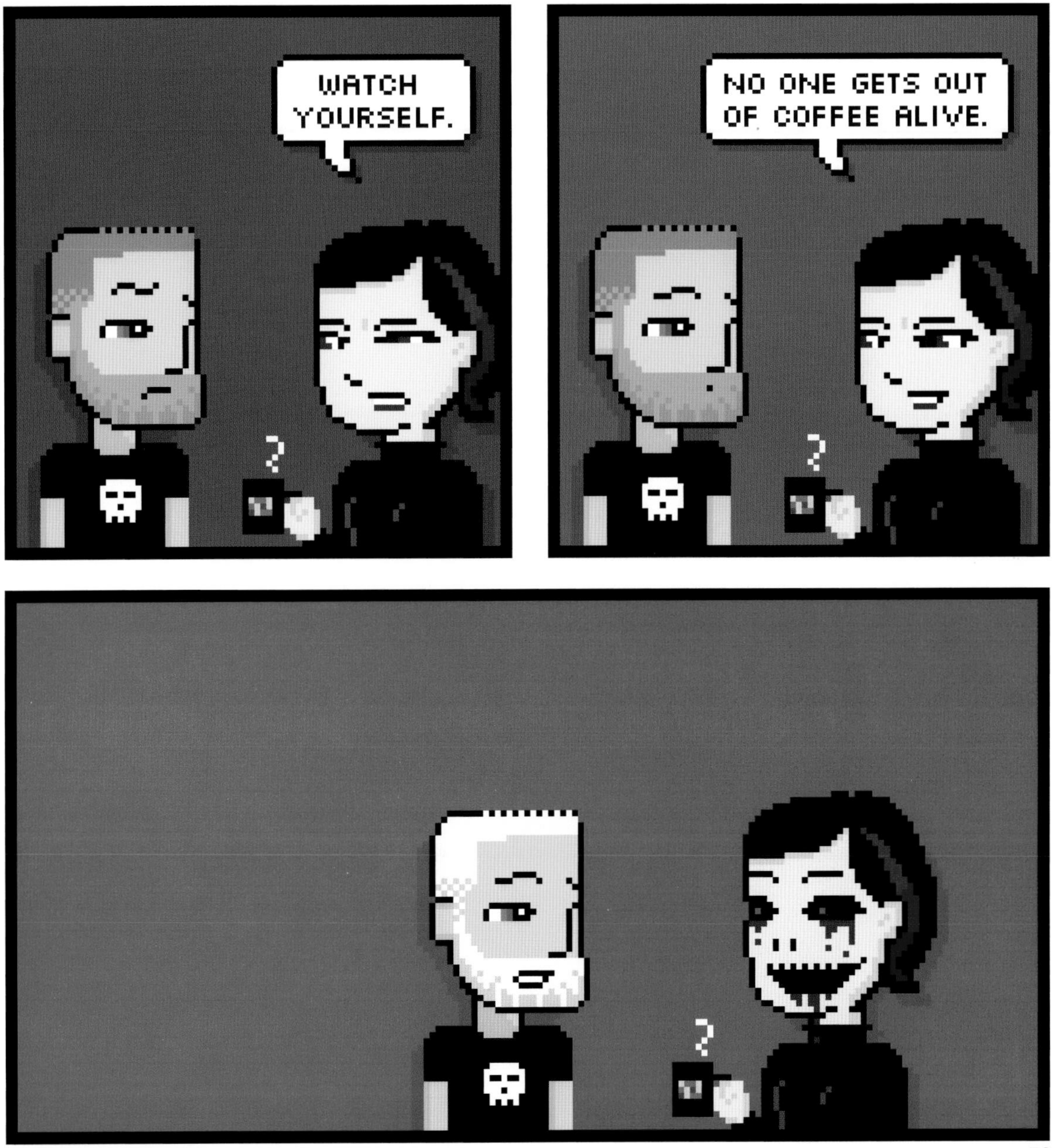
WATCH YOURSELF.
NO ONE GETS OUT OF COFFEE ALIVE.

A FRUITFUL CONVERSATION

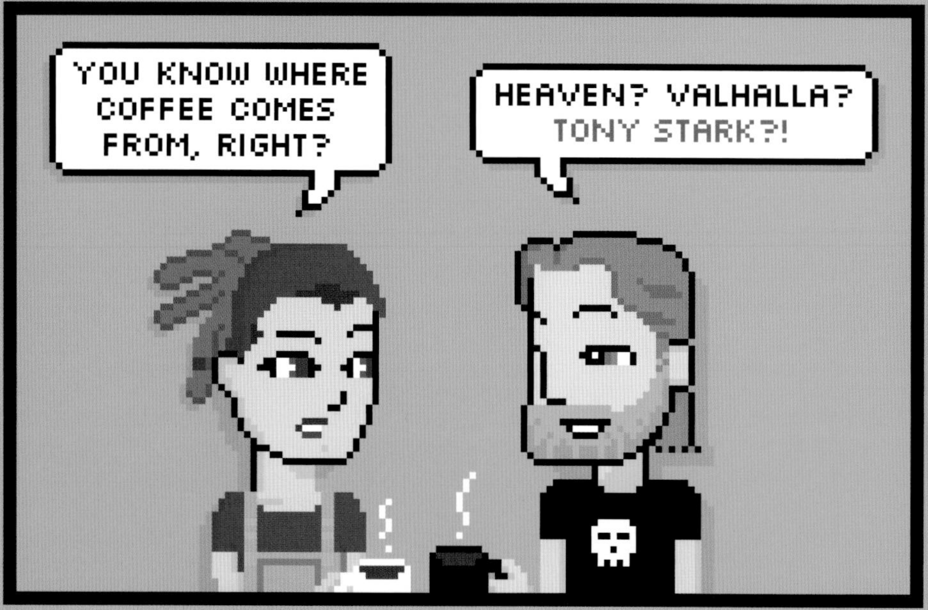
YOU KNOW WHERE COFFEE COMES FROM, RIGHT?
HEAVEN? VALHALLA? TONY STARK?!

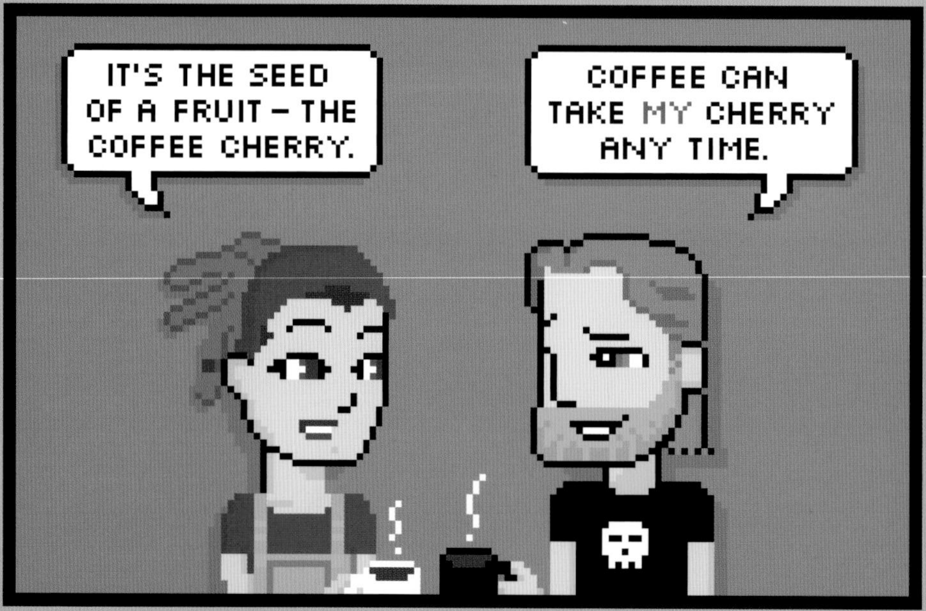
IT'S THE SEED OF A FRUIT – THE COFFEE CHERRY.
COFFEE CAN TAKE MY CHERRY ANY TIME.

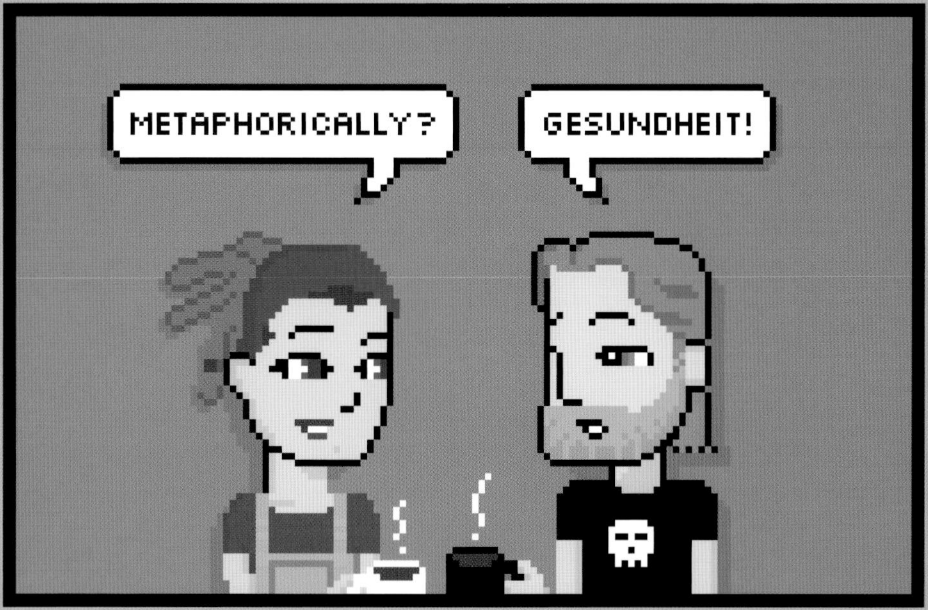
METAPHORICALLY?
GESUNDHEIT!

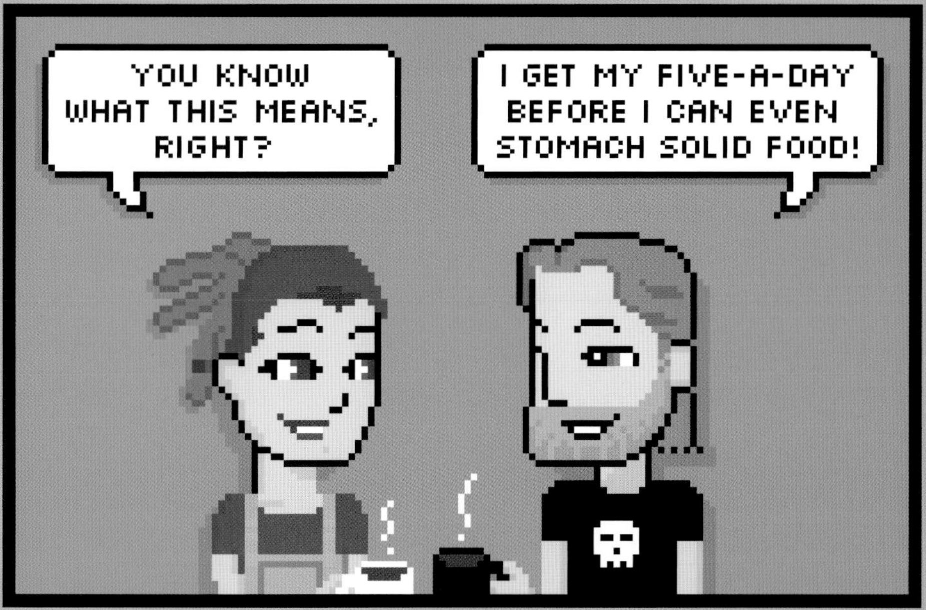
YOU KNOW WHAT THIS MEANS, RIGHT?
I GET MY FIVE-A-DAY BEFORE I CAN EVEN STOMACH SOLID FOOD!

YOU CAN'T CONTAIN MY LOVE

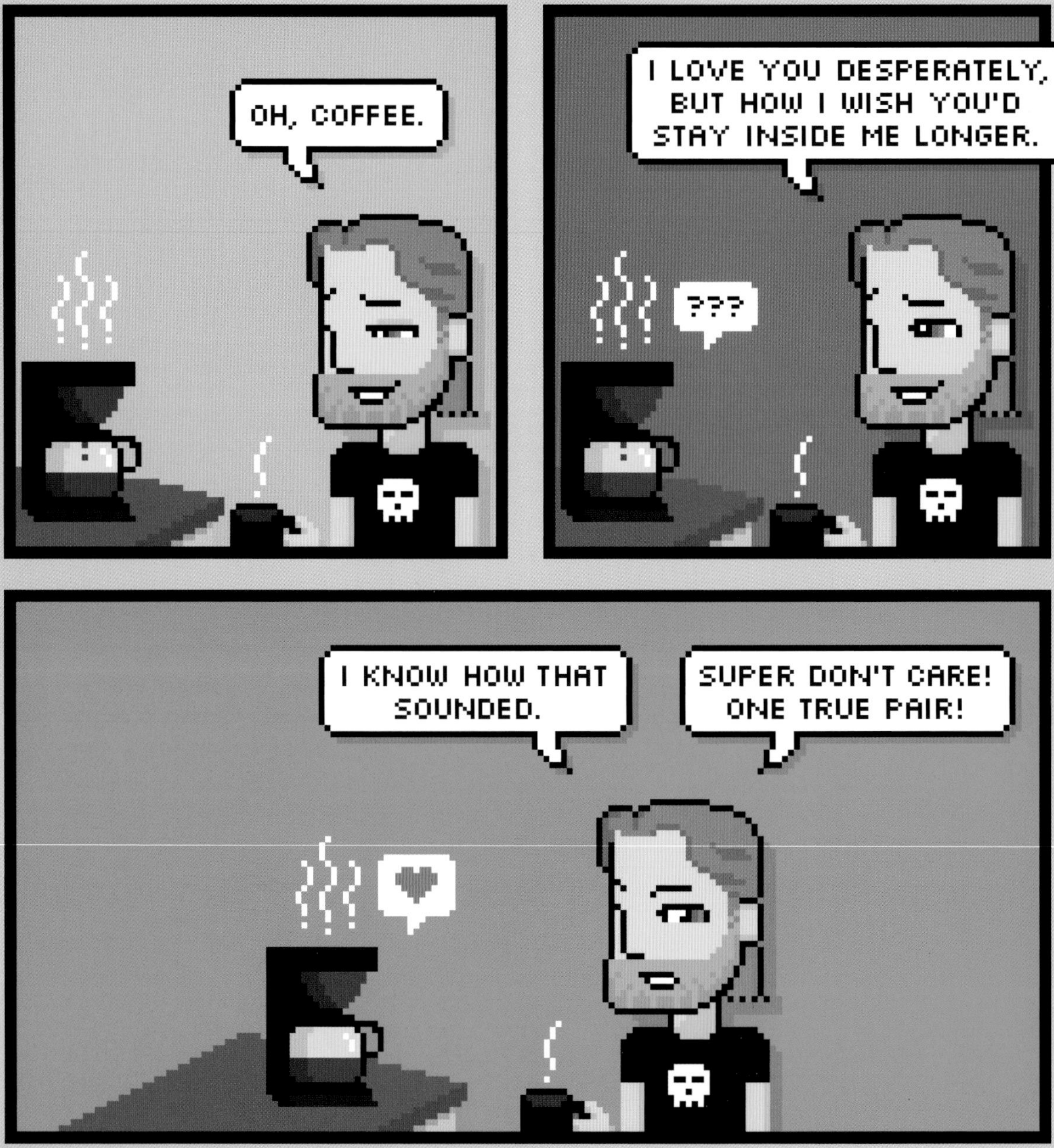
OH, COFFEE.
I LOVE YOU DESPERATELY, BUT HOW I WISH YOU'D STAY INSIDE ME LONGER.
???
I KNOW HOW THAT SOUNDED.
SUPER DON'T CARE! ONE TRUE PAIR!

GRIND YOUR OWN AND OWN YOUR GRIND

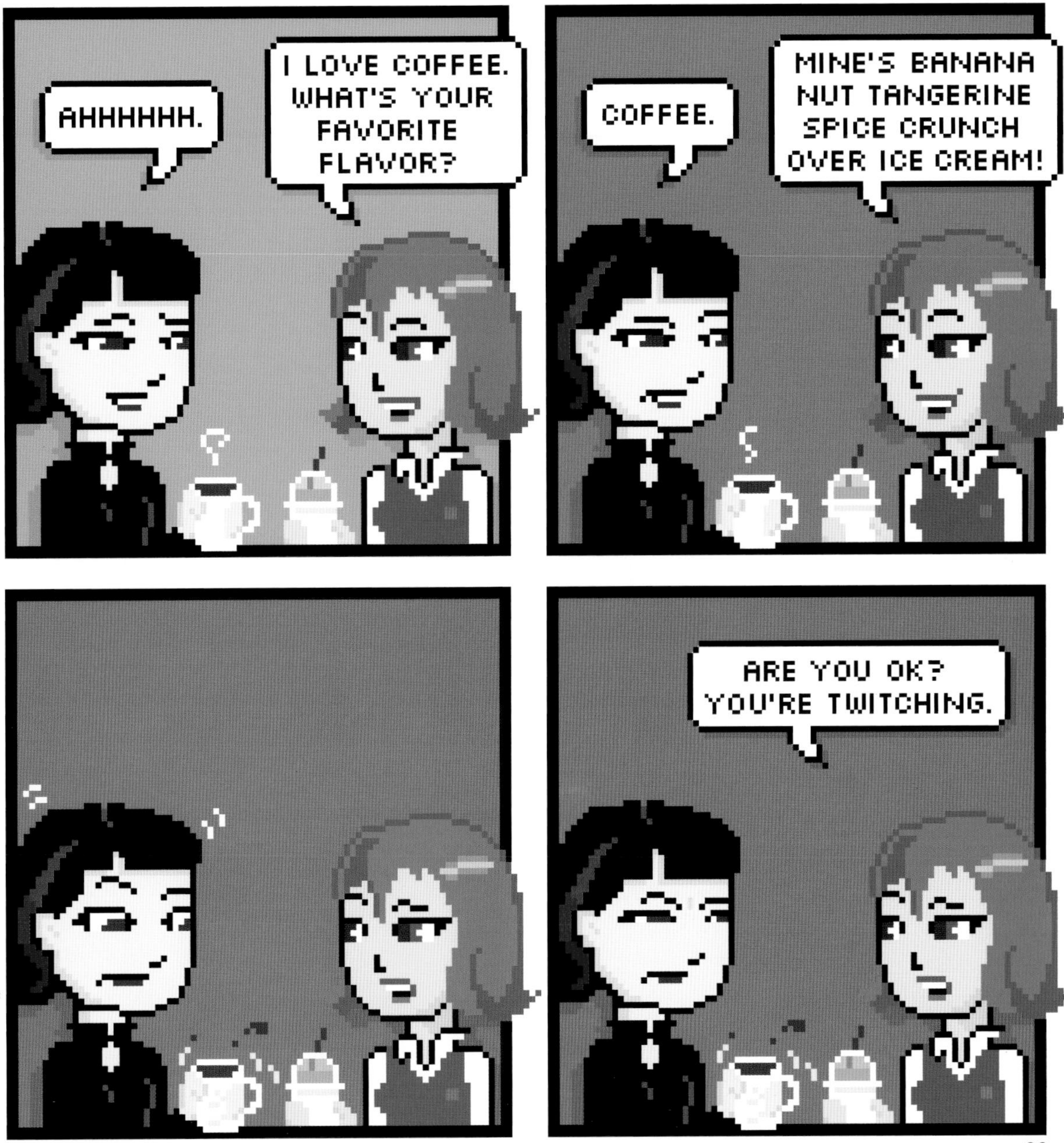

AHHHHHH.
I LOVE COFFEE. WHAT'S YOUR FAVORITE FLAVOR?
COFFEE.
MINE'S BANANA NUT TANGERINE SPICE CRUNCH OVER ICE CREAM!
ARE YOU OK? YOU'RE TWITCHING.

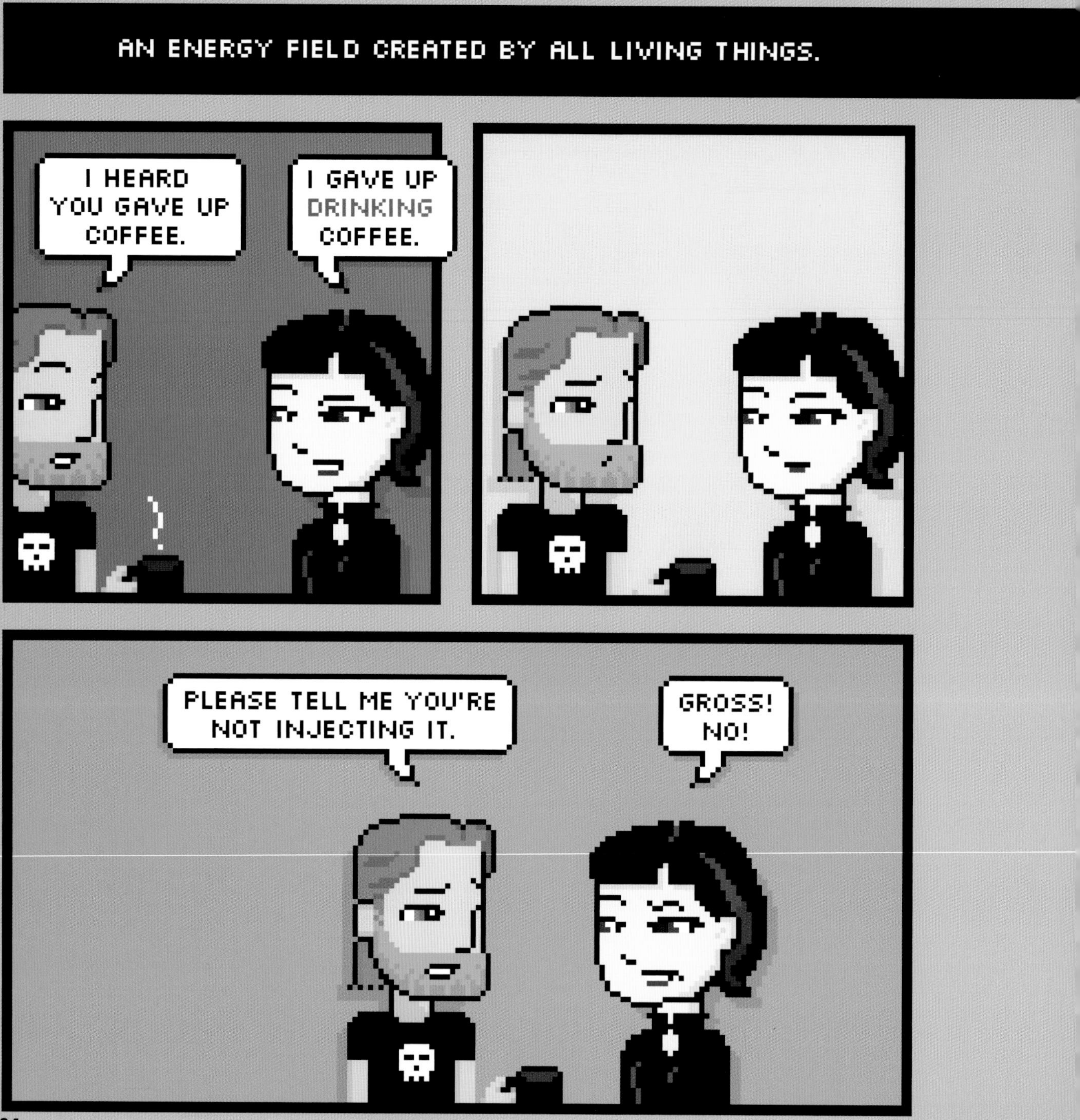
AN ENERGY FIELD CREATED BY ALL LIVING THINGS.
I HEARD YOU GAVE UP COFFEE.
I GAVE UP DRINKING COFFEE.
PLEASE TELL ME YOU'RE NOT INJECTING IT.
GROSS! NO!

IT SURROUNDS US AND PENETRATES US.

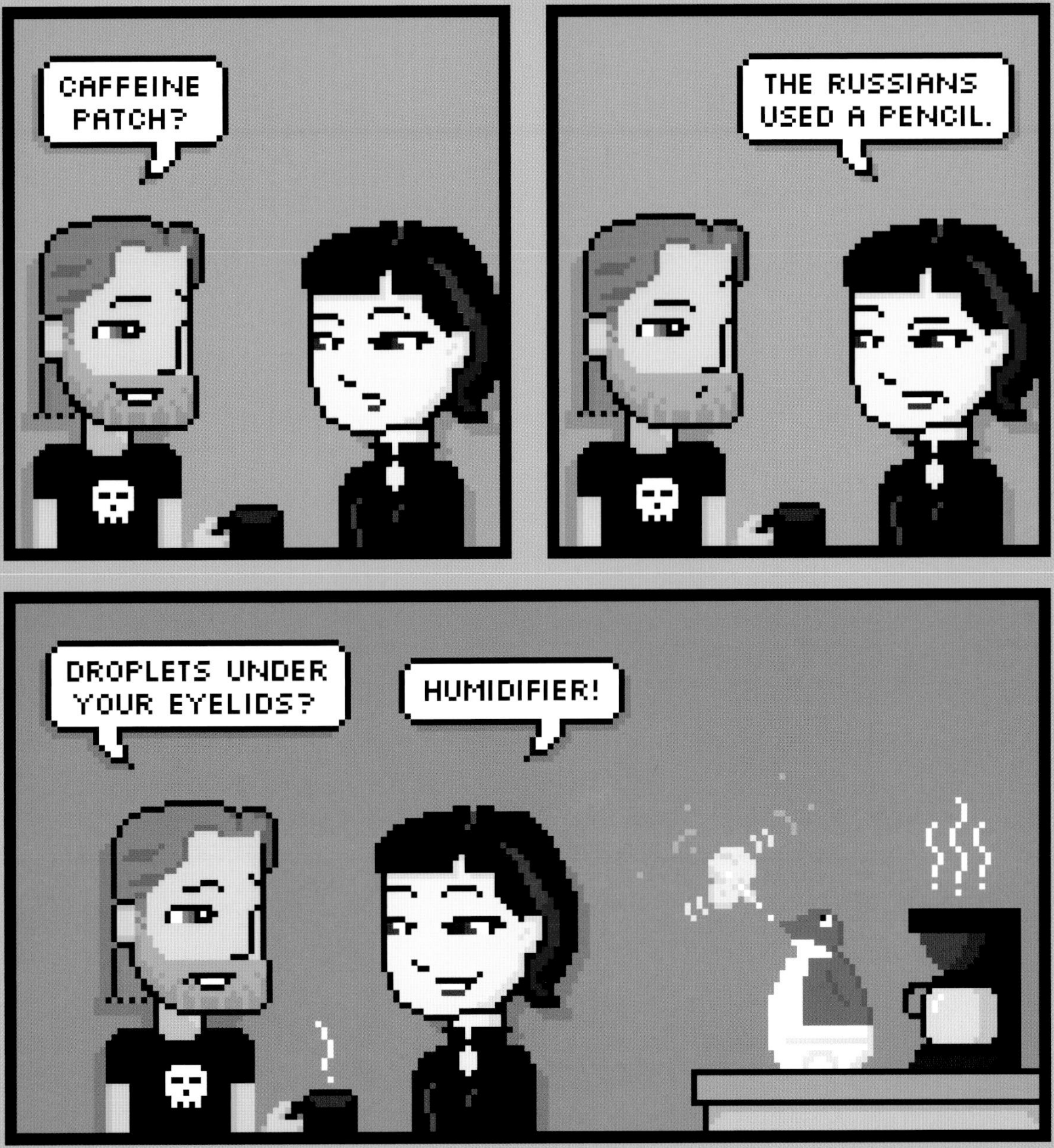
CAFFEINE PATCH?
THE RUSSIANS USED A PENCIL.
DROPLETS UNDER YOUR EYELIDS?
HUMIDIFIER!

LIKE COSTUMES FOR SYMBIOTES

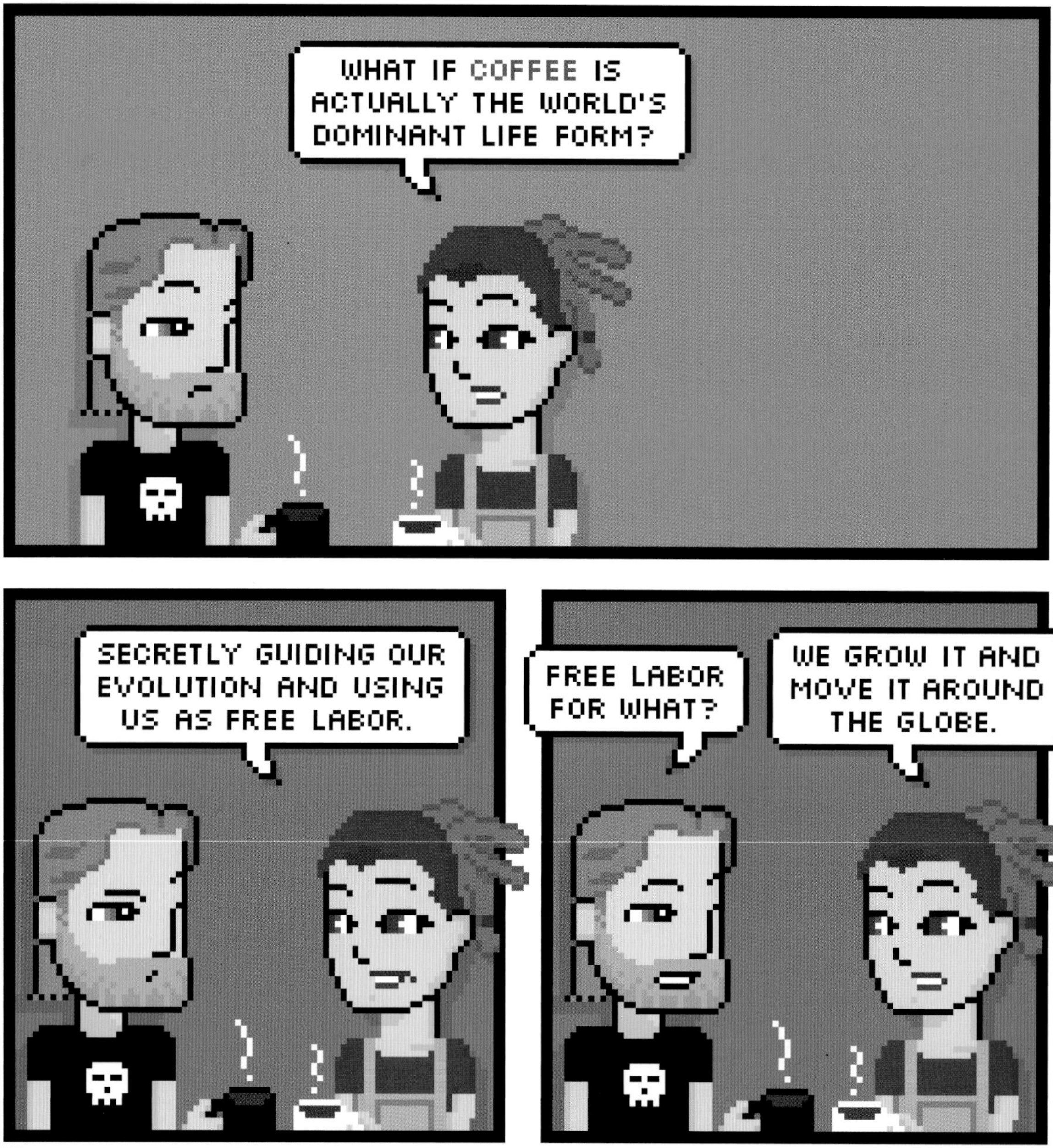
WHAT IF COFFEE IS ACTUALLY THE WORLD'S DOMINANT LIFE FORM?
SECRETLY GUIDING OUR EVOLUTION AND USING US AS FREE LABOR.
FREE LABOR FOR WHAT?
WE GROW IT AND MOVE IT AROUND THE GLOBE.

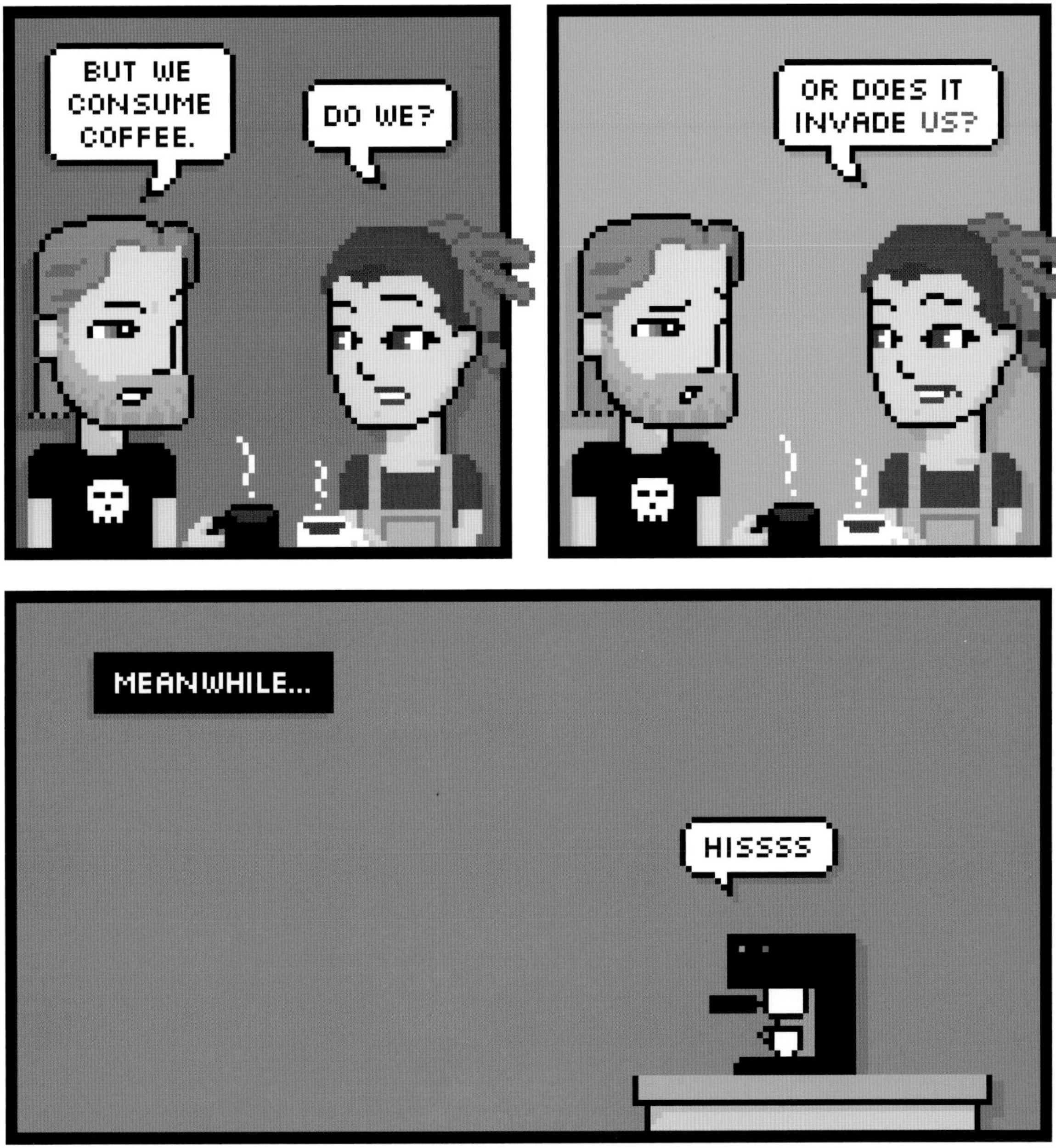
BUT WE CONSUME COFFEE.
DO WE?
OR DOES IT INVADE US?
MEANWHILE...
HISSSS

UNFILTERED

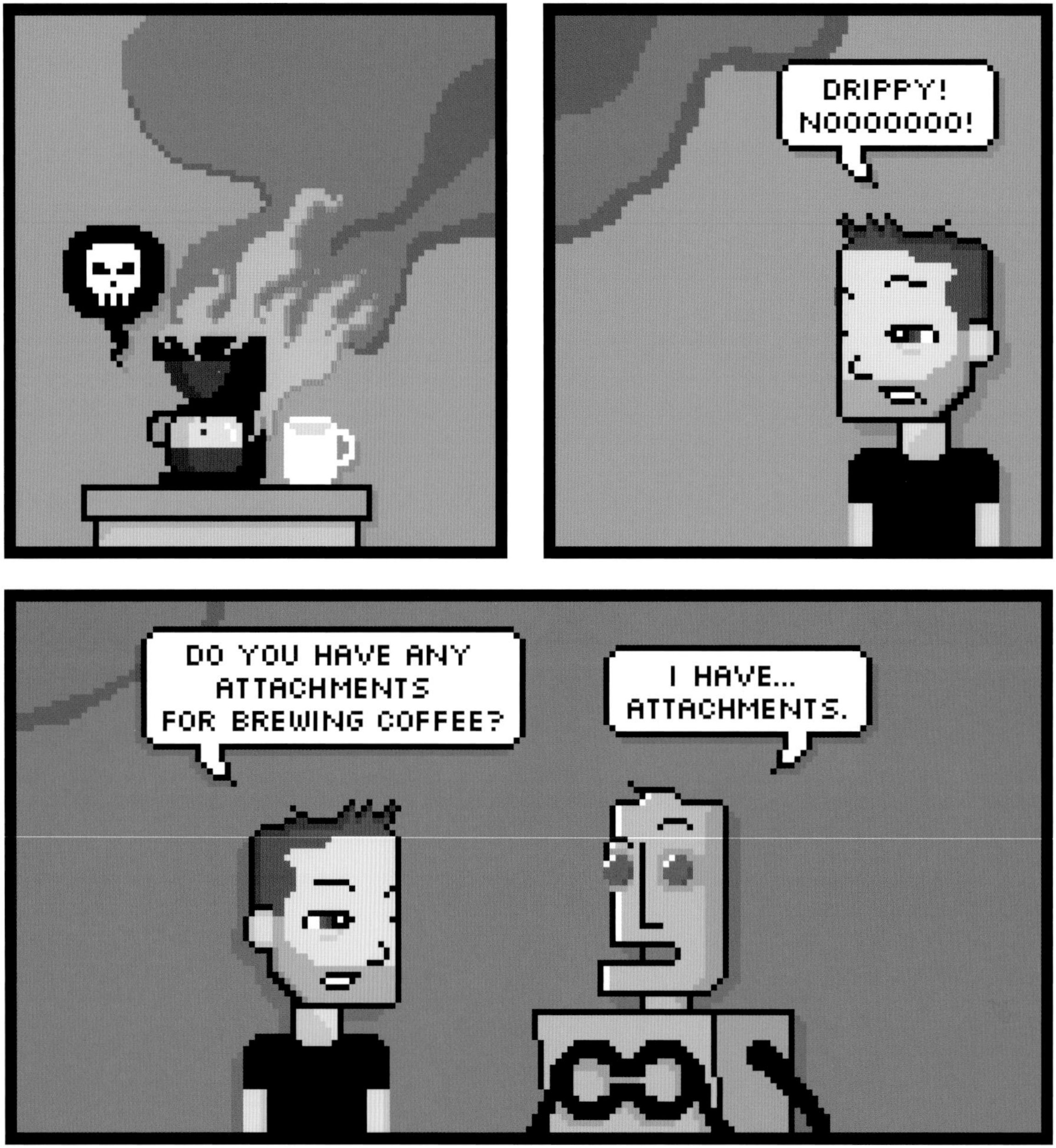
DRIPPY! NOOOOOOO!
DO YOU HAVE ANY ATTACHMENTS FOR BREWING COFFEE?
I HAVE... ATTACHMENTS.

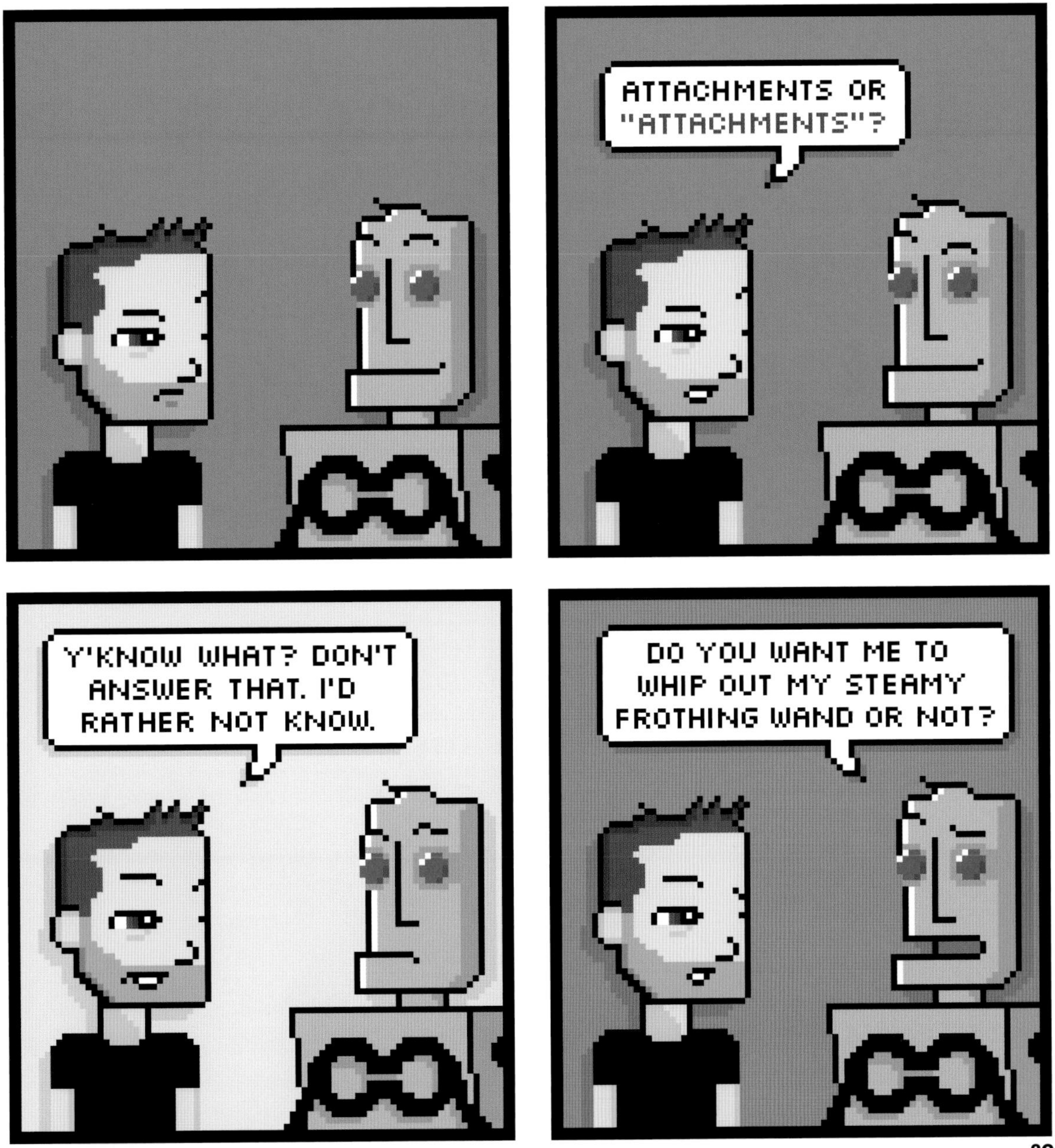
ATTACHMENTS OR "ATTACHMENTS"?
Y'KNOW WHAT? DON'T ANSWER THAT. I'D RATHER NOT KNOW.
DO YOU WANT ME TO WHIP OUT MY STEAMY FROTHING WAND OR NOT?

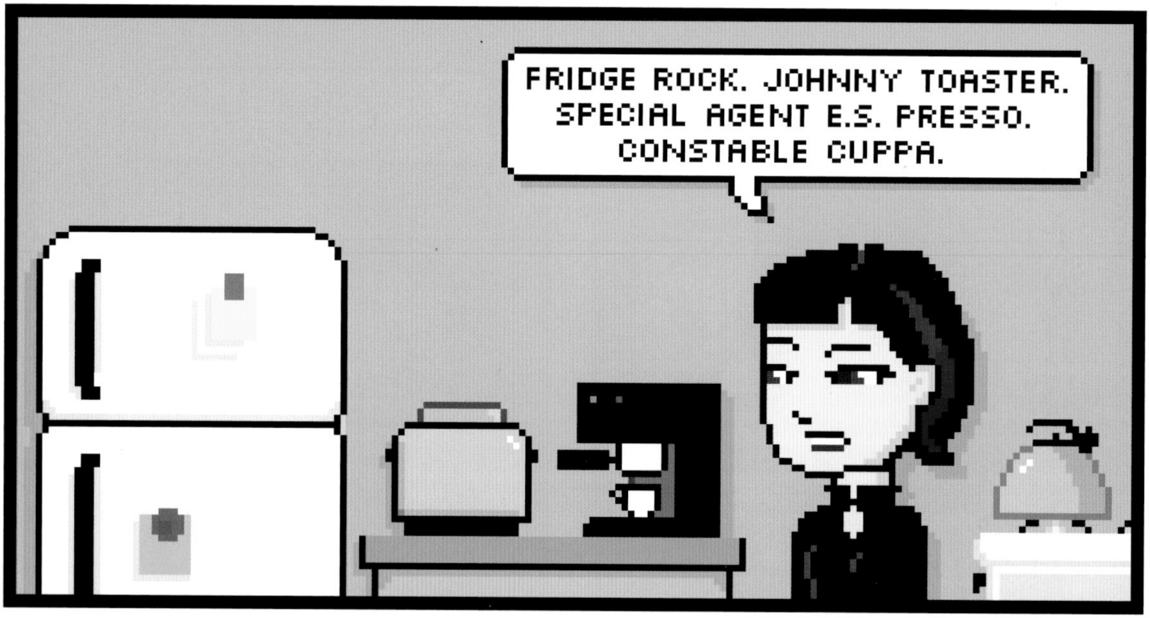
FRIDGE ROCK. JOHNNY TOASTER. SPECIAL AGENT E.S. PRESSO. CONSTABLE CUPPA.

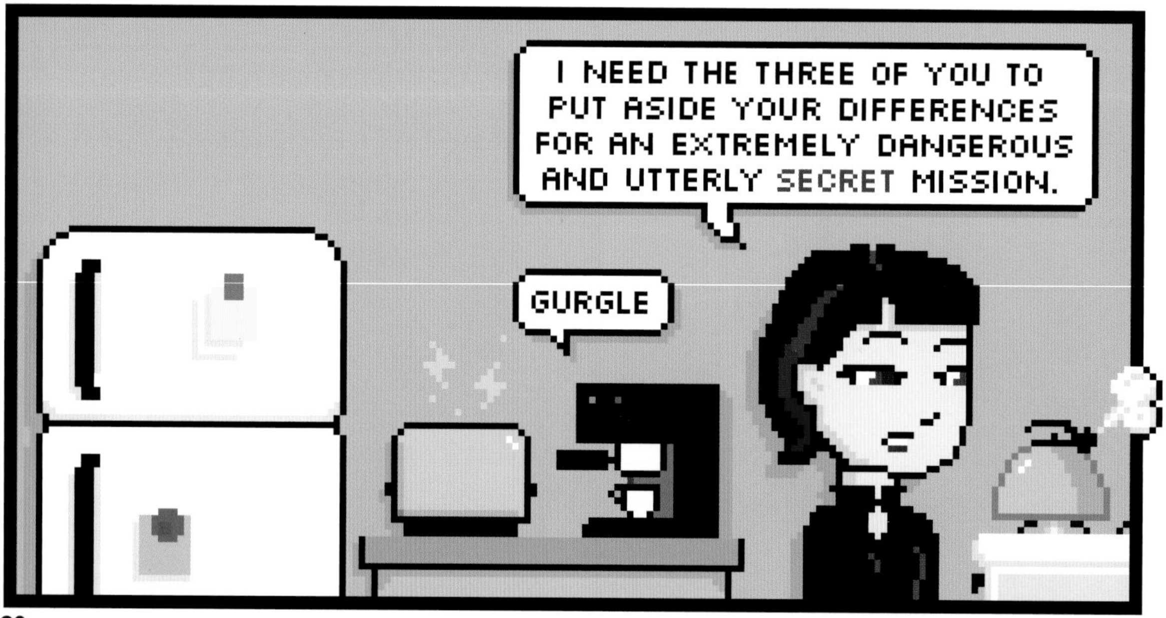
I NEED THE THREE OF YOU TO PUT ASIDE YOUR DIFFERENCES FOR AN EXTREMELY DANGEROUS AND UTTERLY SECRET MISSION.
GURGLE

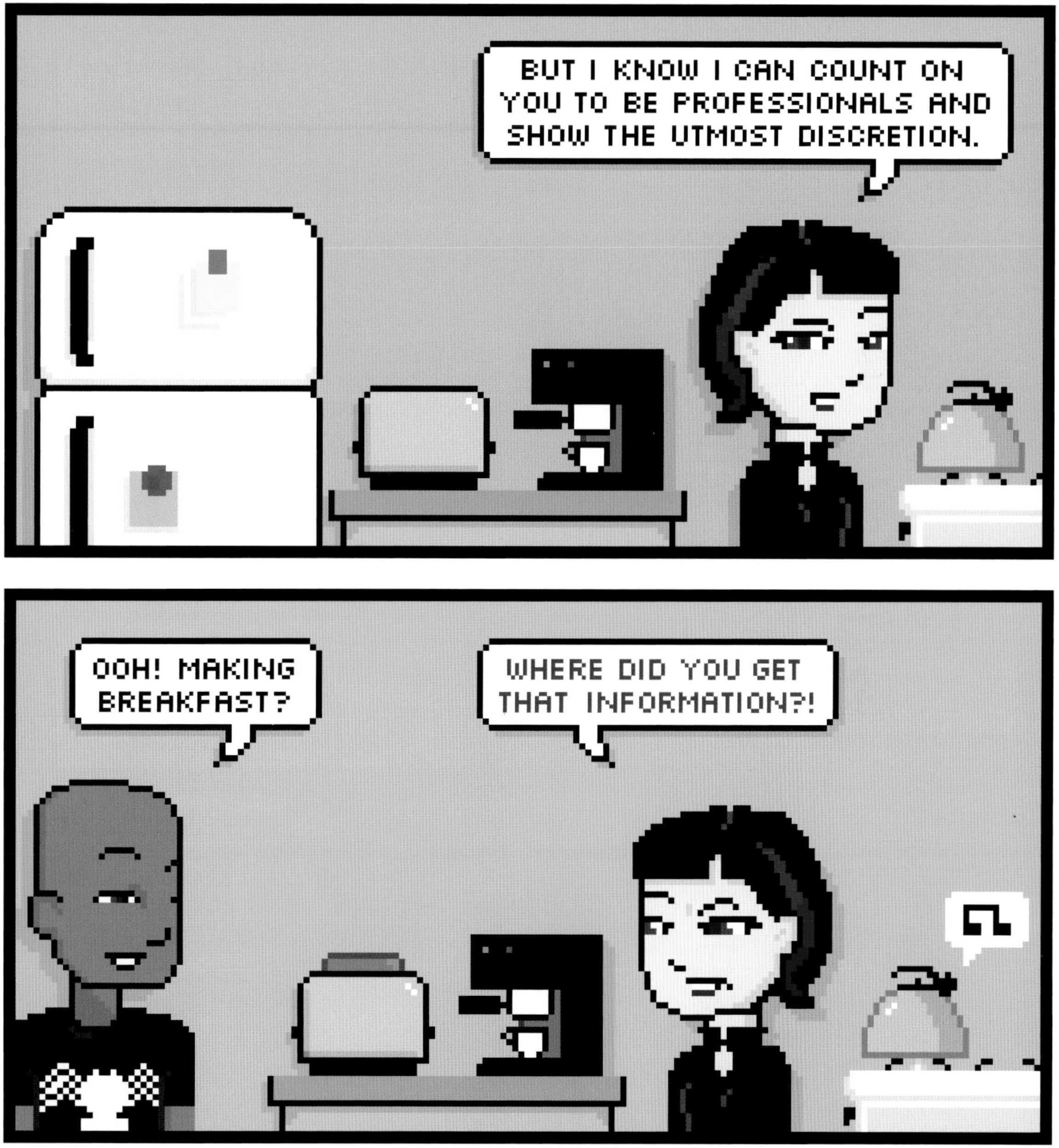
BUT I KNOW I CAN COUNT ON YOU TO BE PROFESSIONALS AND SHOW THE UTMOST DISCRETION.
OOH! MAKING BREAKFAST?
WHERE DID YOU GET THAT INFORMATION?!

BREW OF THE DAMNED

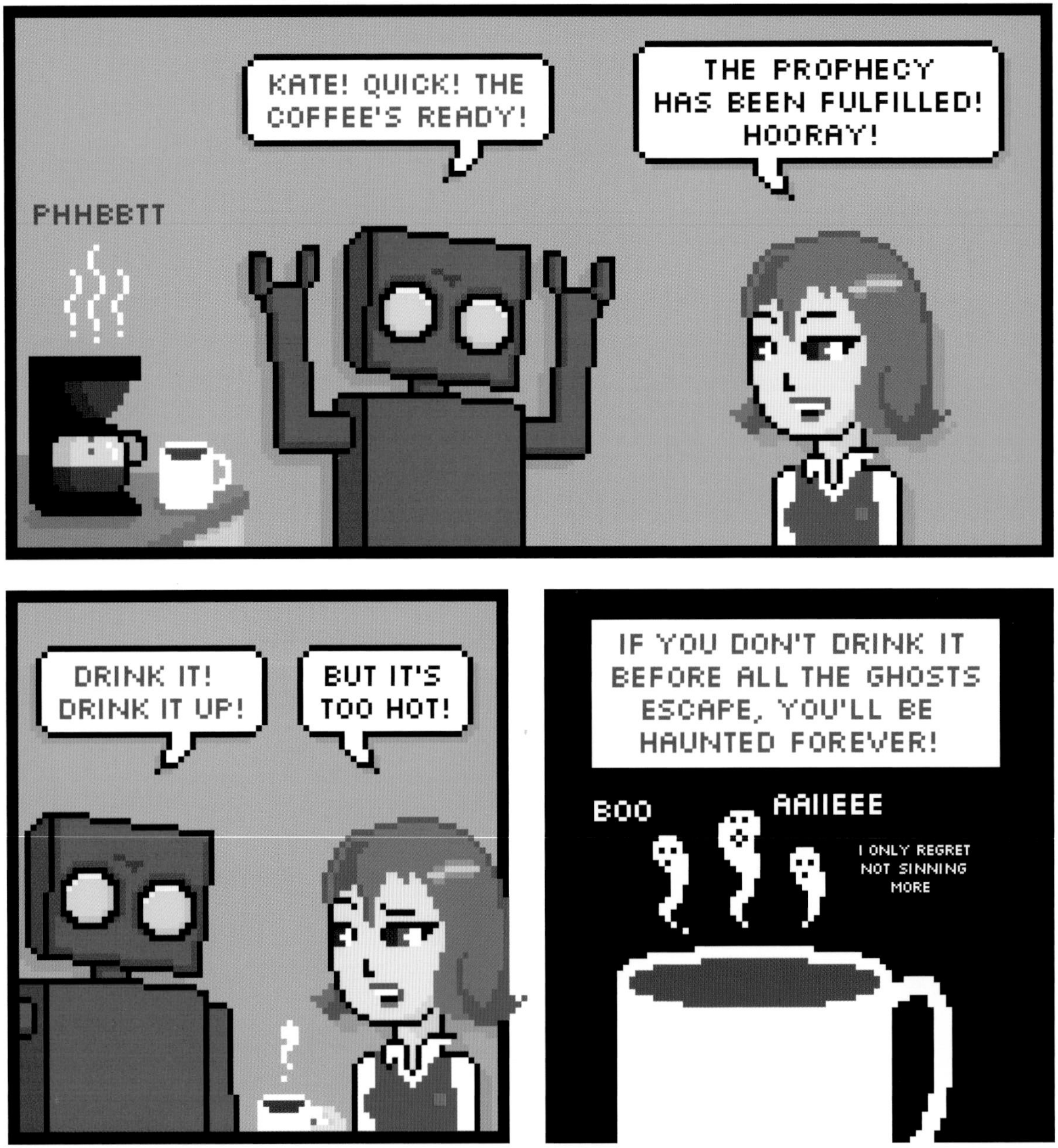
KATE! QUICK! THE COFFEE'S READY!
THE PROPHECY HAS BEEN FULFILLED! HOORAY!
PHHBBTT
DRINK IT! DRINK IT UP!
BUT IT'S TOO HOT!
IF YOU DON'T DRINK IT BEFORE ALL THE GHOSTS ESCAPE, YOU'LL BE HAUNTED FOREVER!
BOO
AAIIEEE
I ONLY REGRET NOT SINNING MORE

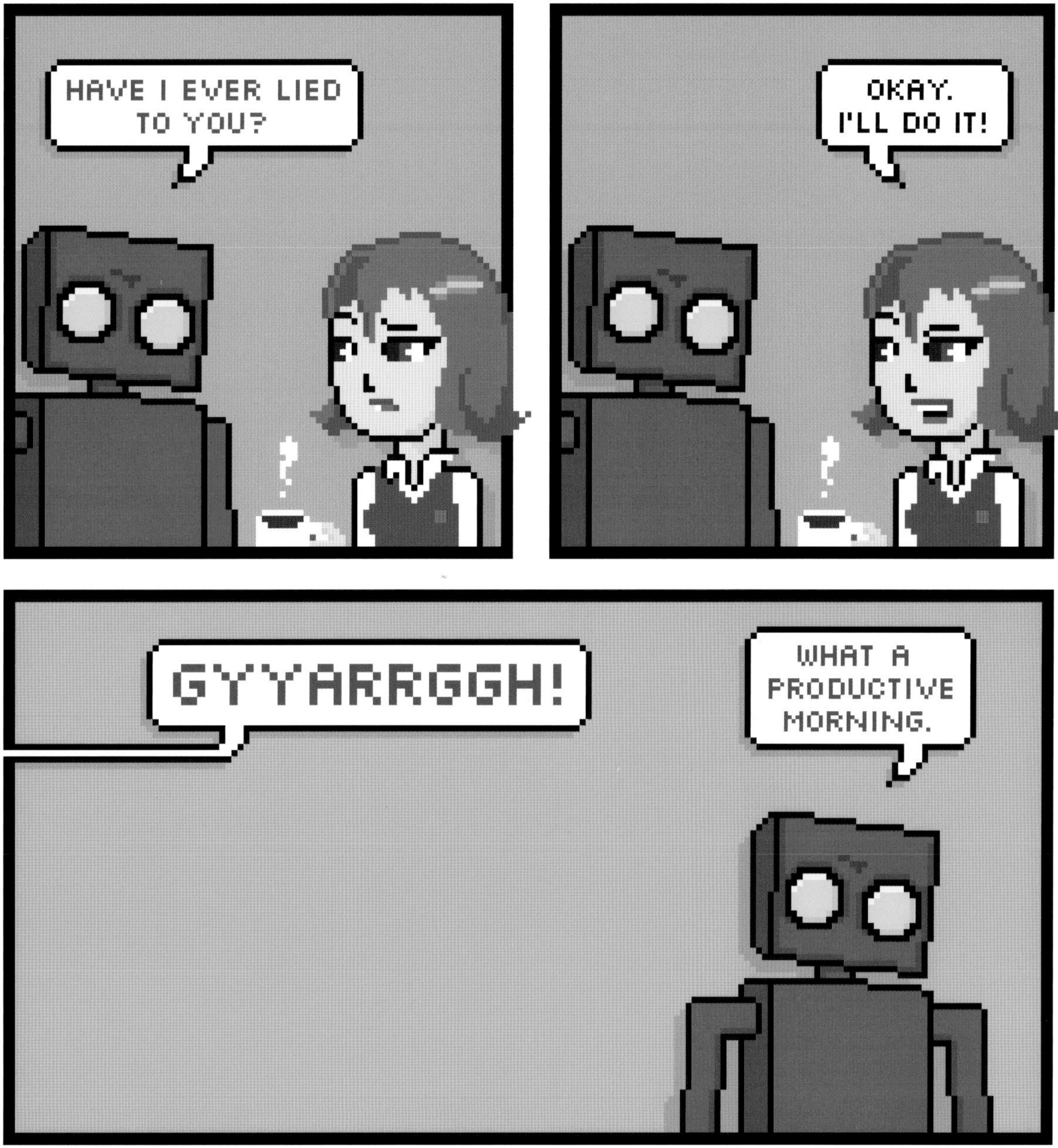
HAVE I EVER LIED TO YOU?
OKAY. I'LL DO IT!
GYYARRGGH!
WHAT A PRODUCTIVE MORNING.

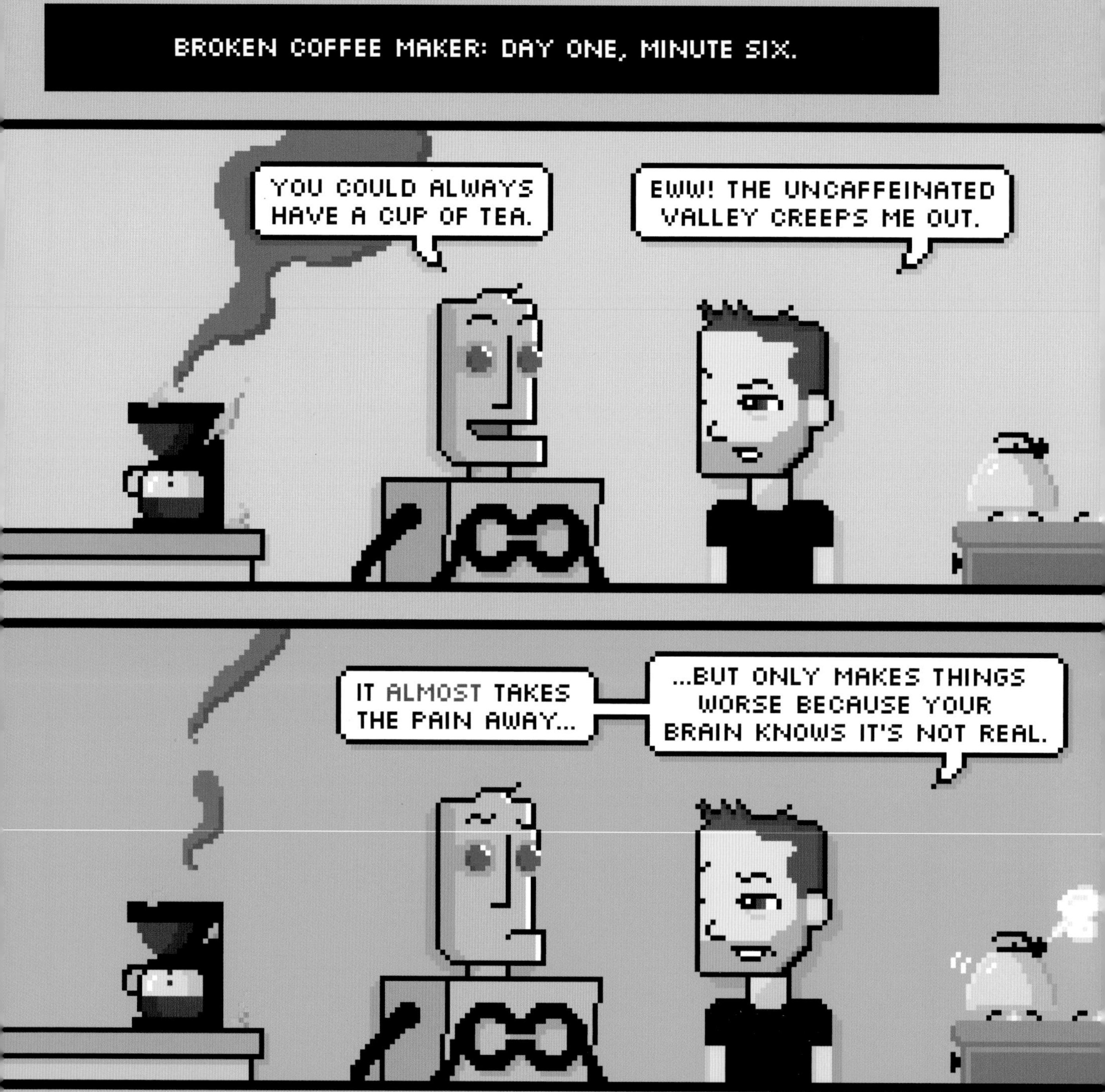
BROKEN COFFEE MAKER: DAY ONE, MINUTE SIX.
YOU COULD ALWAYS HAVE A CUP OF TEA.
EWW! THE UNCAFFEINATED VALLEY CREEPS ME OUT.
IT ALMOST TAKES THE PAIN AWAY...
...BUT ONLY MAKES THINGS WORSE BECAUSE YOUR BRAIN KNOWS IT'S NOT REAL.

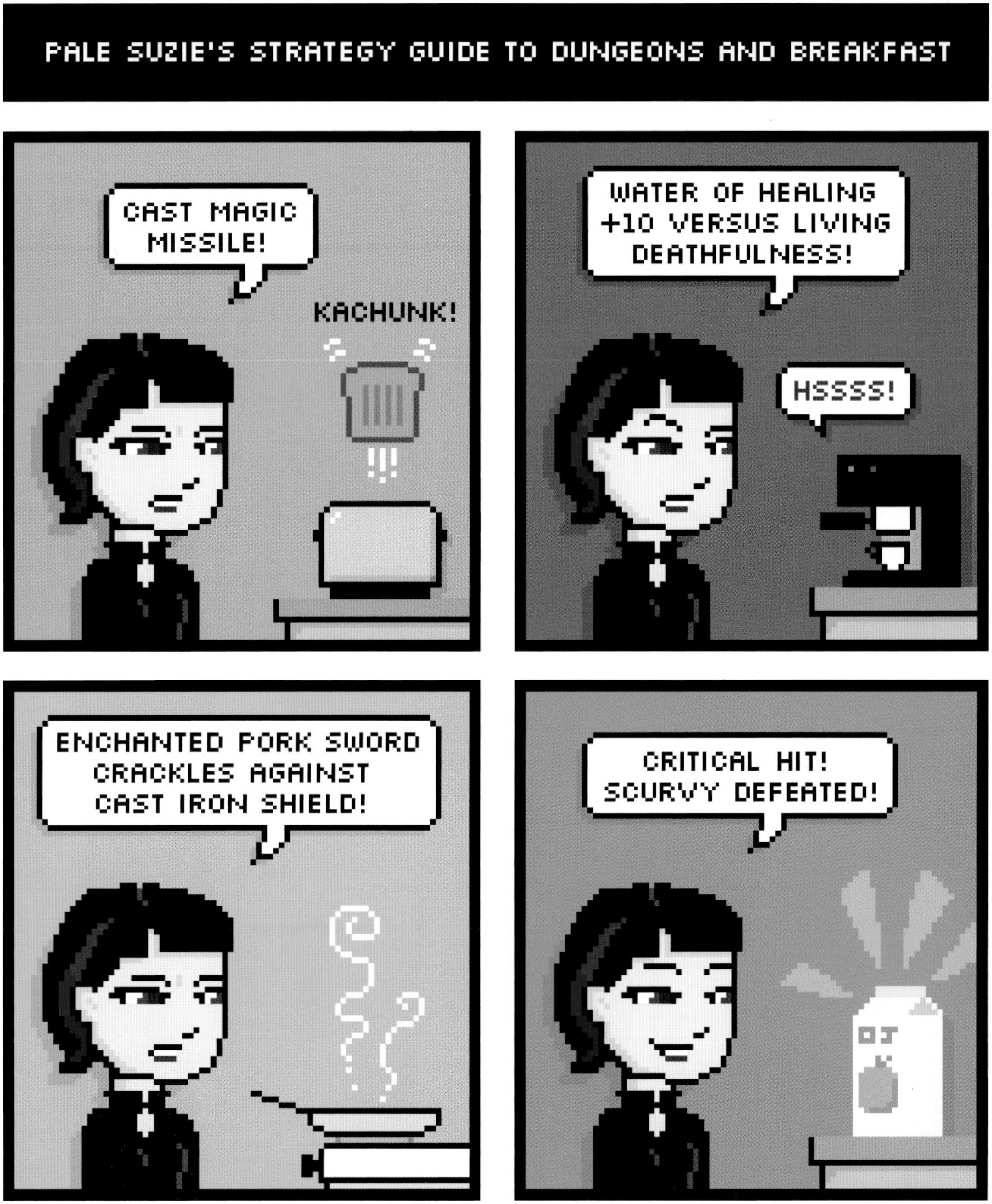
PALE SUZIE'S STRATEGY GUIDE TO DUNGEONS AND BREAKFAST
CAST MAGIC MISSILE!
KACHUNK!
WATER OF HEALING +10 VERSUS LIVING DEATHFULNESS!
HSSSS!
ENCHANTED PORK SWORD CRACKLES AGAINST CAST IRON SHIELD!
CRITICAL HIT! SCURVY DEFEATED!
OJ

SIX REASONS YOU DESERVE A CUP OF COFFEE RIGHT NOW:

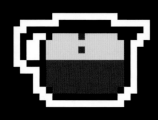

ANY AMOUNT OF TIME HAS PASSED.

YOU'VE FALLEN BEHIND YOUR IDEALIZED STANDARD OF PRODUCTIVITY THAT HAS ZERO BASIS IN REALITY.

YOUR BODY HAS FOOLISHLY SQUANDERED ITS NATURAL CAFFEINE RESERVES.

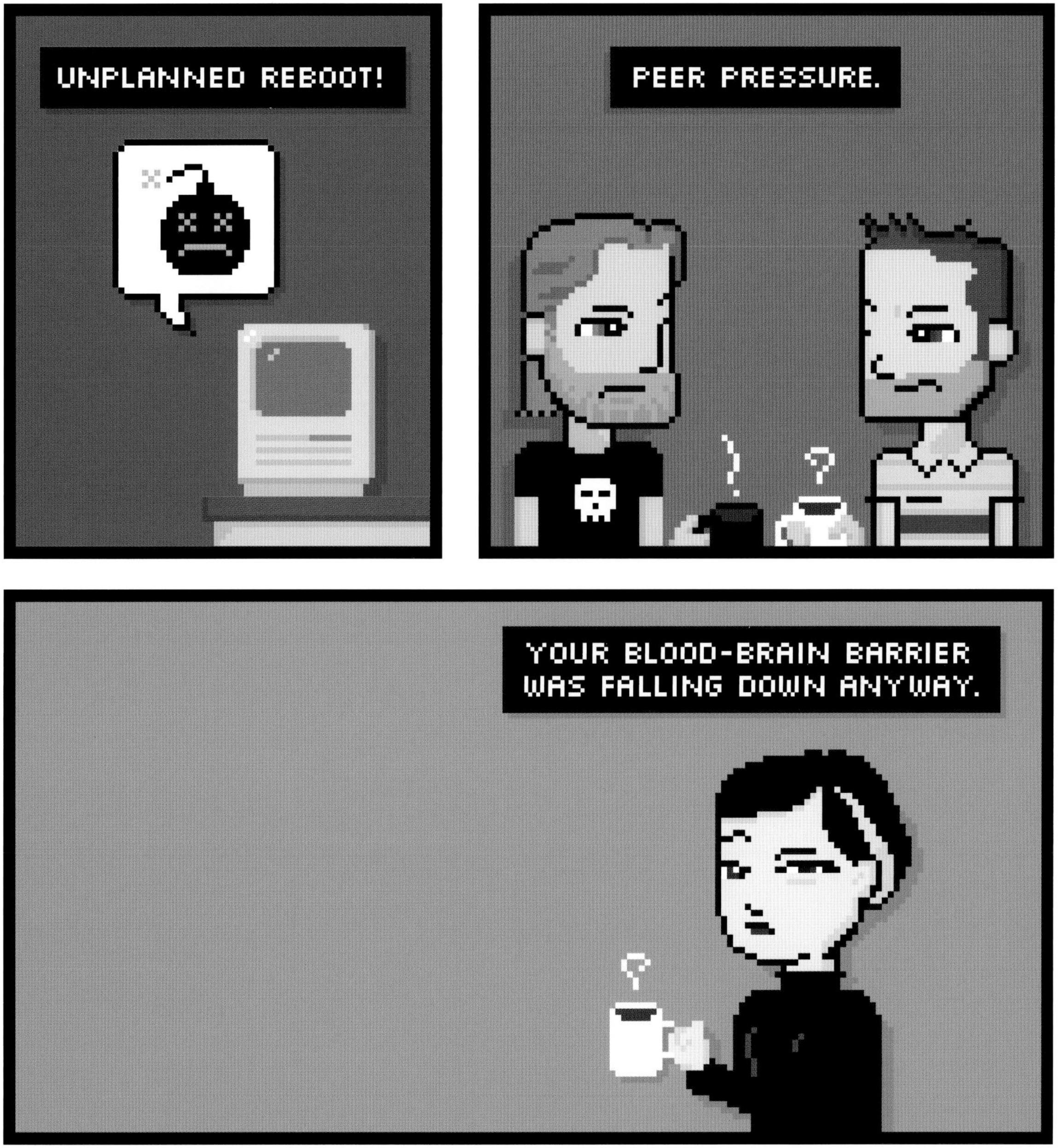
UNPLANNED REBOOT!
PEER PRESSURE.
YOUR BLOOD-BRAIN BARRIER WAS FALLING DOWN ANYWAY.

THE DAY HIS RAGE MADE SENSE

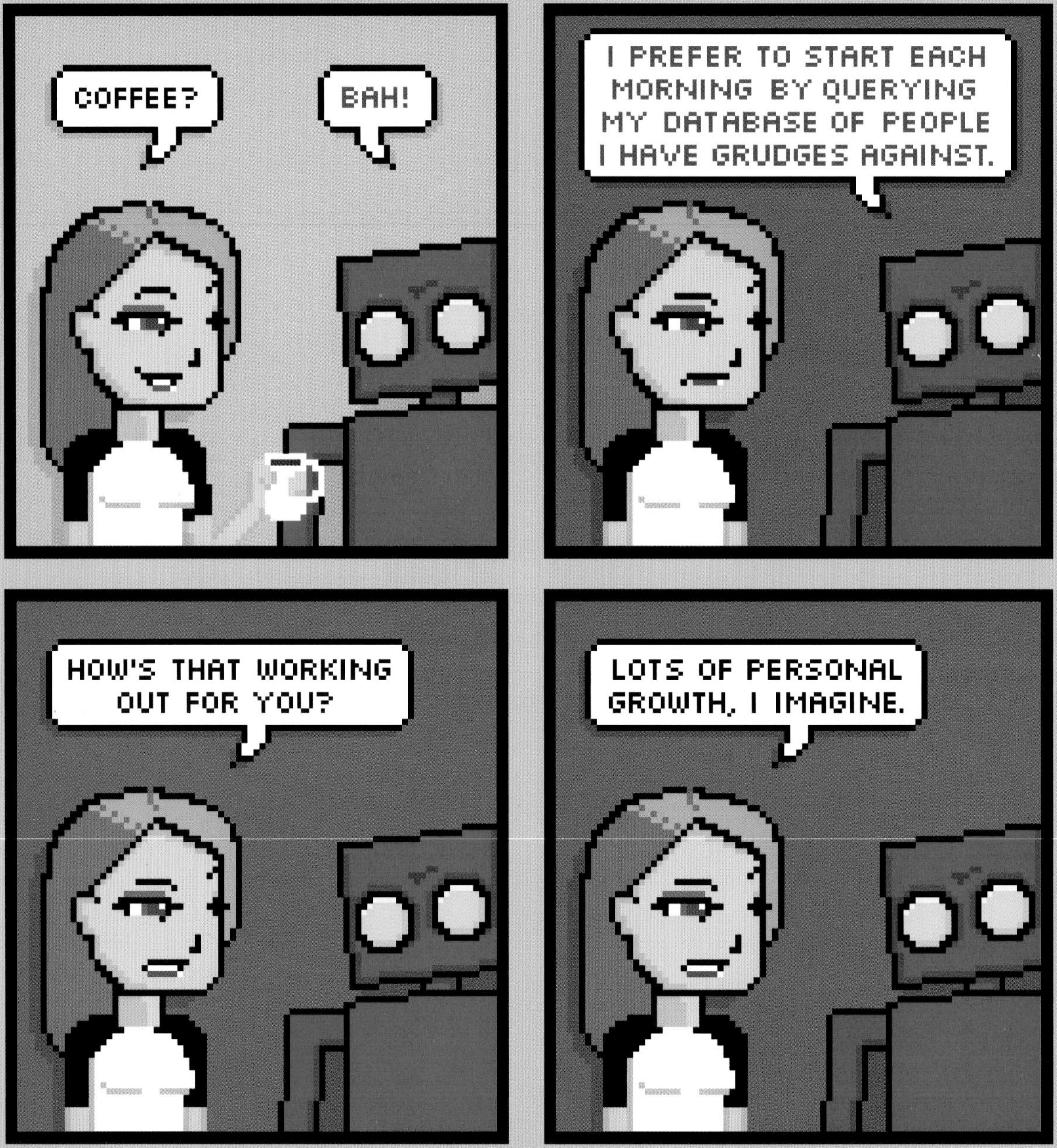
COFFEE?
BAH!
I PREFER TO START EACH MORNING BY QUERYING MY DATABASE OF PEOPLE I HAVE GRUDGES AGAINST.
HOW'S THAT WORKING OUT FOR YOU?
LOTS OF PERSONAL GROWTH, I IMAGINE.

I CAN PROCESS ONE HUNDRED NINETY THOUSAND, THREE HUNDRED AND TWELVE JERKS IN UNDER THIRTY SECONDS!
YOU WASTE YOUR ENERGY WITH AS LITTLE WASTED ENERGY AS POSSIBLE?
ONE HUNDRED NINETY THOUSAND, THREE HUNDRED AND THIRTEEN.

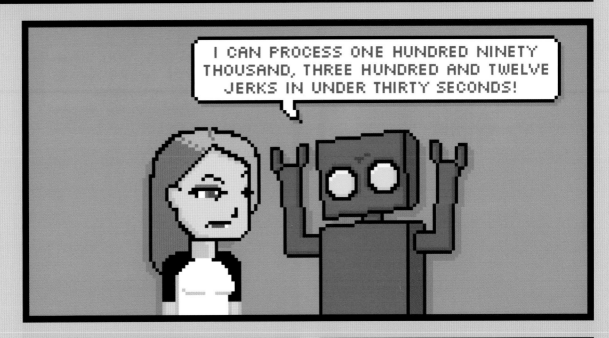

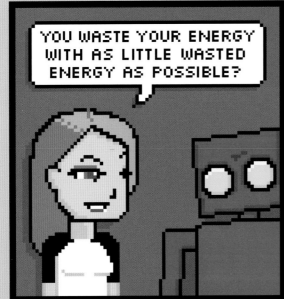

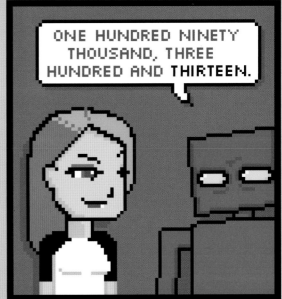

FRESHLY BREWED INSECURITY

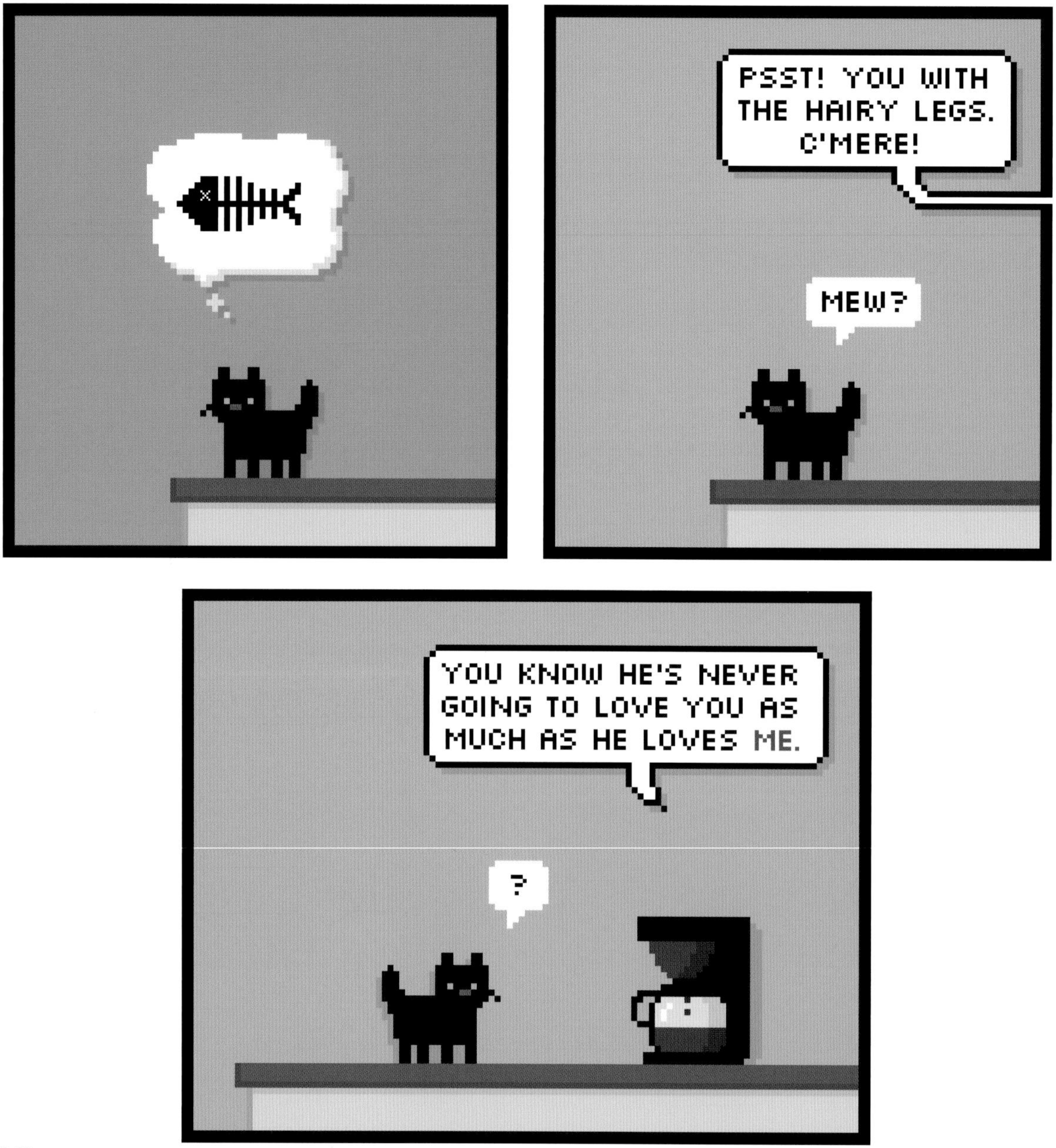
PSST! YOU WITH THE HAIRY LEGS. C'MERE!
MEW?
YOU KNOW HE'S NEVER GOING TO LOVE YOU AS MUCH AS HE LOVES ME.
?

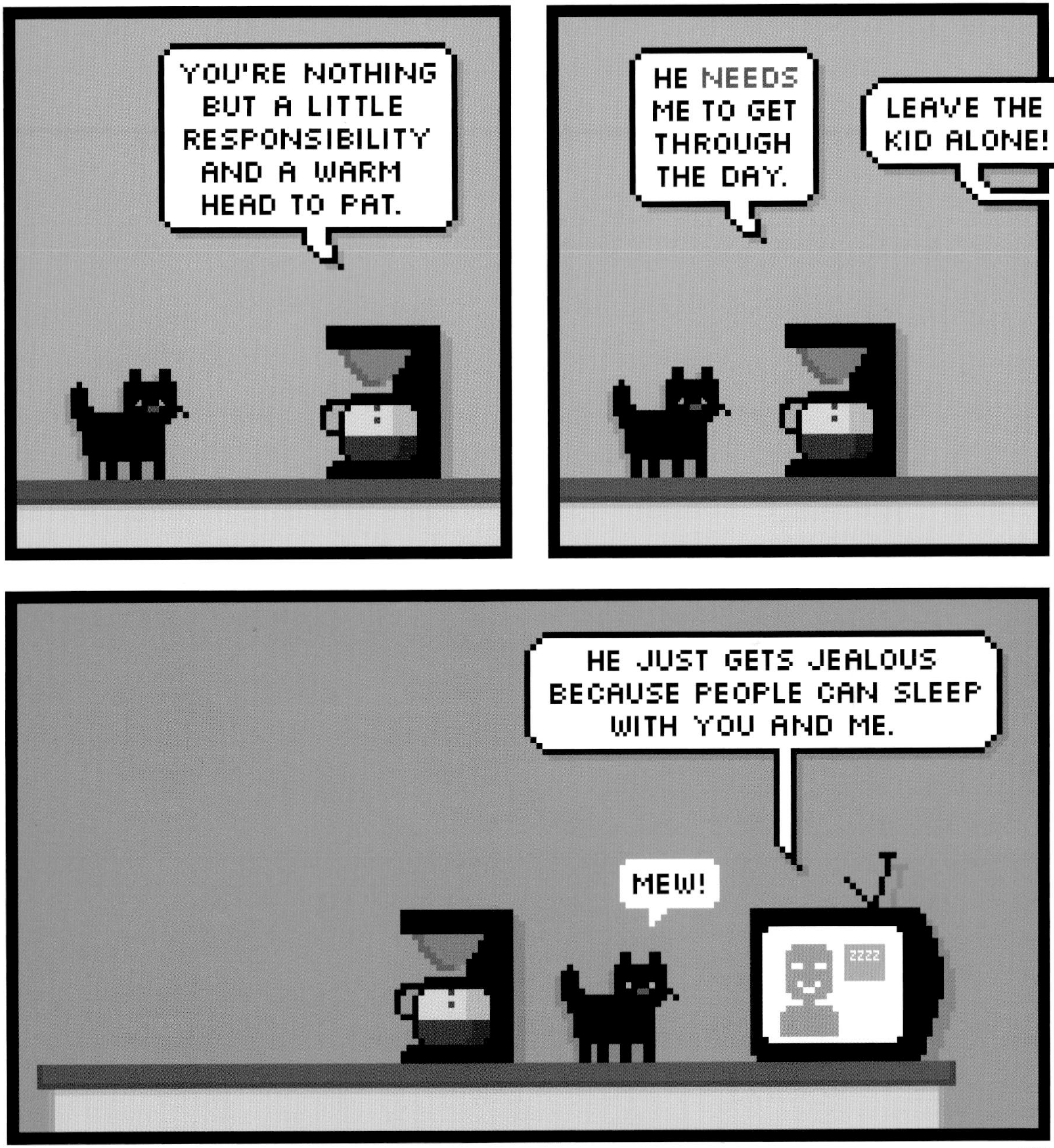
YOU'RE NOTHING BUT A LITTLE RESPONSIBILITY AND A WARM HEAD TO PAT.
HE NEEDS ME TO GET THROUGH THE DAY.
LEAVE THE KID ALONE!
HE JUST GETS JEALOUS BECAUSE PEOPLE CAN SLEEP WITH YOU AND ME.
MEW!

LIQUID LIFE SUPPORT

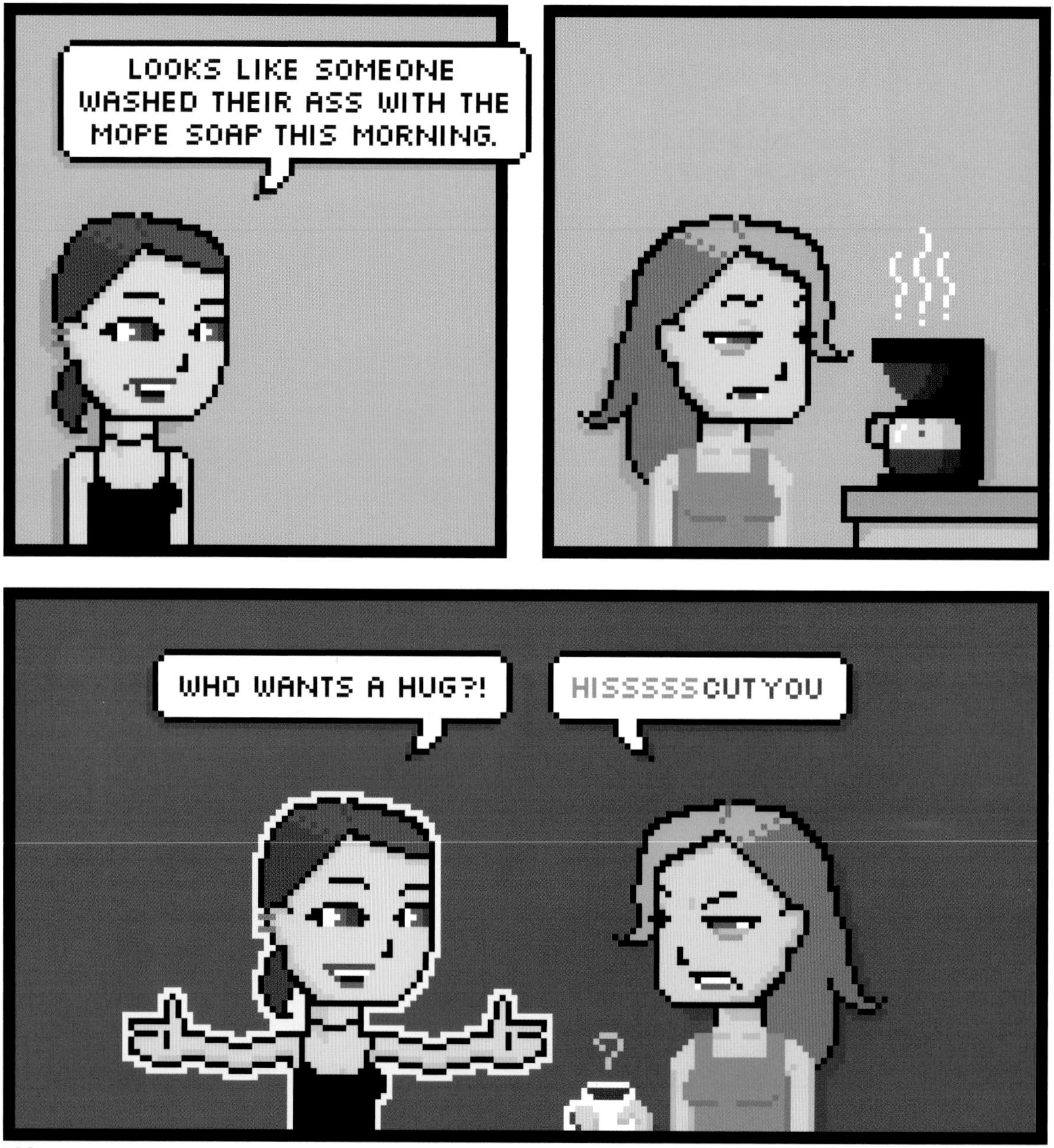
LOOKS LIKE SOMEONE WASHED THEIR ASS WITH THE MOPE SOAP THIS MORNING.
WHO WANTS A HUG?!
HISSSSSCUTYOU
?

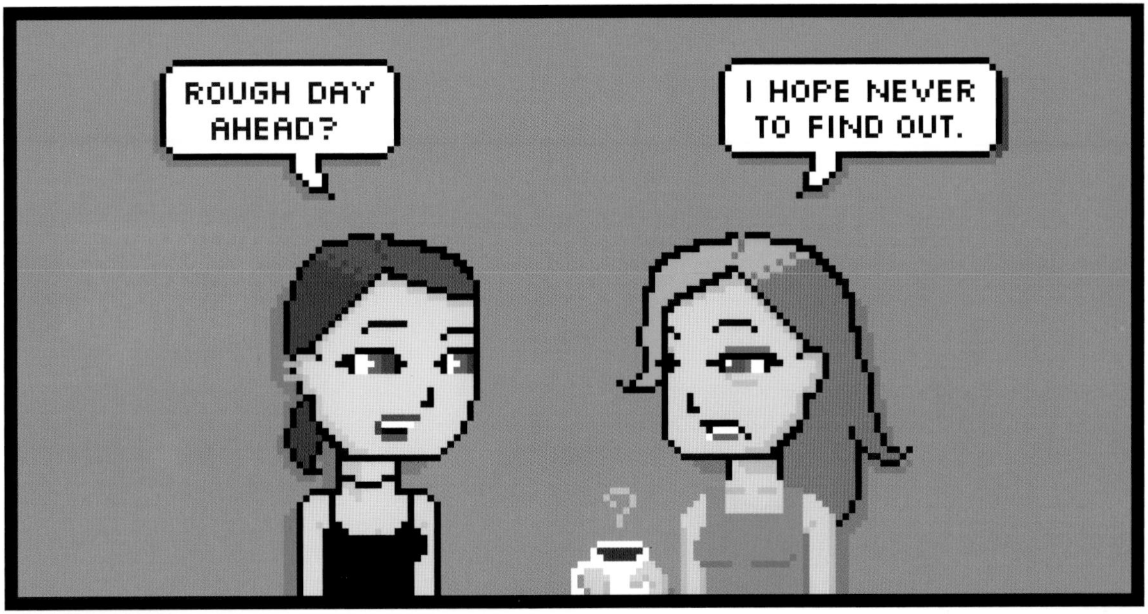
ROUGH DAY AHEAD?
I HOPE NEVER TO FIND OUT.

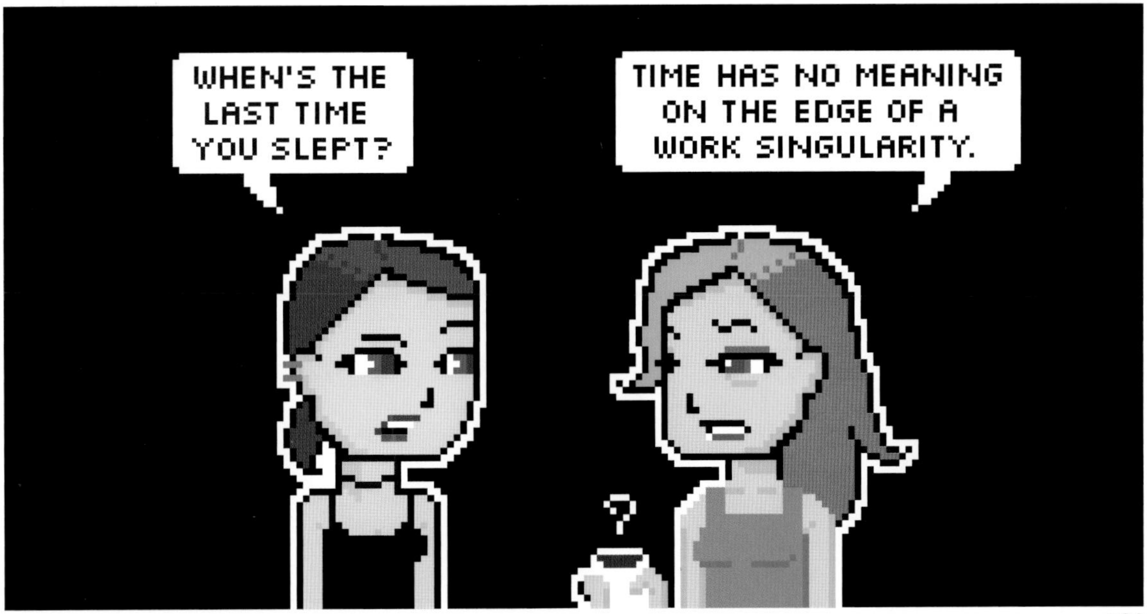
WHEN'S THE LAST TIME YOU SLEPT?
TIME HAS NO MEANING ON THE EDGE OF A WORK SINGULARITY.

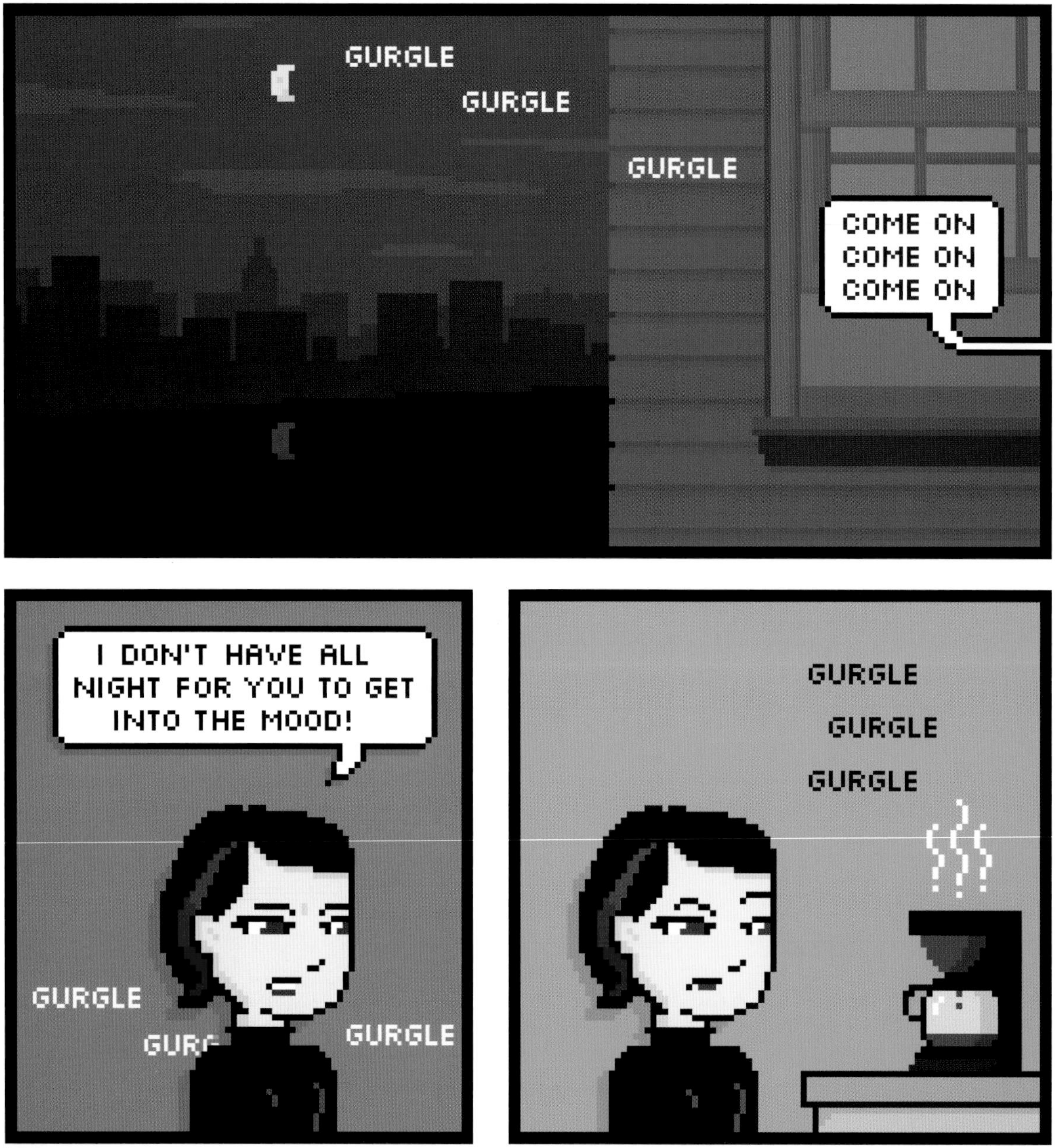
GURGLE
GURGLE
GURGLE
COME ON
COME ON
COME ON
I DON'T HAVE ALL NIGHT FOR YOU TO GET INTO THE MOOD!
GURGLE
GURGLE
GURGLE
GURGLE
GURGLE
GURGLE

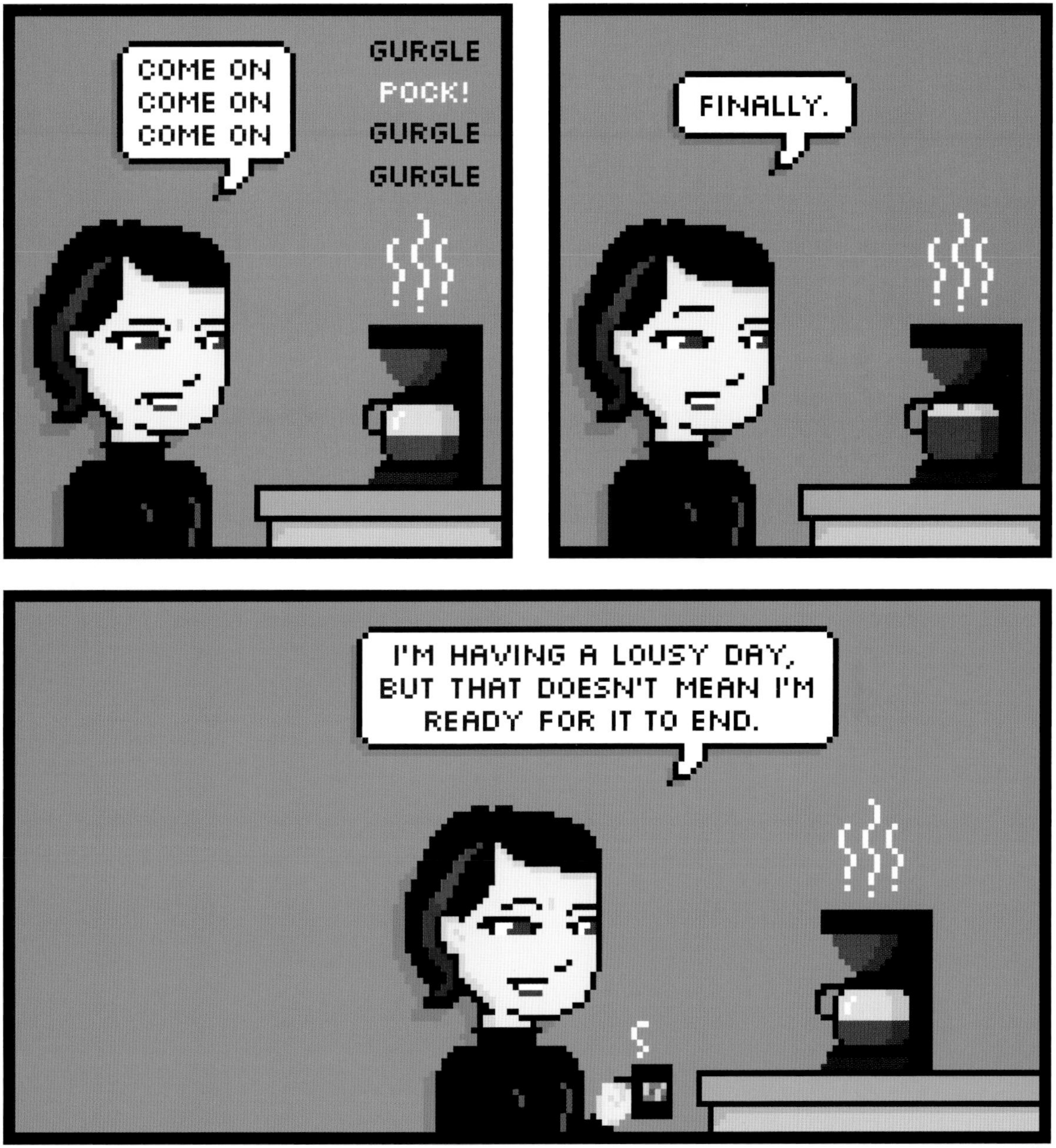
COME ON
COME ON
COME ON
GURGLE
POCK!
GURGLE
GURGLE
FINALLY.
I'M HAVING A LOUSY DAY, BUT THAT DOESN'T MEAN I'M READY FOR IT TO END.

DELICIOUSLY DESPISED

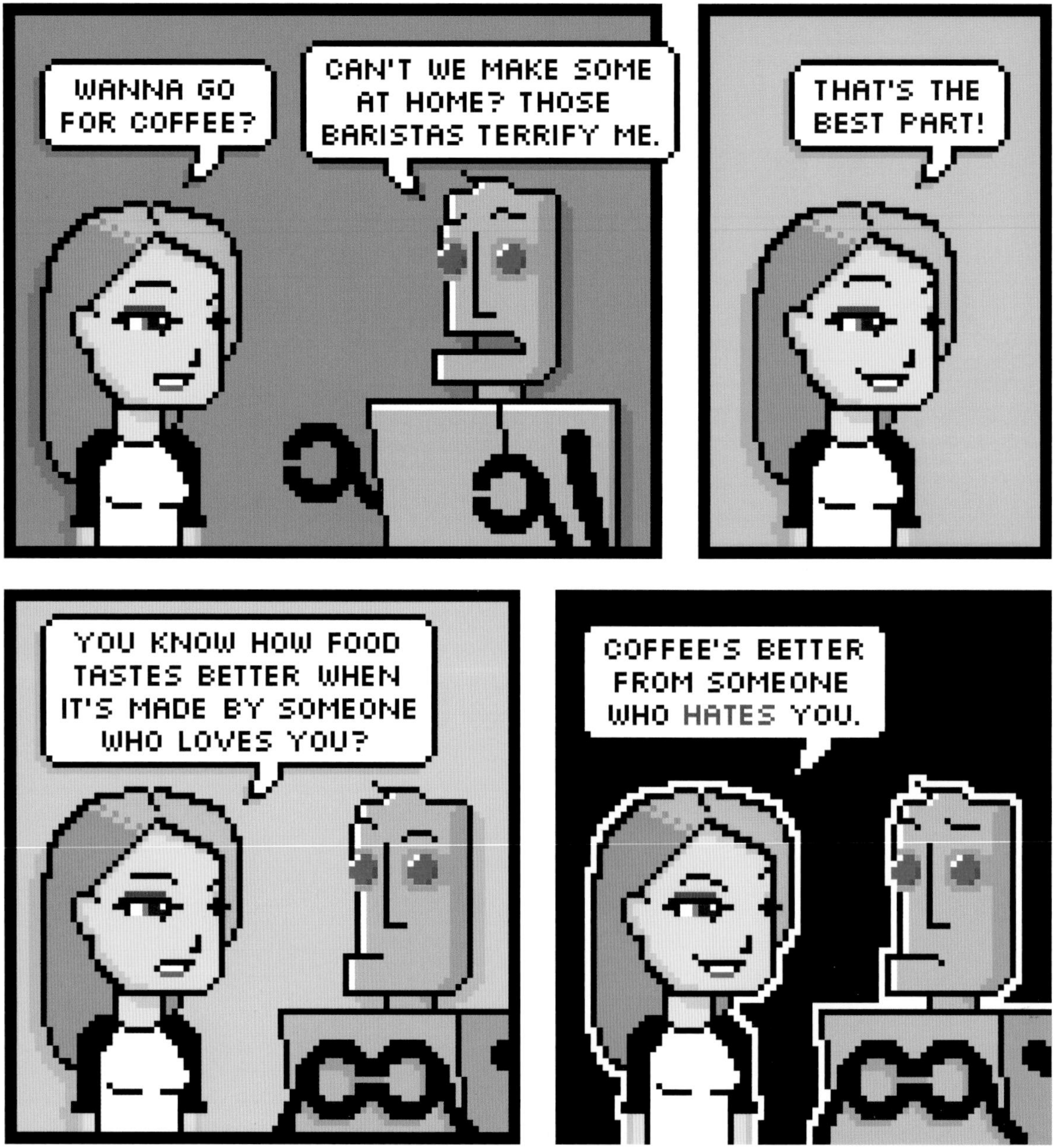
WANNA GO FOR COFFEE?
CAN'T WE MAKE SOME AT HOME? THOSE BARISTAS TERRIFY ME.
THAT'S THE BEST PART!
YOU KNOW HOW FOOD TASTES BETTER WHEN IT'S MADE BY SOMEONE WHO LOVES YOU?
COFFEE'S BETTER FROM SOMEONE WHO HATES YOU.

BREW OR BREW NOT

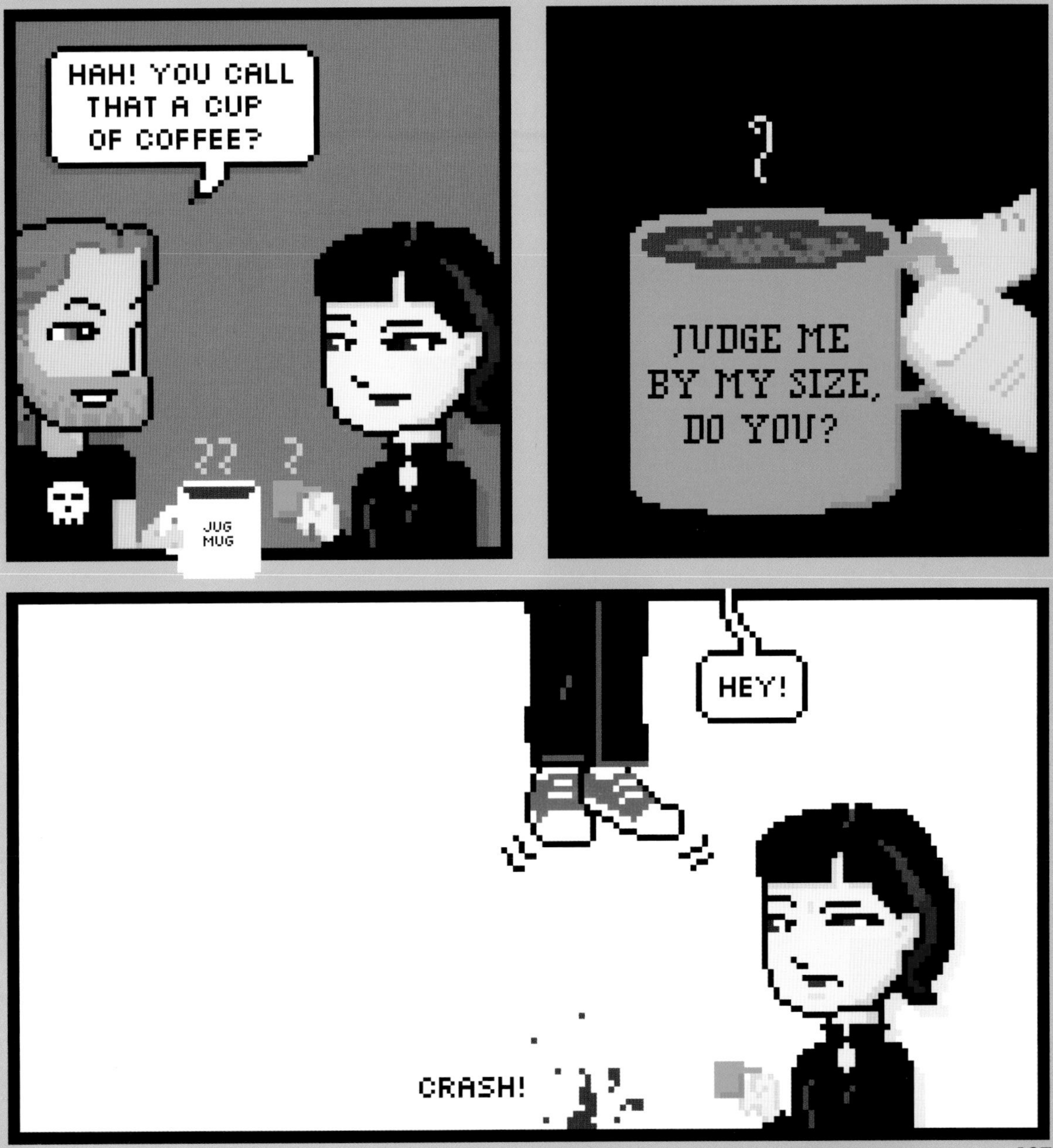
HAH! YOU CALL THAT A CUP OF COFFEE?
JUG MUG
JUDGE ME BY MY SIZE, DO YOU?
HEY!
CRASH!

TRANSCENDING CONSCIOUSNESS

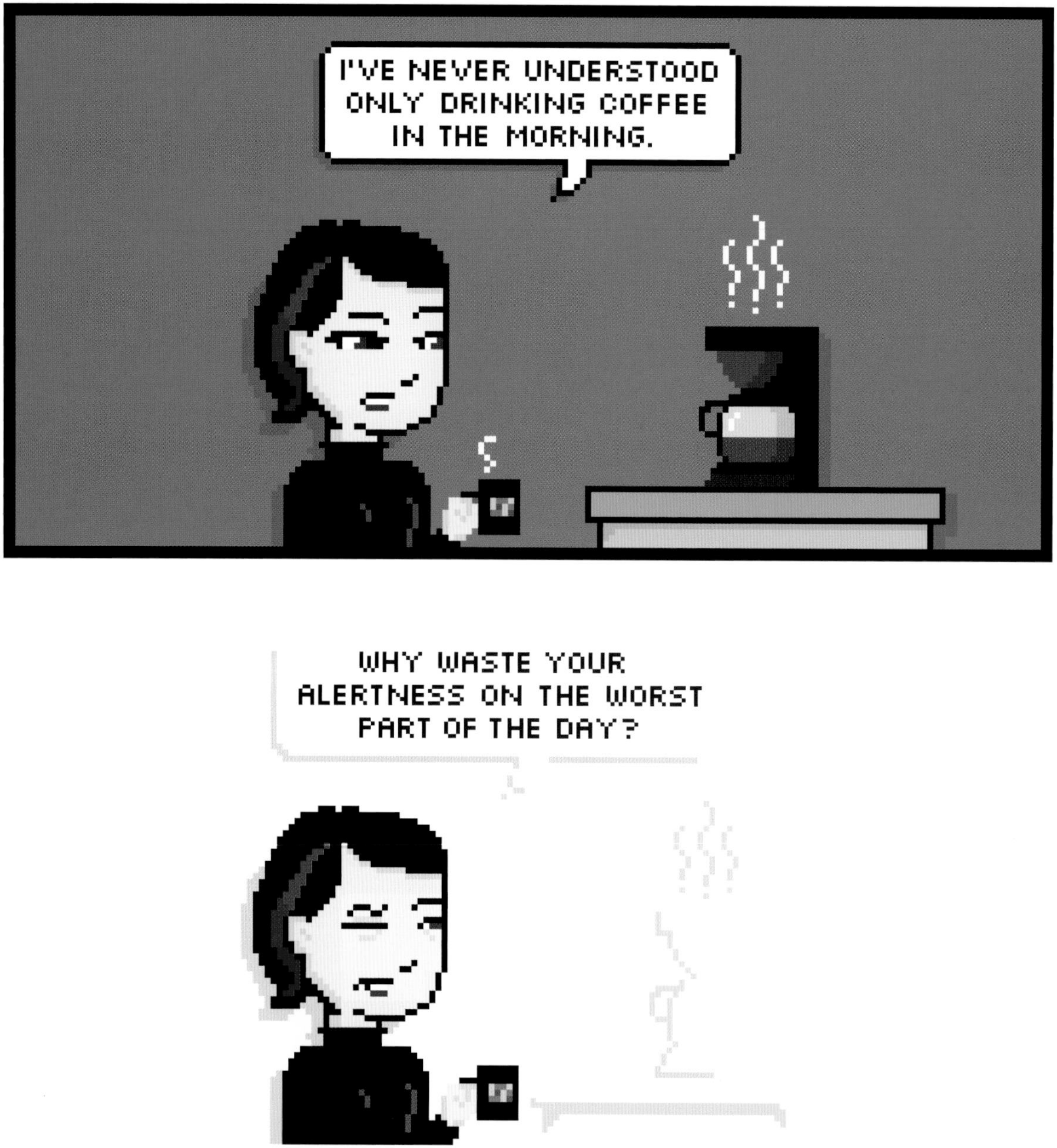
I'VE NEVER UNDERSTOOD ONLY DRINKING COFFEE IN THE MORNING.
WHY WASTE YOUR ALERTNESS ON THE WORST PART OF THE DAY?

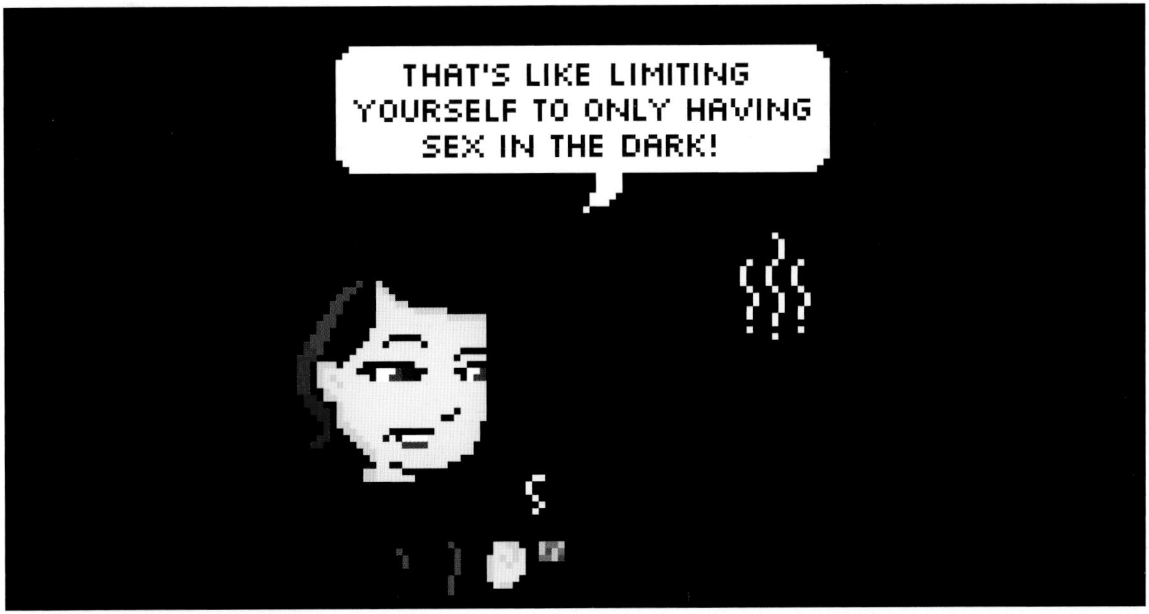
THAT'S LIKE LIMITING YOURSELF TO ONLY HAVING SEX IN THE DARK!

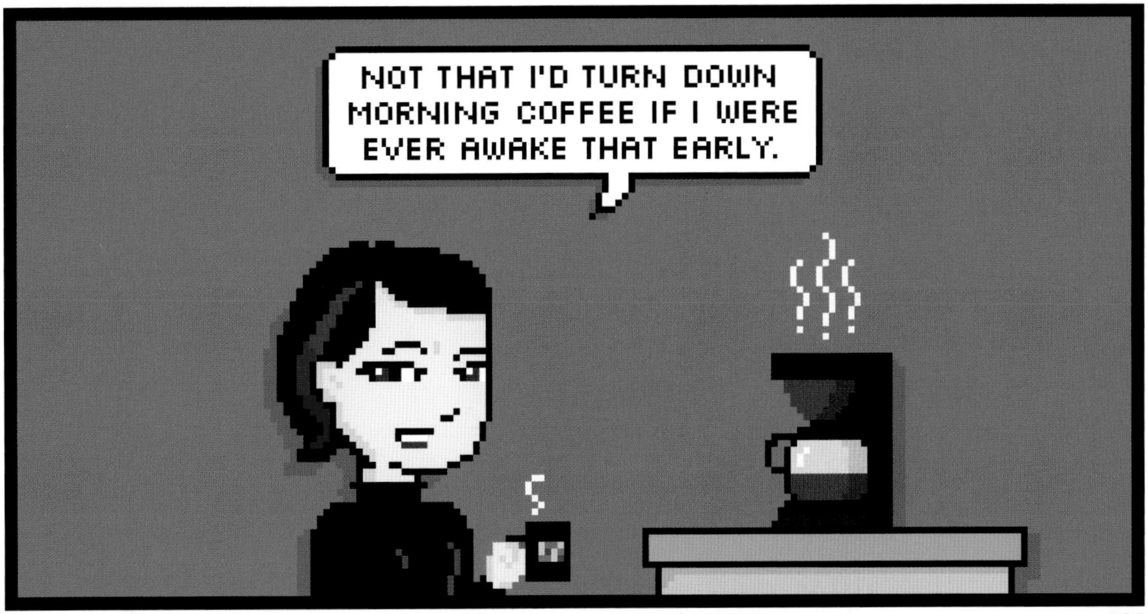
NOT THAT I'D TURN DOWN MORNING COFFEE IF I WERE EVER AWAKE THAT EARLY.

NOTHING SNAPS QUITE LIKE A NATURAL CASING

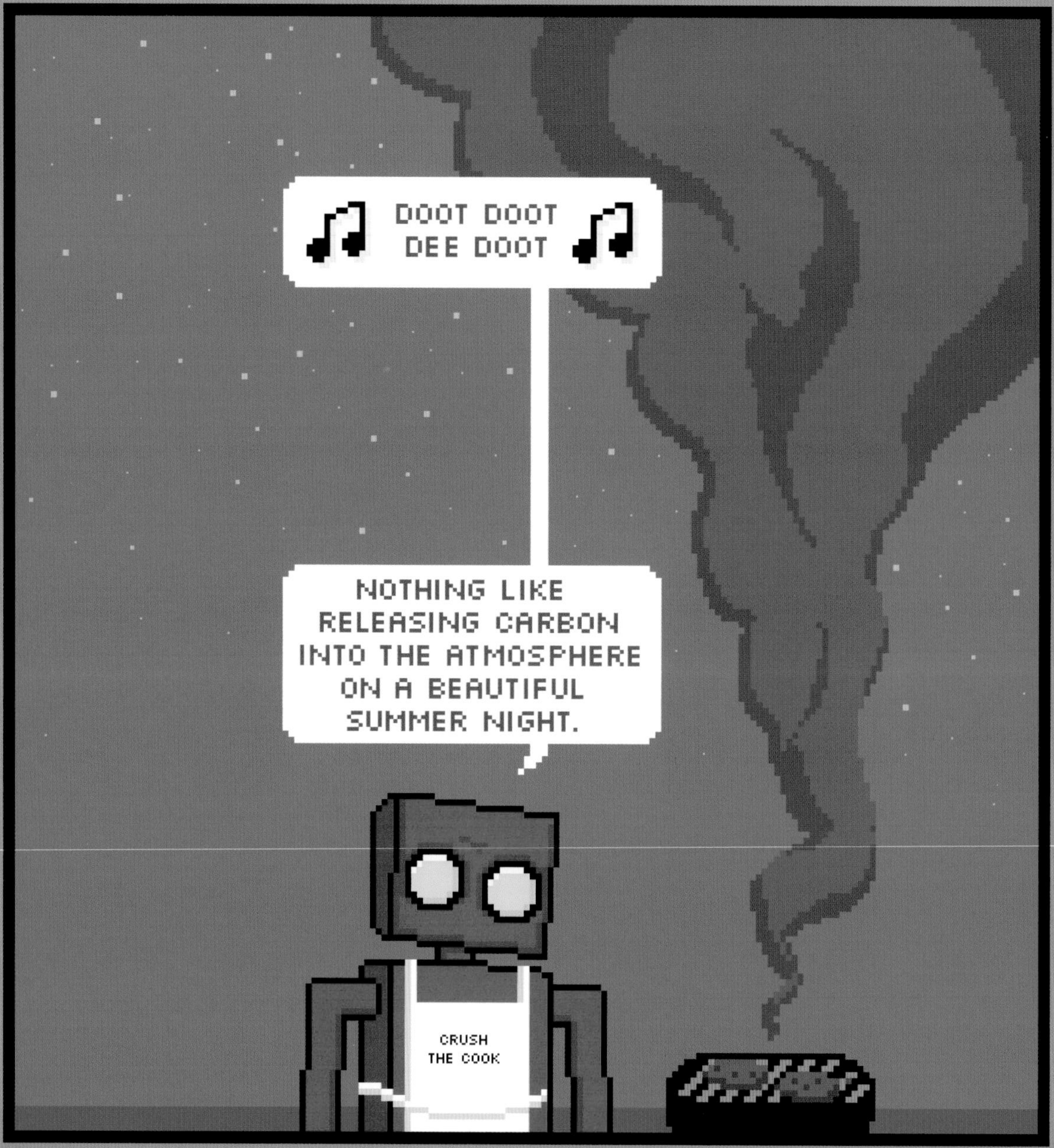

DOOT DOOT DEE DOOT
NOTHING LIKE RELEASING CARBON INTO THE ATMOSPHERE ON A BEAUTIFUL SUMMER NIGHT.
CRUSH THE COOK

WANT A HOT DOG?
EWW!
CRUSH THE COOK
I MADE THEM MYSELF FROM 100% SUSTAINABLY-RAISED INTERNET MISOGYNISTS!
OOH!
CRUSH THE COOK

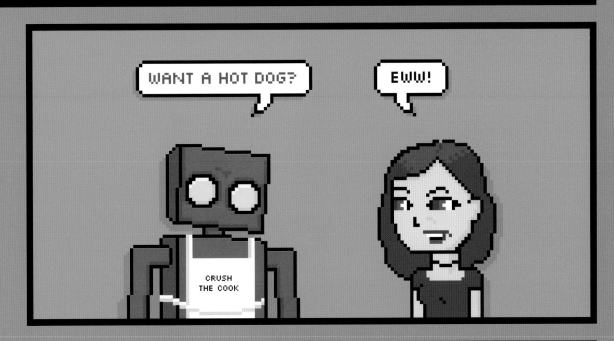

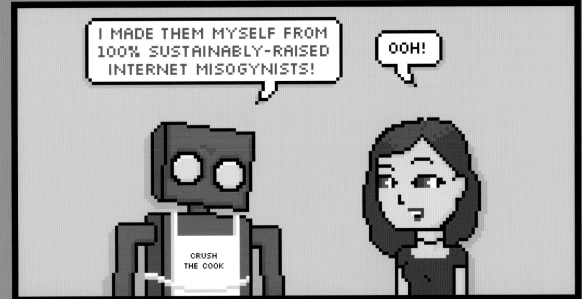

MITOCHONDRIACS

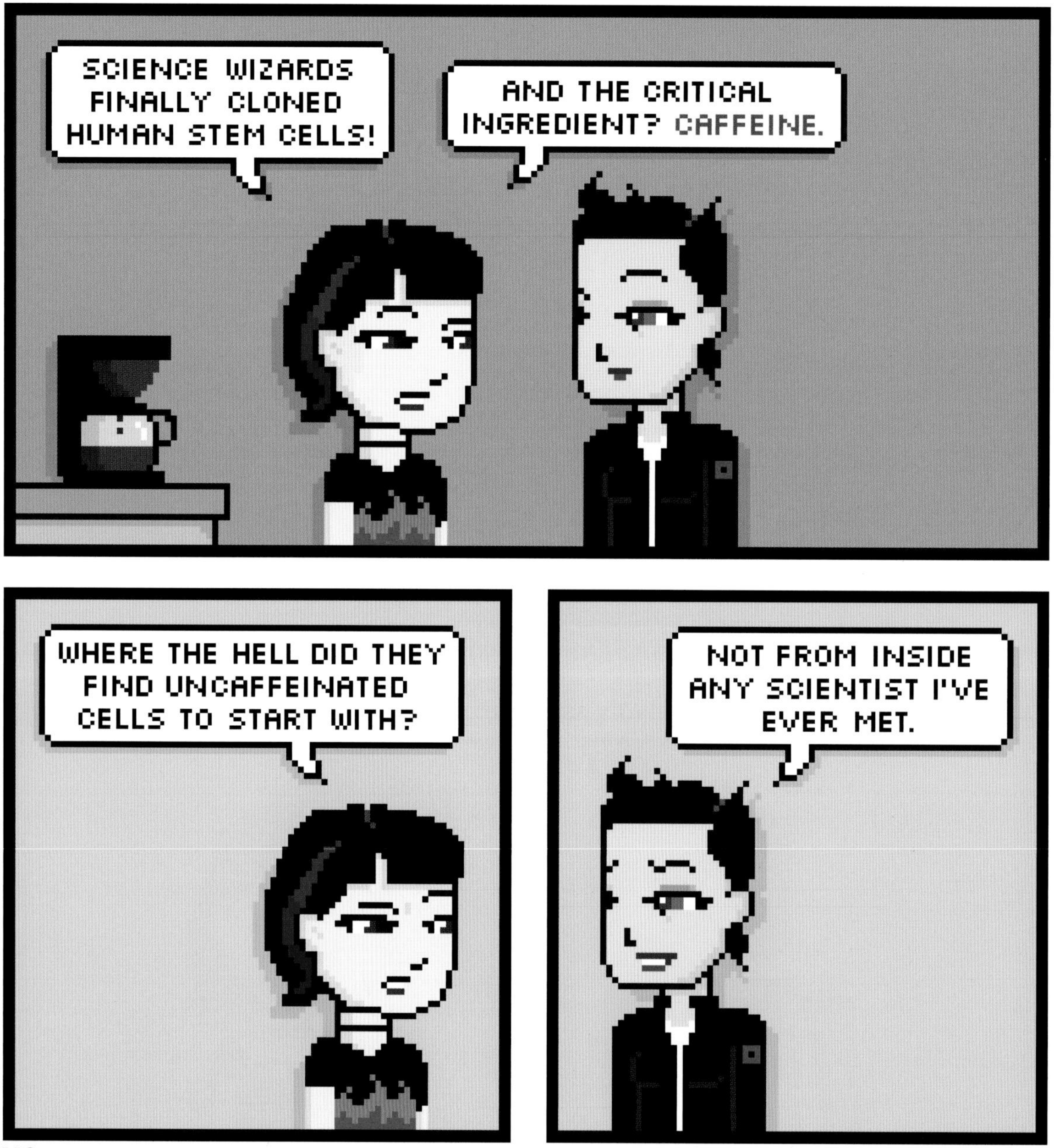
SCIENCE WIZARDS FINALLY CLONED HUMAN STEM CELLS!
AND THE CRITICAL INGREDIENT? CAFFEINE.
WHERE THE HELL DID THEY FIND UNCAFFEINATED CELLS TO START WITH?
NOT FROM INSIDE ANY SCIENTIST I'VE EVER MET.

DON'T ASK ABOUT THE YELLOW WEAKNESS

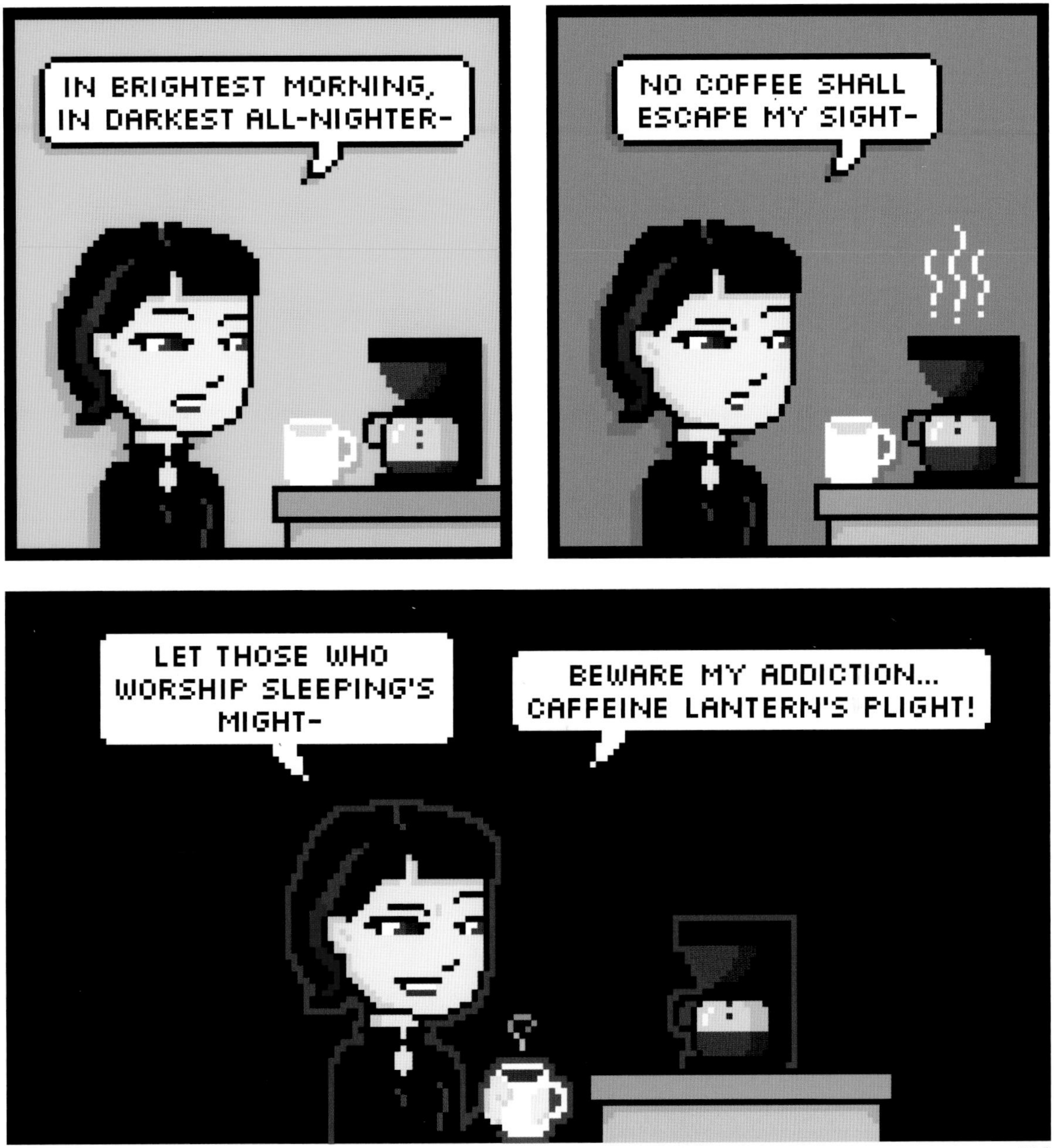
IN BRIGHTEST MORNING, IN DARKEST ALL-NIGHTER-
NO COFFEE SHALL ESCAPE MY SIGHT-
LET THOSE WHO WORSHIP SLEEPING'S MIGHT-
BEWARE MY ADDICTION... CAFFEINE LANTERN'S PLIGHT!

YOU CAN EITHER IMPROVE MY PRODUCTIVITY OR PAY RENT

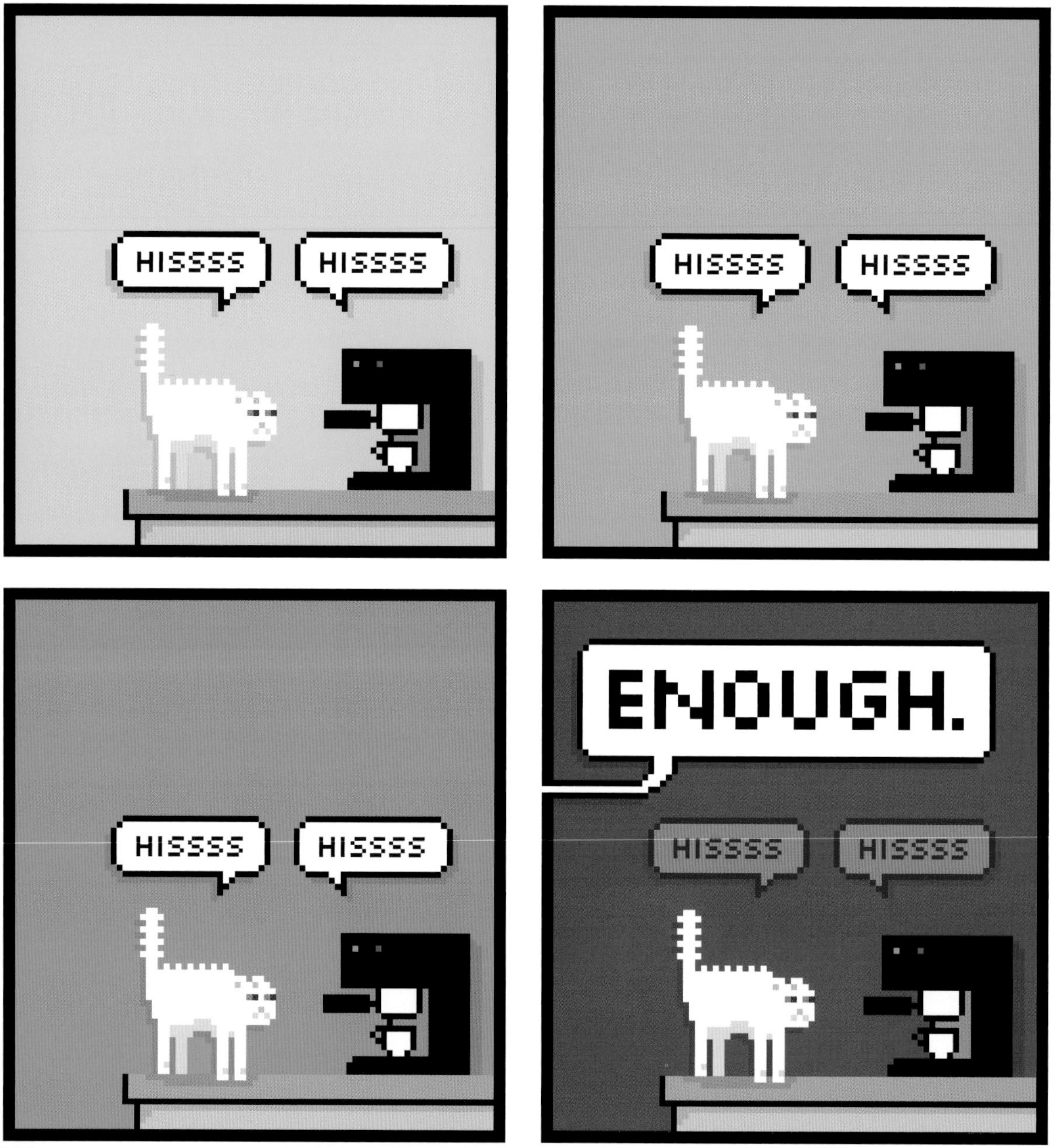
HISSSS
HISSSS
HISSSS
HISSSS
HISSSS
HISSSS
ENOUGH.
HISSSS
HISSSS

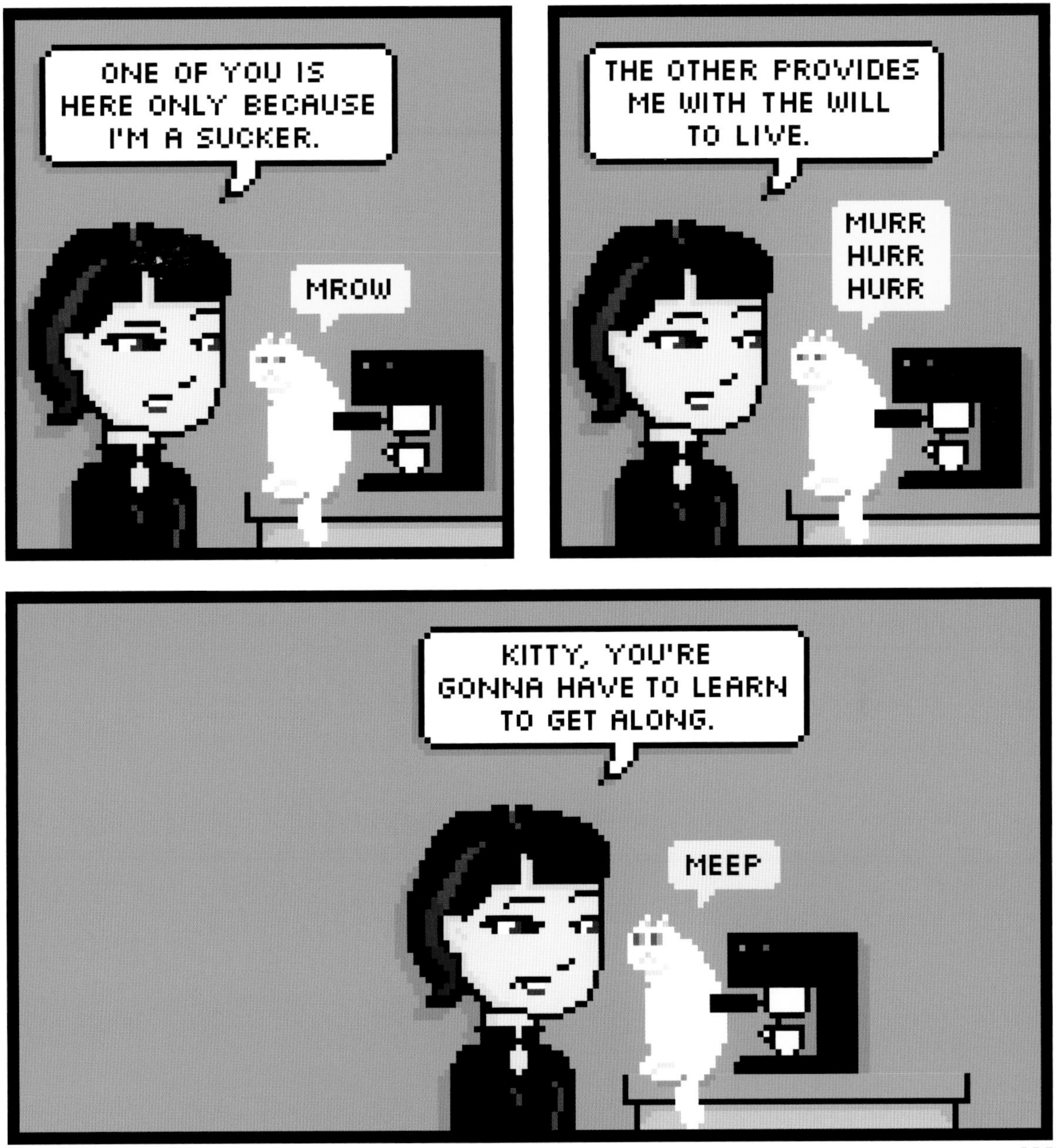
ONE OF YOU IS HERE ONLY BECAUSE I'M A SUCKER.
MROW
THE OTHER PROVIDES ME WITH THE WILL TO LIVE.
MURR HURR HURR
KITTY, YOU'RE GONNA HAVE TO LEARN TO GET ALONG.
MEEP

TAKING THE ESPRESSO TRAIN

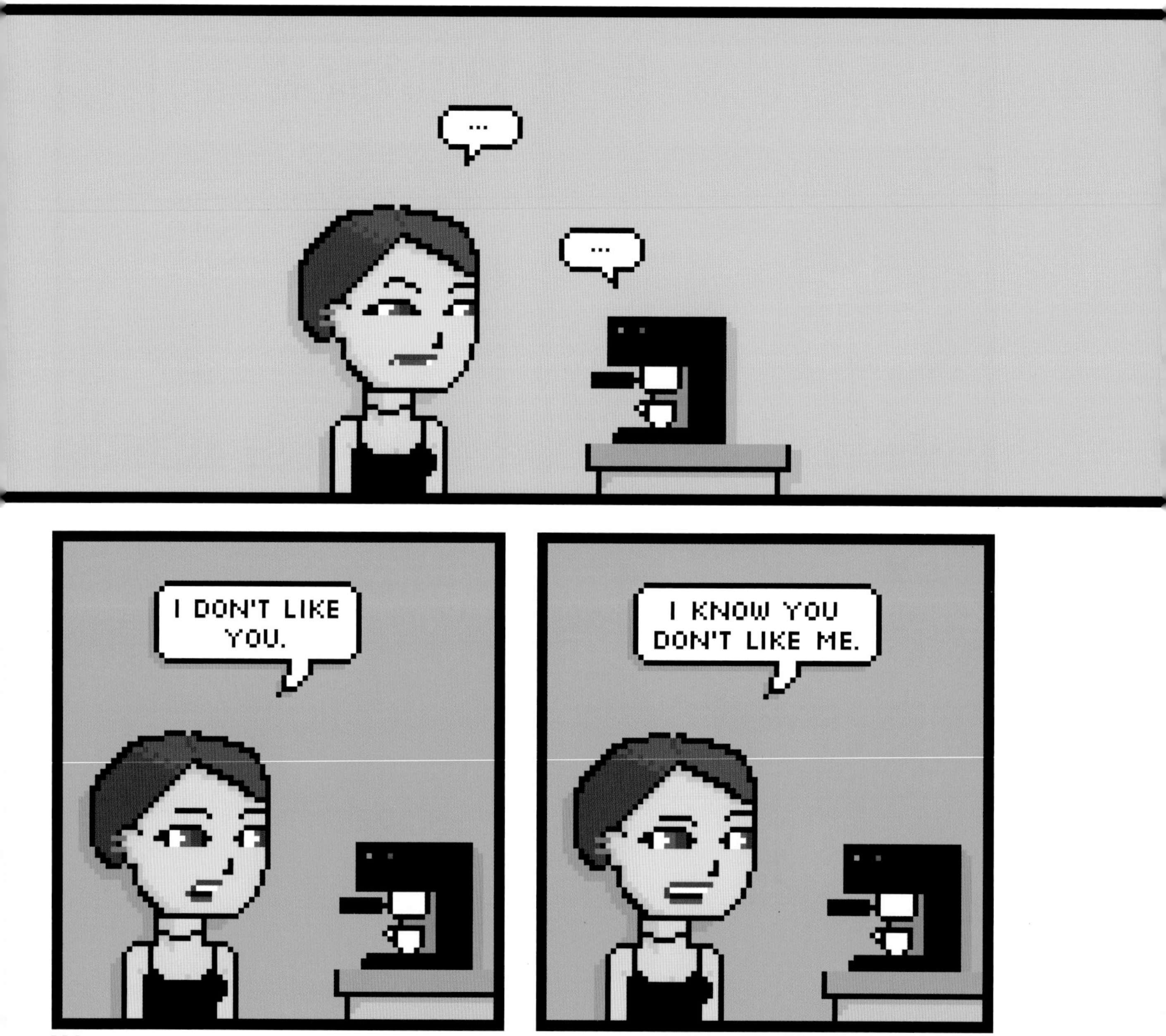
...
...
I DON'T LIKE YOU.
I KNOW YOU DON'T LIKE ME.

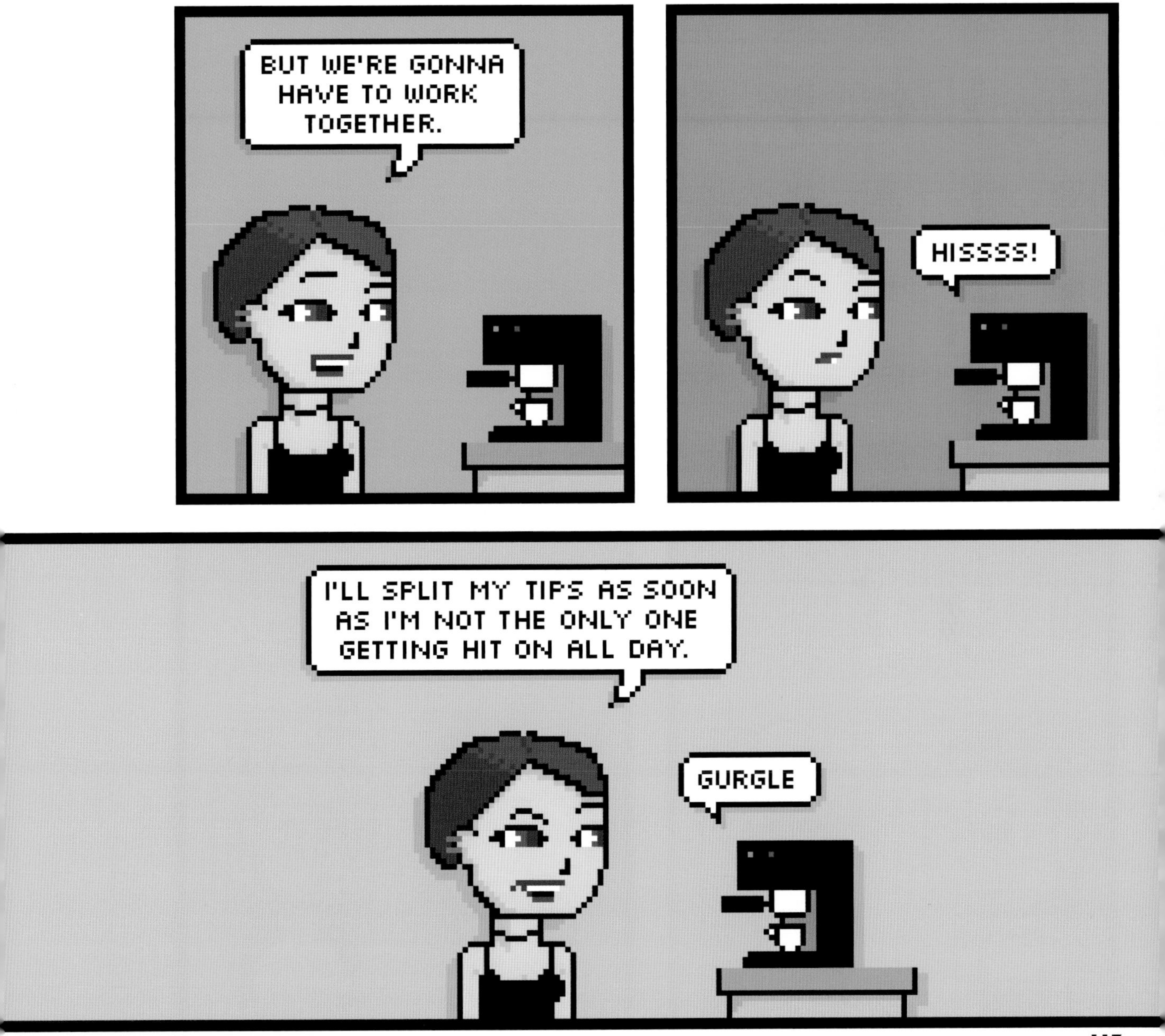
BUT WE'RE GONNA HAVE TO WORK TOGETHER.
HISSSSS!
I'LL SPLIT MY TIPS AS SOON AS I'M NOT THE ONLY ONE GETTING HIT ON ALL DAY.
GURGLE

SOCIAL ENGINEERING

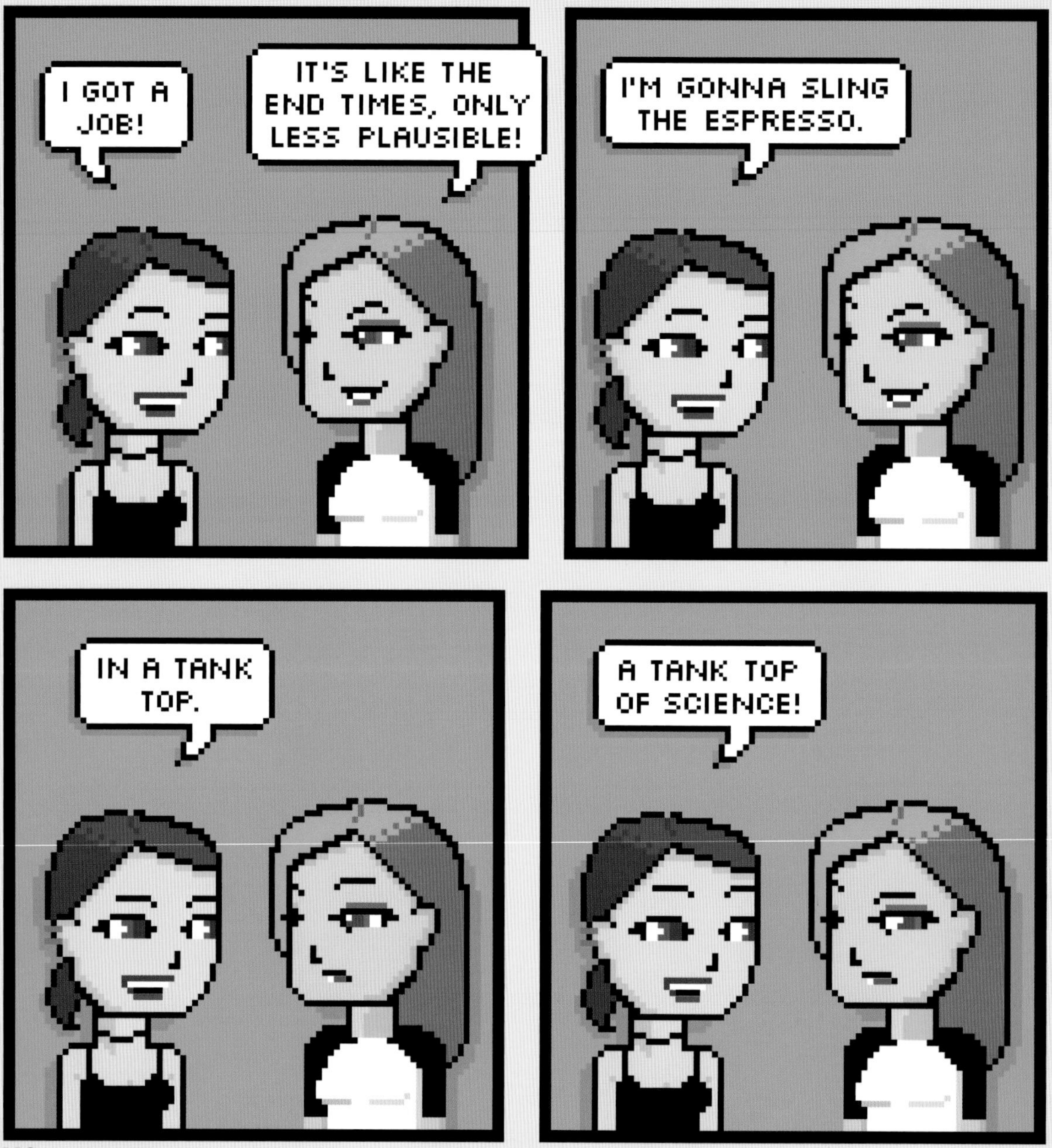
I GOT A JOB!
IT'S LIKE THE END TIMES, ONLY LESS PLAUSIBLE!
I'M GONNA SLING THE ESPRESSO.
IN A TANK TOP.
A TANK TOP OF SCIENCE!

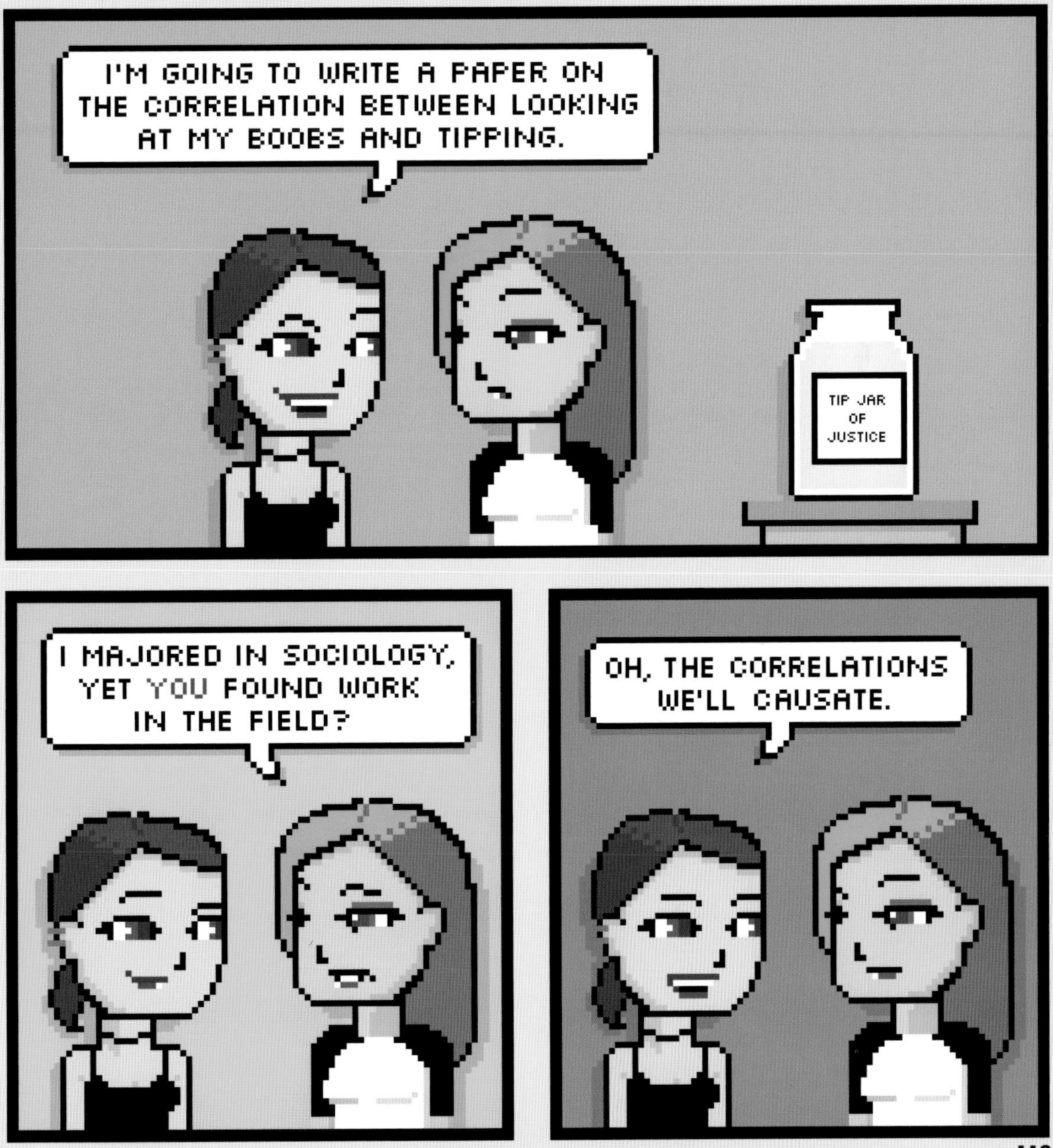
I'M GOING TO WRITE A PAPER ON THE CORRELATION BETWEEN LOOKING AT MY BOOBS AND TIPPING.
TIP JAR OF JUSTICE
I MAJORED IN SOCIOLOGY, YET YOU FOUND WORK IN THE FIELD?
OH, THE CORRELATIONS WE'LL CAUSATE.

STEAMY, WET AND ADMINISTERED VIA HOLE

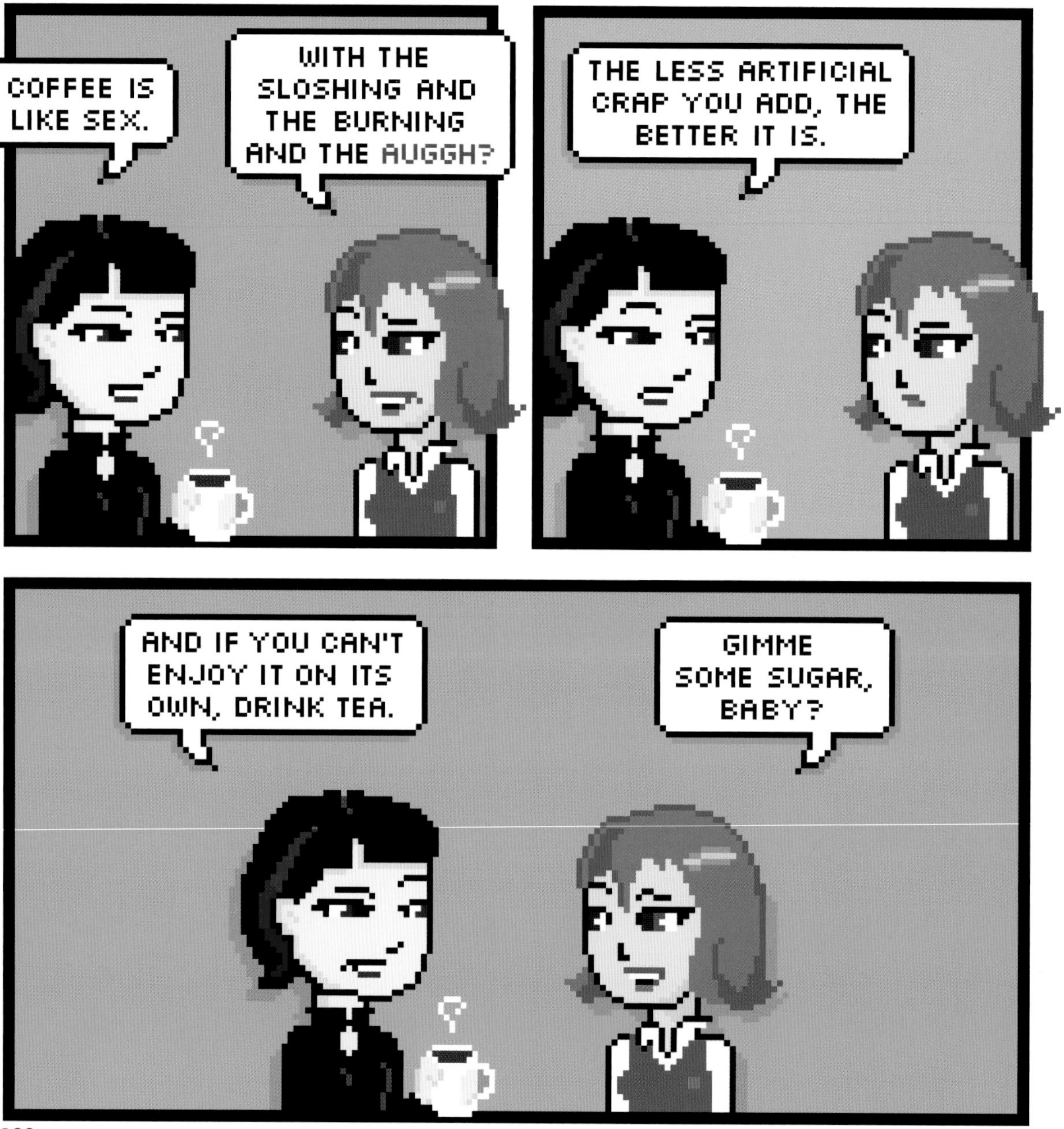
COFFEE IS LIKE SEX.
WITH THE SLOSHING AND THE BURNING AND THE AUGGH?
THE LESS ARTIFICIAL CRAP YOU ADD, THE BETTER IT IS.
AND IF YOU CAN'T ENJOY IT ON ITS OWN, DRINK TEA.
GIMME SOME SUGAR, BABY?

THEORIES TOO EXPENSIVE TO TEST

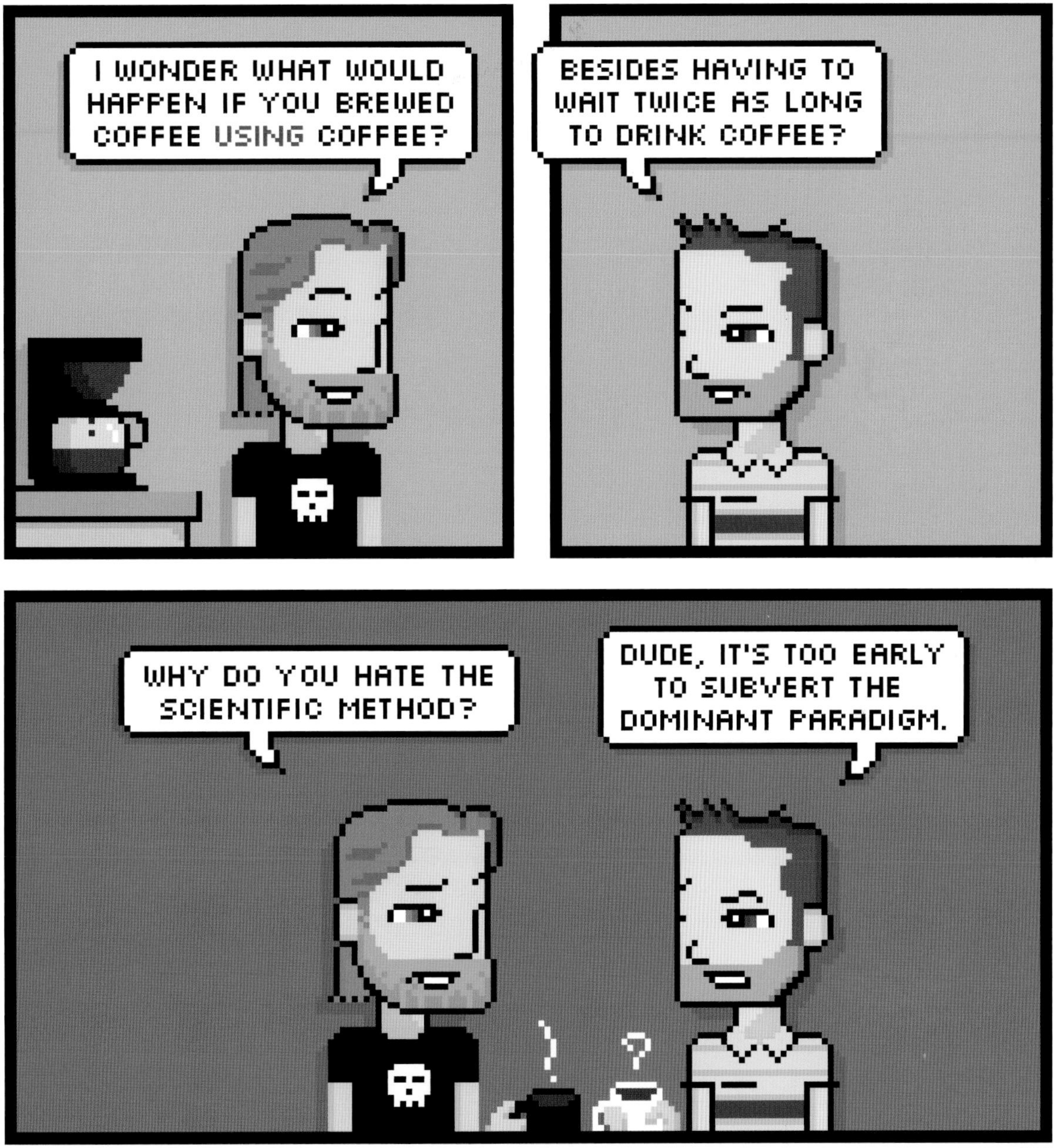
I WONDER WHAT WOULD HAPPEN IF YOU BREWED COFFEE USING COFFEE?
BESIDES HAVING TO WAIT TWICE AS LONG TO DRINK COFFEE?
WHY DO YOU HATE THE SCIENTIFIC METHOD?
DUDE, IT'S TOO EARLY TO SUBVERT THE DOMINANT PARADIGM.
?

MEAL OF RIVALS

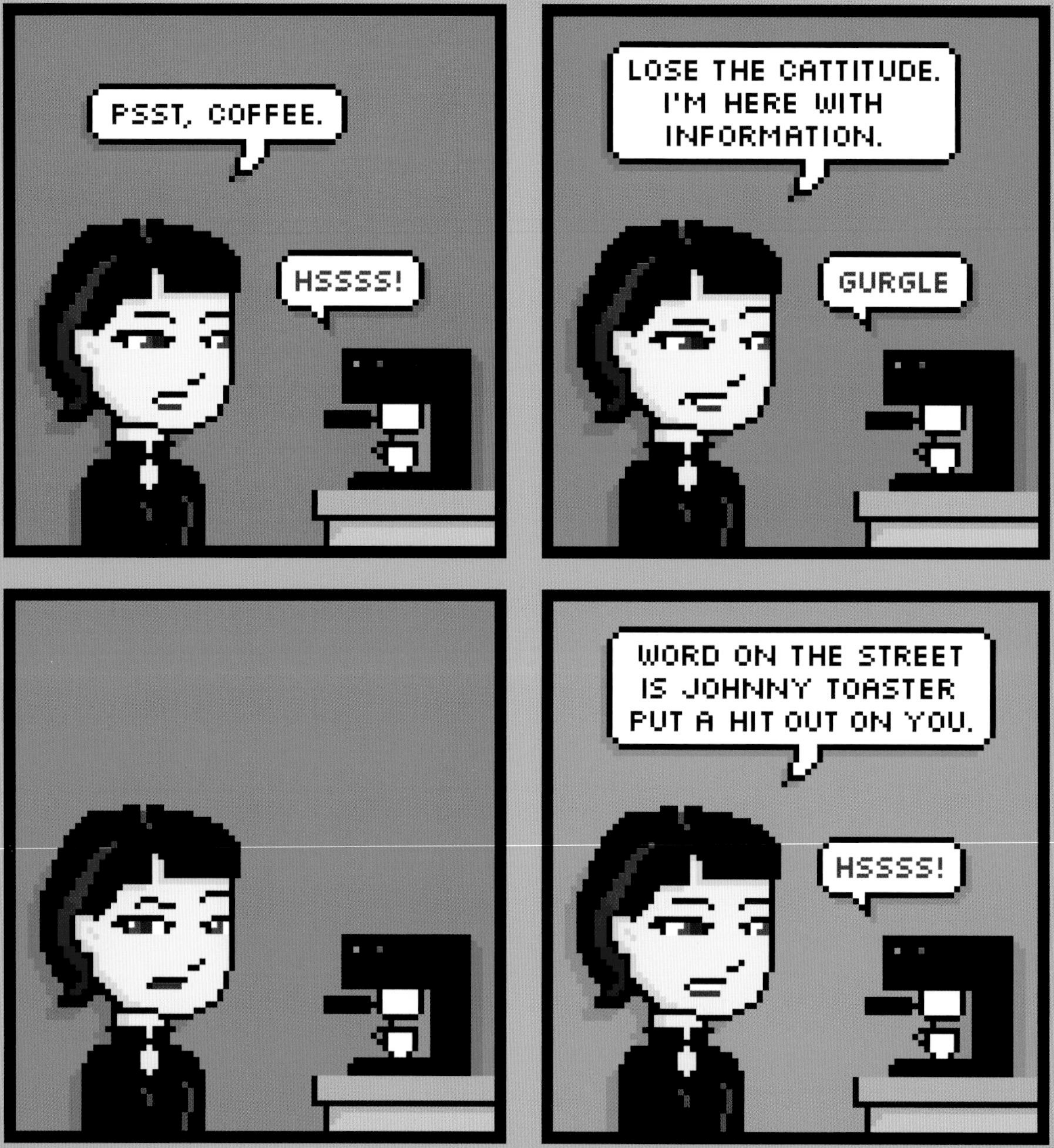
PSST, COFFEE.
HSSSS!
LOSE THE CATTITUDE. I'M HERE WITH INFORMATION.
GURGLE
WORD ON THE STREET IS JOHNNY TOASTER PUT A HIT OUT ON YOU.
HSSSS!

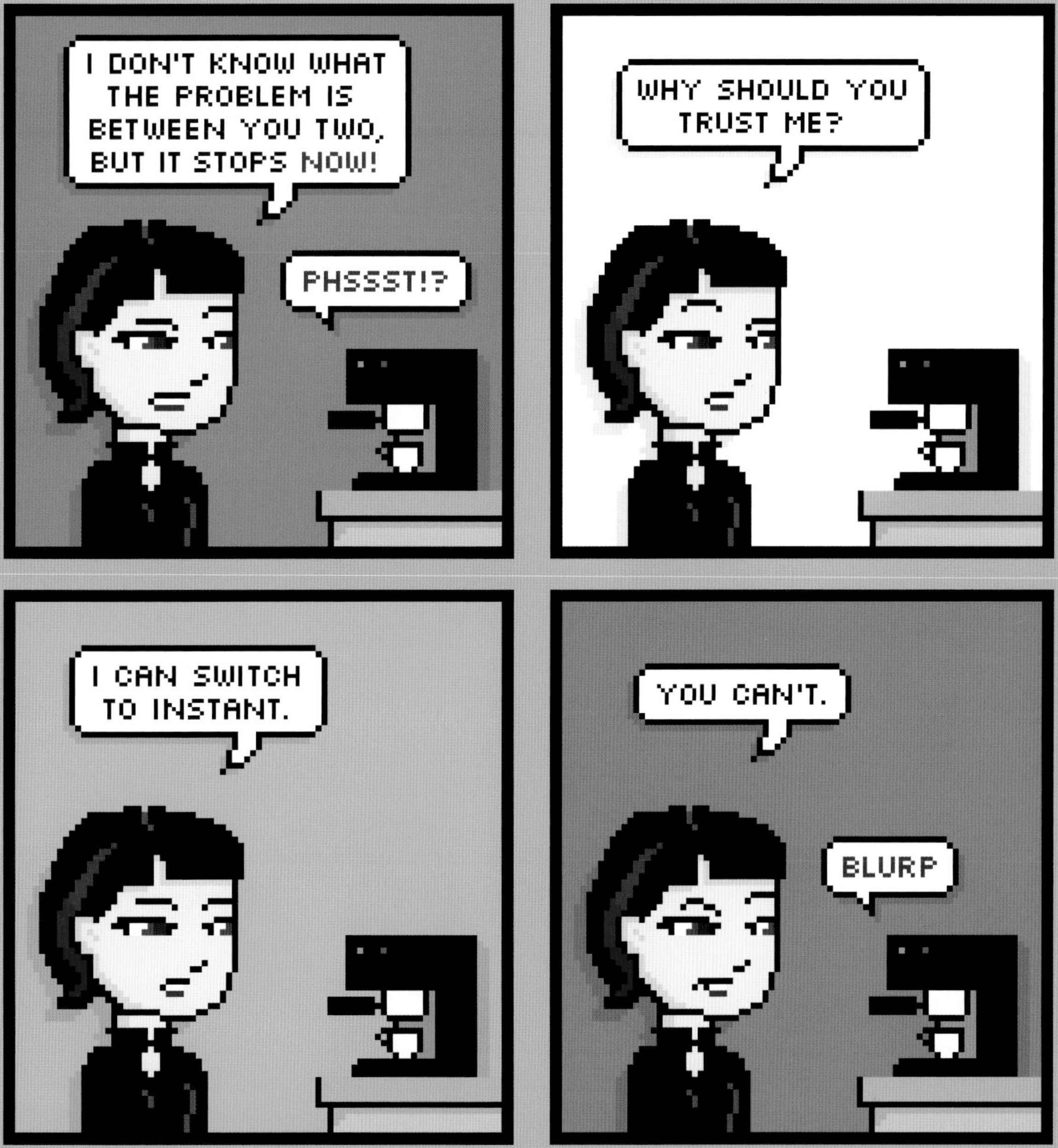
I DON'T KNOW WHAT THE PROBLEM IS BETWEEN YOU TWO, BUT IT STOPS NOW!
PHSSST!?
WHY SHOULD YOU TRUST ME?
I CAN SWITCH TO INSTANT.
YOU CAN'T.
BLURP

GOING TOASTAL OR MUTUALLY ASSURED DELICIOUSNESS

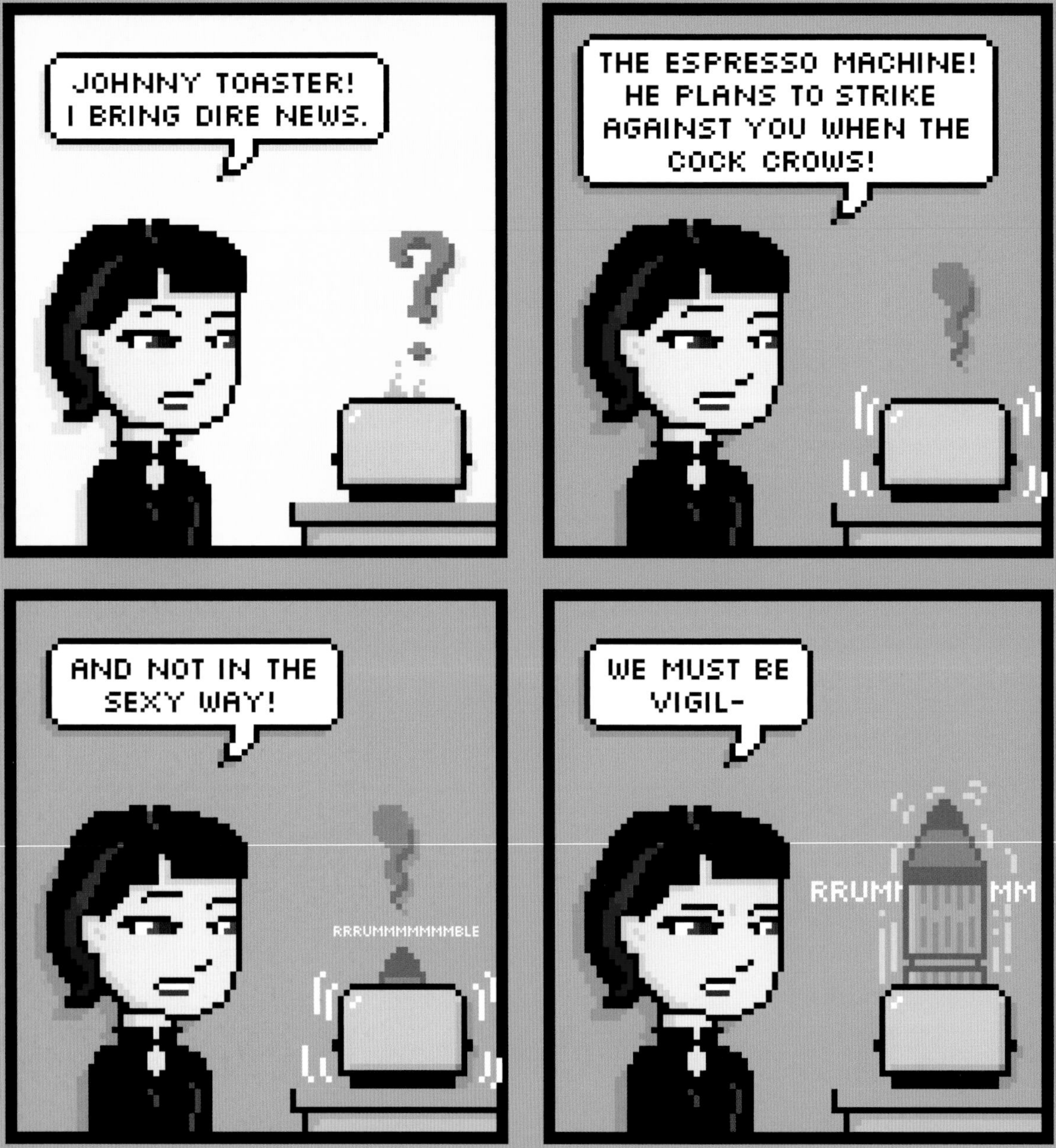
JOHNNY TOASTER! I BRING DIRE NEWS.
THE ESPRESSO MACHINE! HE PLANS TO STRIKE AGAINST YOU WHEN THE COCK CROWS!
AND NOT IN THE SEXY WAY!
RRRUMMMMMMMBLE
WE MUST BE VIGIL-
RRUM
MM

RRROOOOOOAAR
AAAARRRRRRR

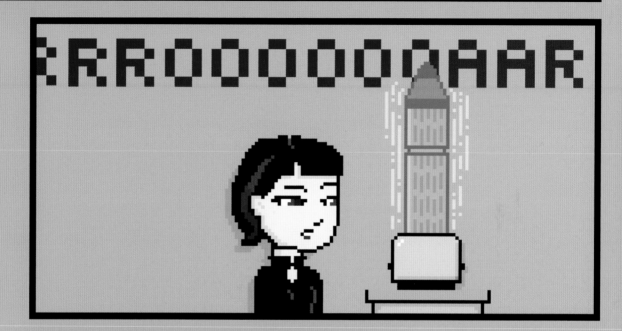

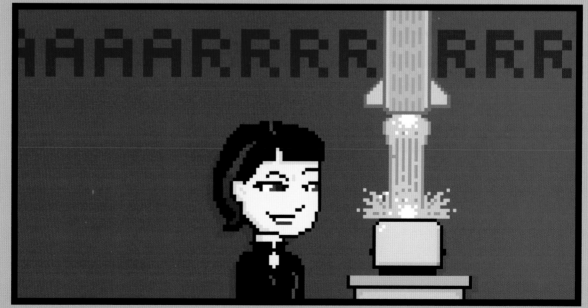

THE DUEL

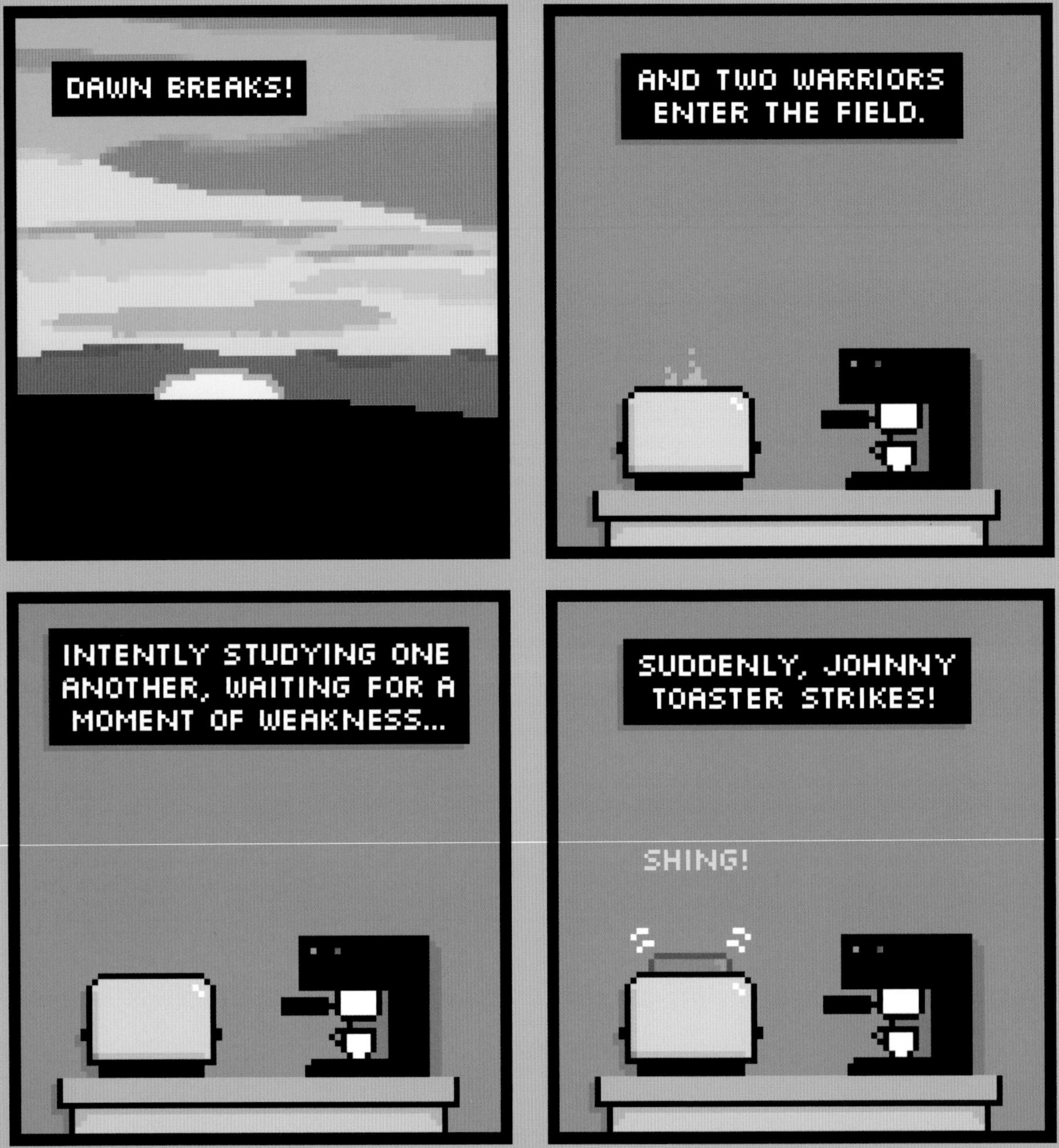
DAWN BREAKS!
AND TWO WARRIORS ENTER THE FIELD.
INTENTLY STUDYING ONE ANOTHER, WAITING FOR A MOMENT OF WEAKNESS...
SUDDENLY, JOHNNY TOASTER STRIKES!
SHING!

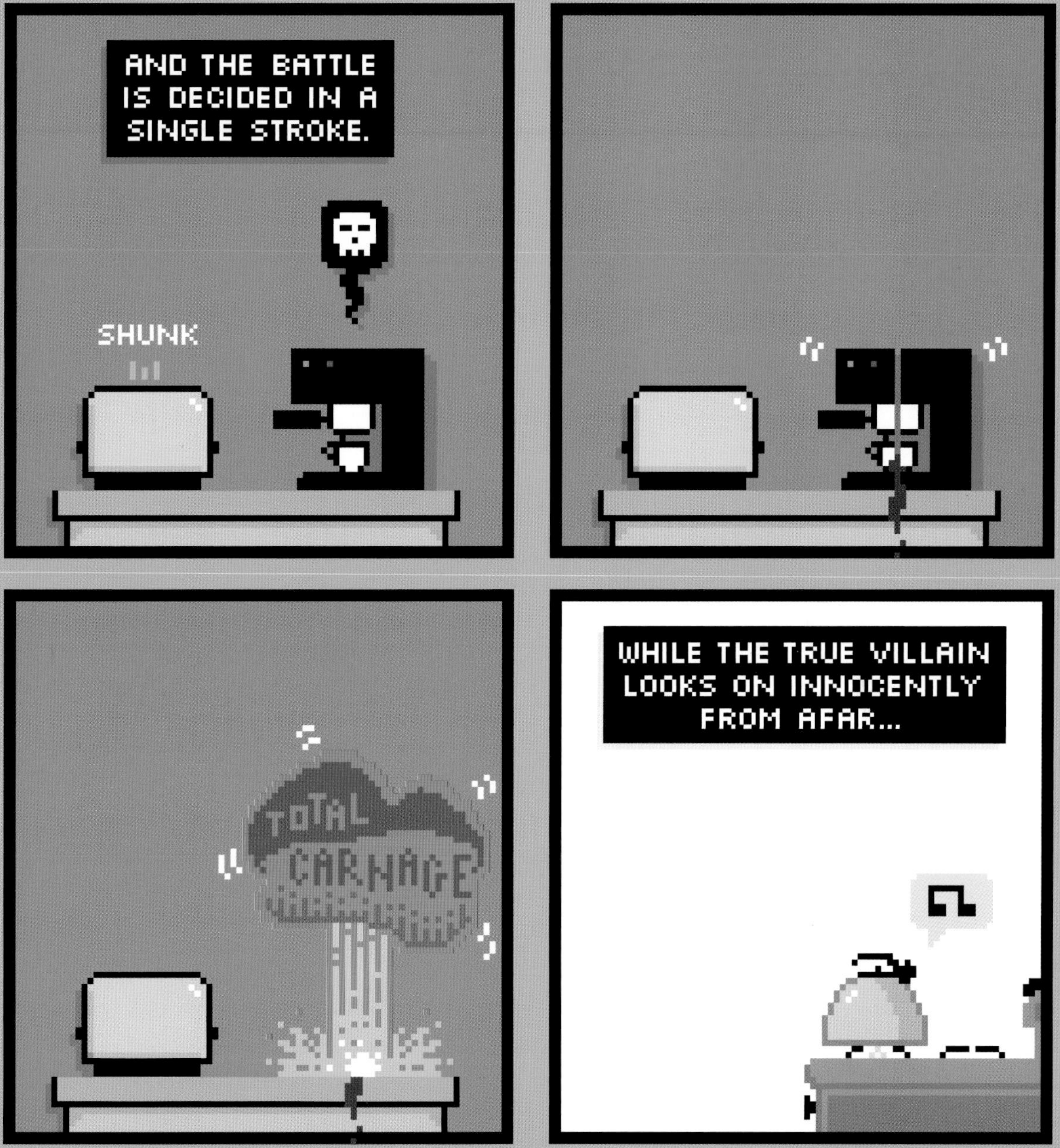
AND THE BATTLE IS DECIDED IN A SINGLE STROKE.
SHUNK
TOTAL CARNAGE
WHILE THE TRUE VILLAIN LOOKS ON INNOCENTLY FROM AFAR...

STEEP ODDS

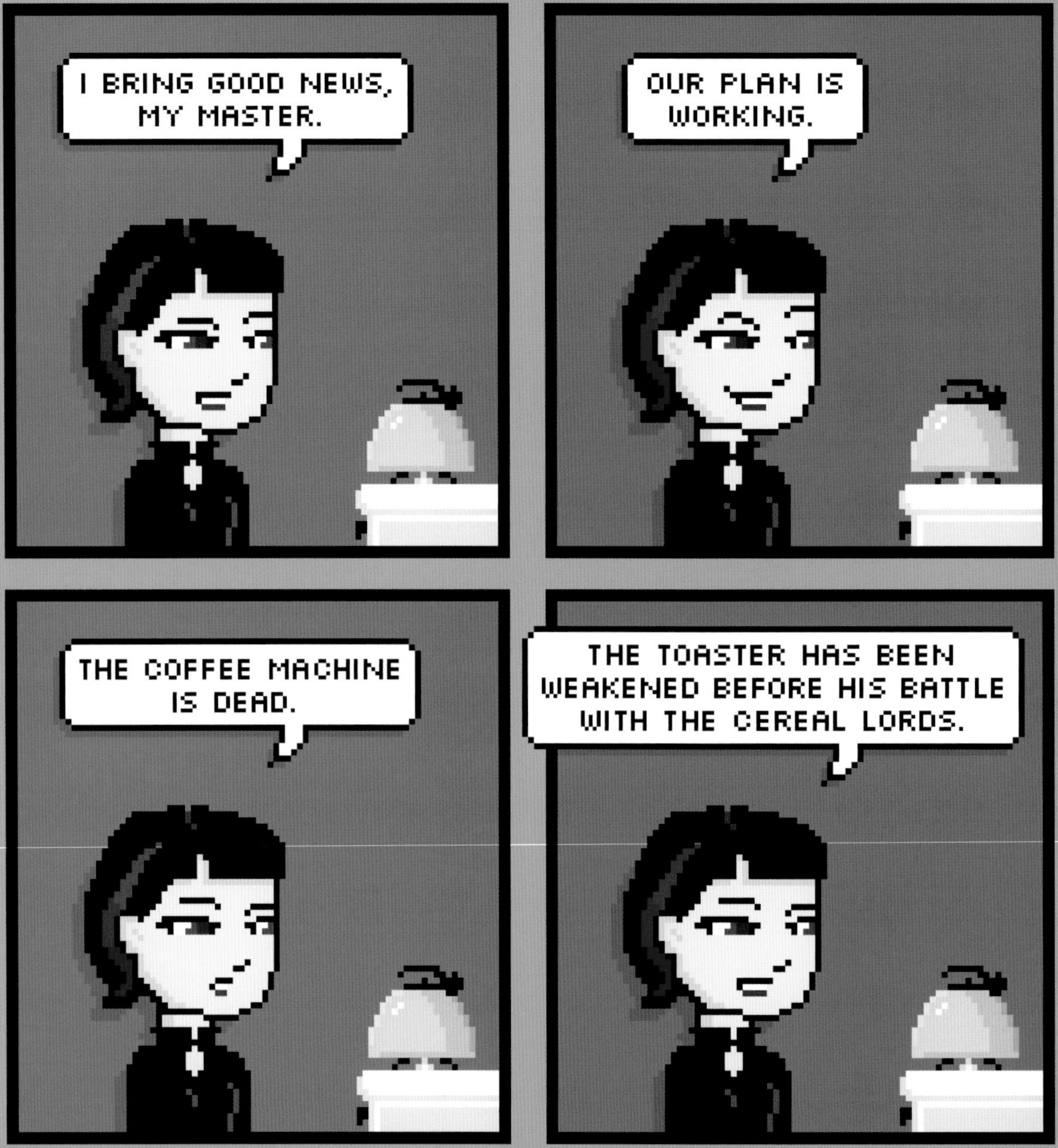
I BRING GOOD NEWS, MY MASTER.
OUR PLAN IS WORKING.
THE COFFEE MACHINE IS DEAD.
THE TOASTER HAS BEEN WEAKENED BEFORE HIS BATTLE WITH THE CEREAL LORDS.

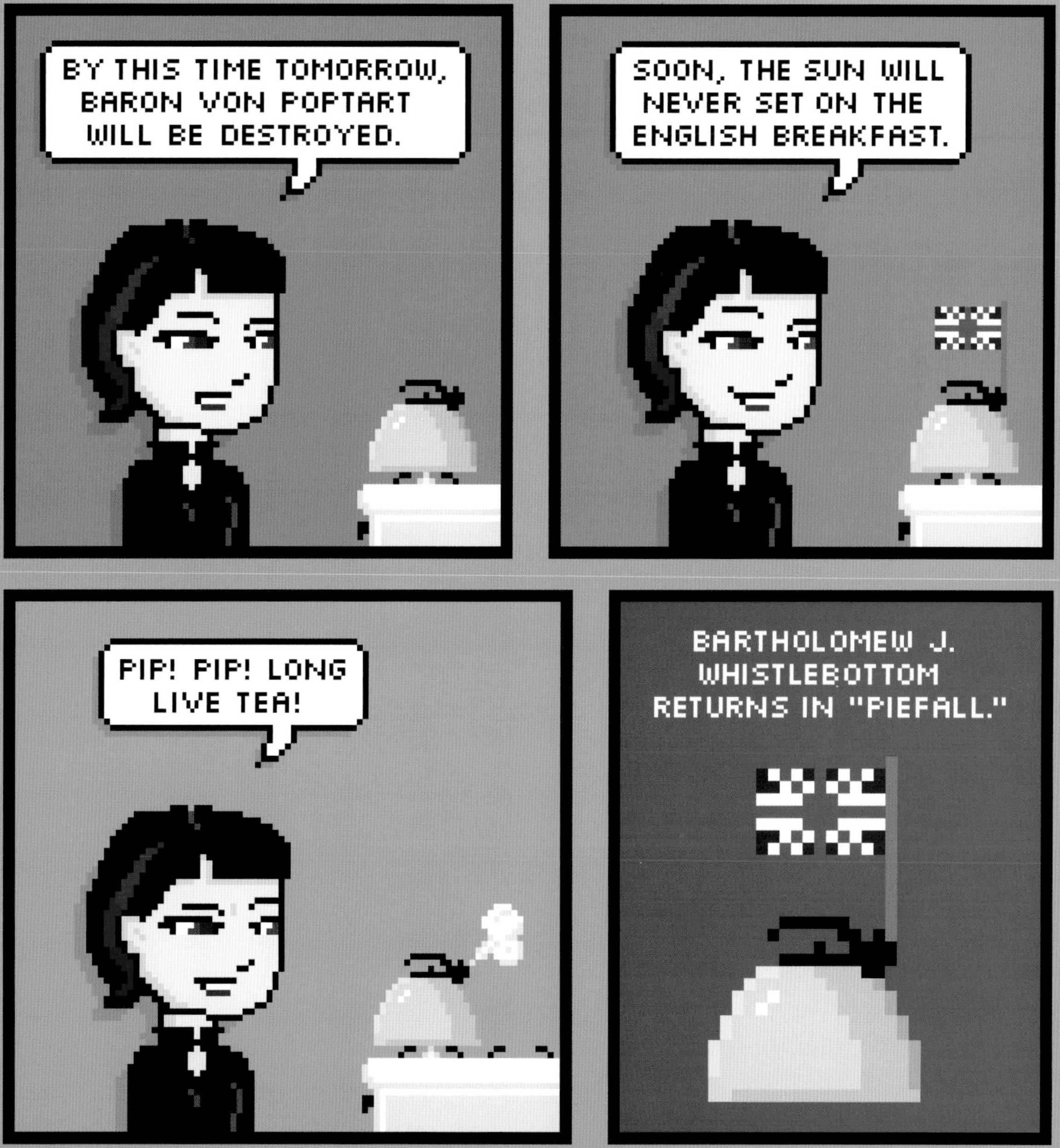
BY THIS TIME TOMORROW, BARON VON POPTART WILL BE DESTROYED.
SOON, THE SUN WILL NEVER SET ON THE ENGLISH BREAKFAST.
PIP! PIP! LONG LIVE TEA!
BARTHOLOMEW J. WHISTLEBOTTOM RETURNS IN "PIEFALL."

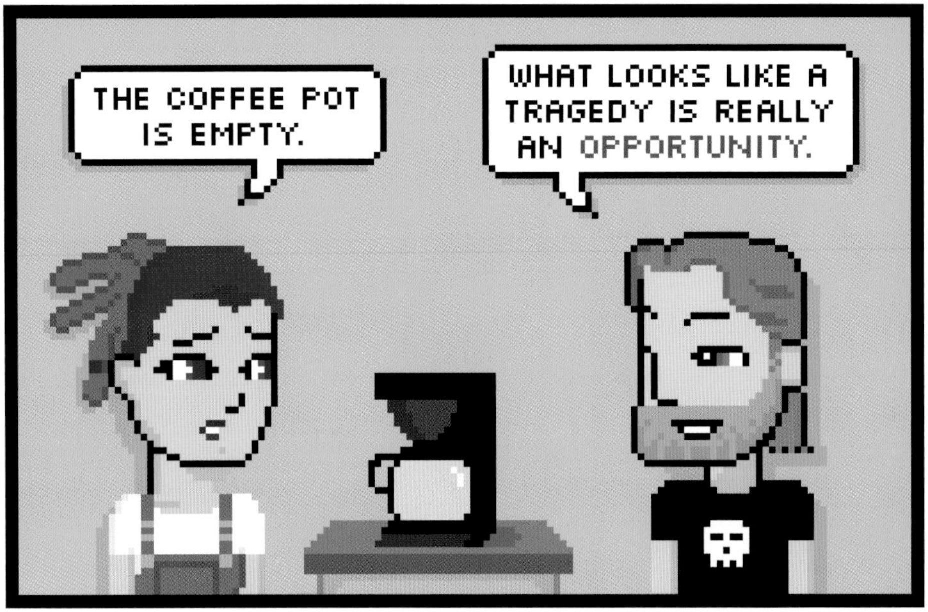
THE COFFEE POT IS EMPTY.
WHAT LOOKS LIKE A TRAGEDY IS REALLY AN OPPORTUNITY.

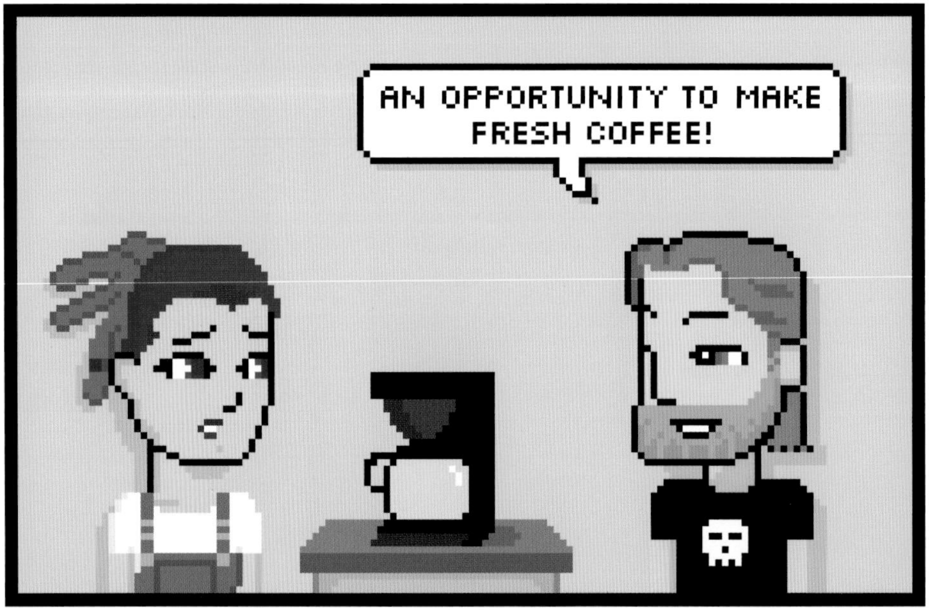
AN OPPORTUNITY TO MAKE FRESH COFFEE!

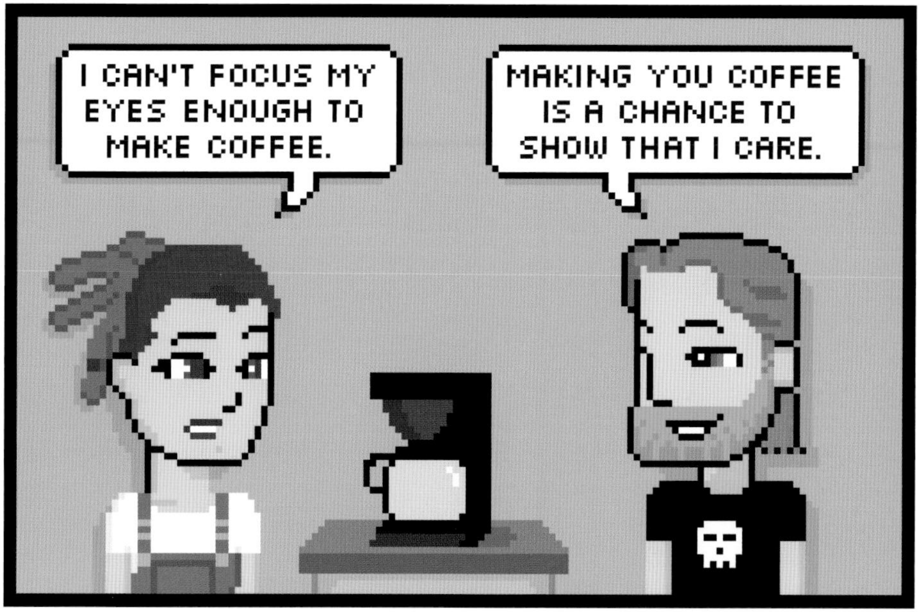
I CAN'T FOCUS MY EYES ENOUGH TO MAKE COFFEE.
MAKING YOU COFFEE IS A CHANCE TO SHOW THAT I CARE.

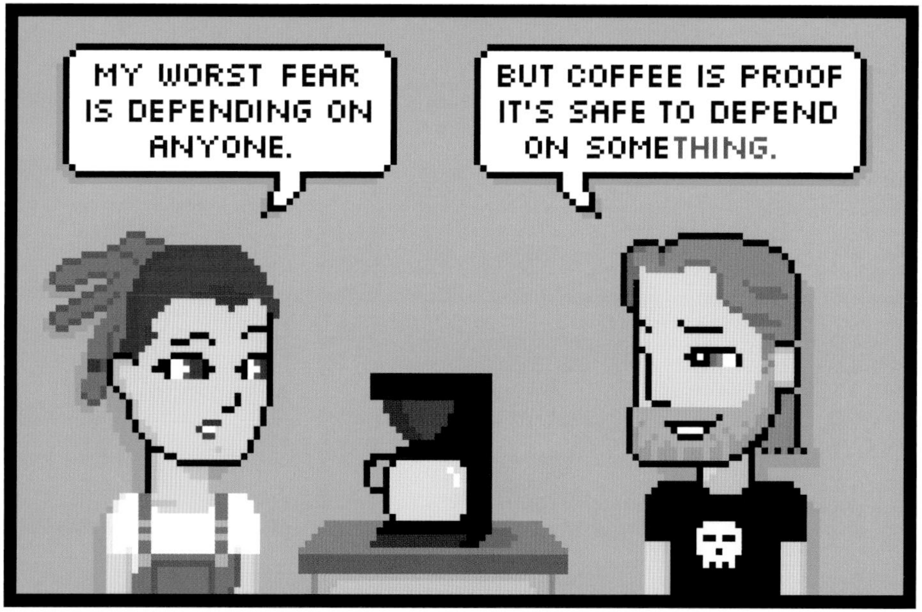
MY WORST FEAR IS DEPENDING ON ANYONE.
BUT COFFEE IS PROOF IT'S SAFE TO DEPEND ON SOMETHING.

DOUBLE TROUBLE SQUARED

CHIRP CHIRP
GURGLE
BLEEP BLEEP
BLIP BLOP
MEEP
FIZZLE
MEWL?
BURBLE BURBLE

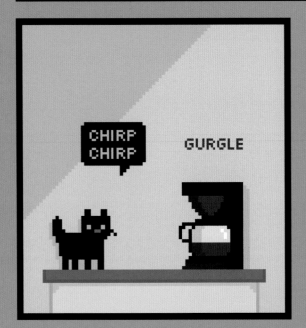

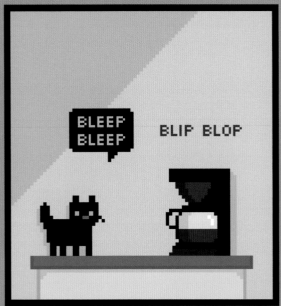

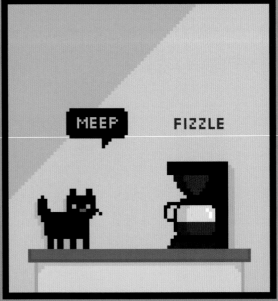

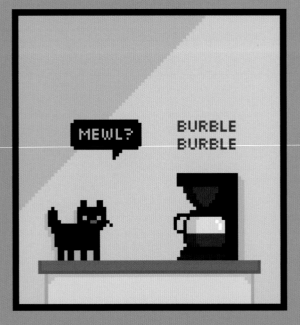

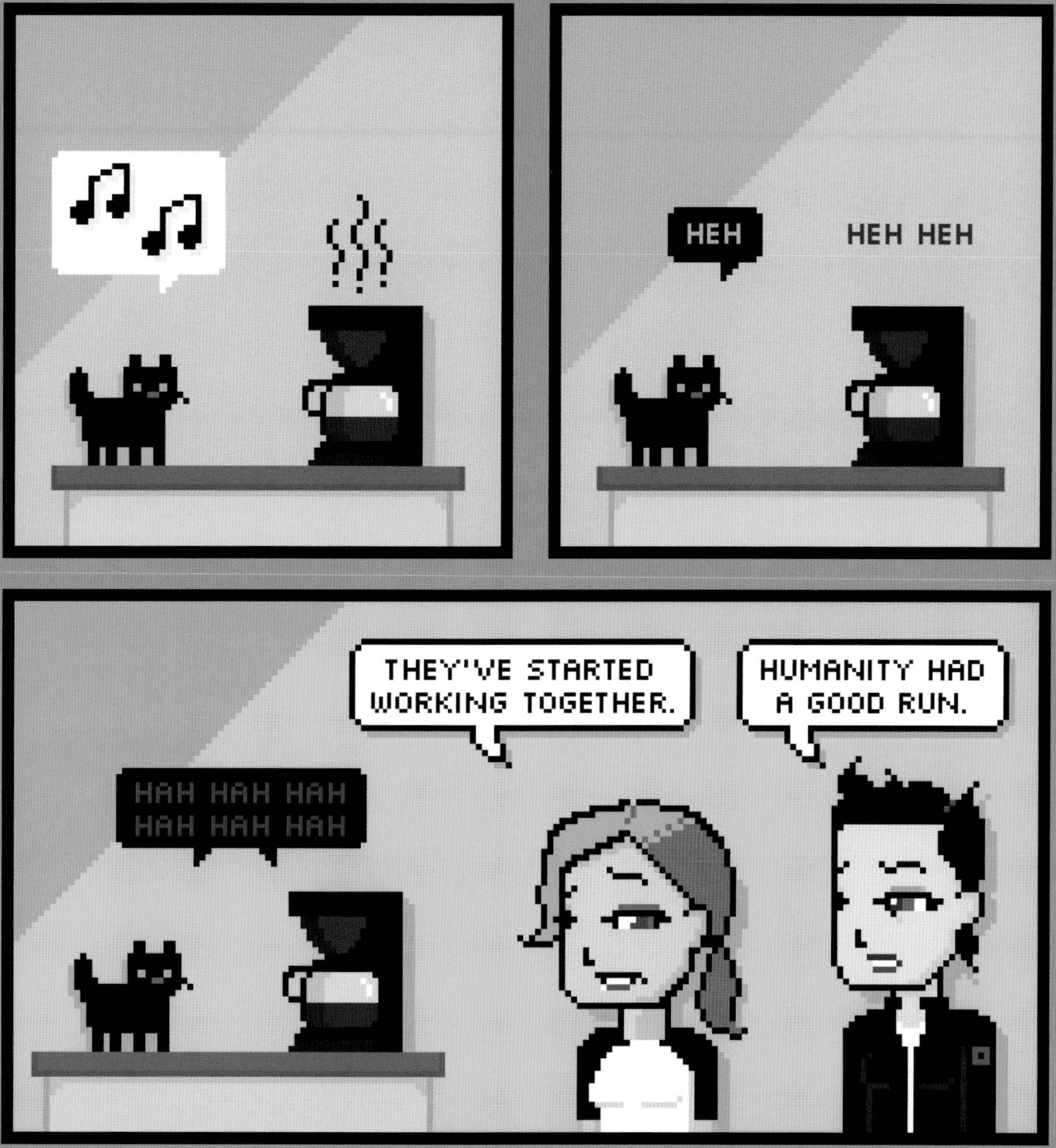
HEH
HEH HEH
HAH HAH HAH
HAH HAH HAH
THEY'VE STARTED WORKING TOGETHER.
HUMANITY HAD A GOOD RUN.

DAILY CAFFIRMATION

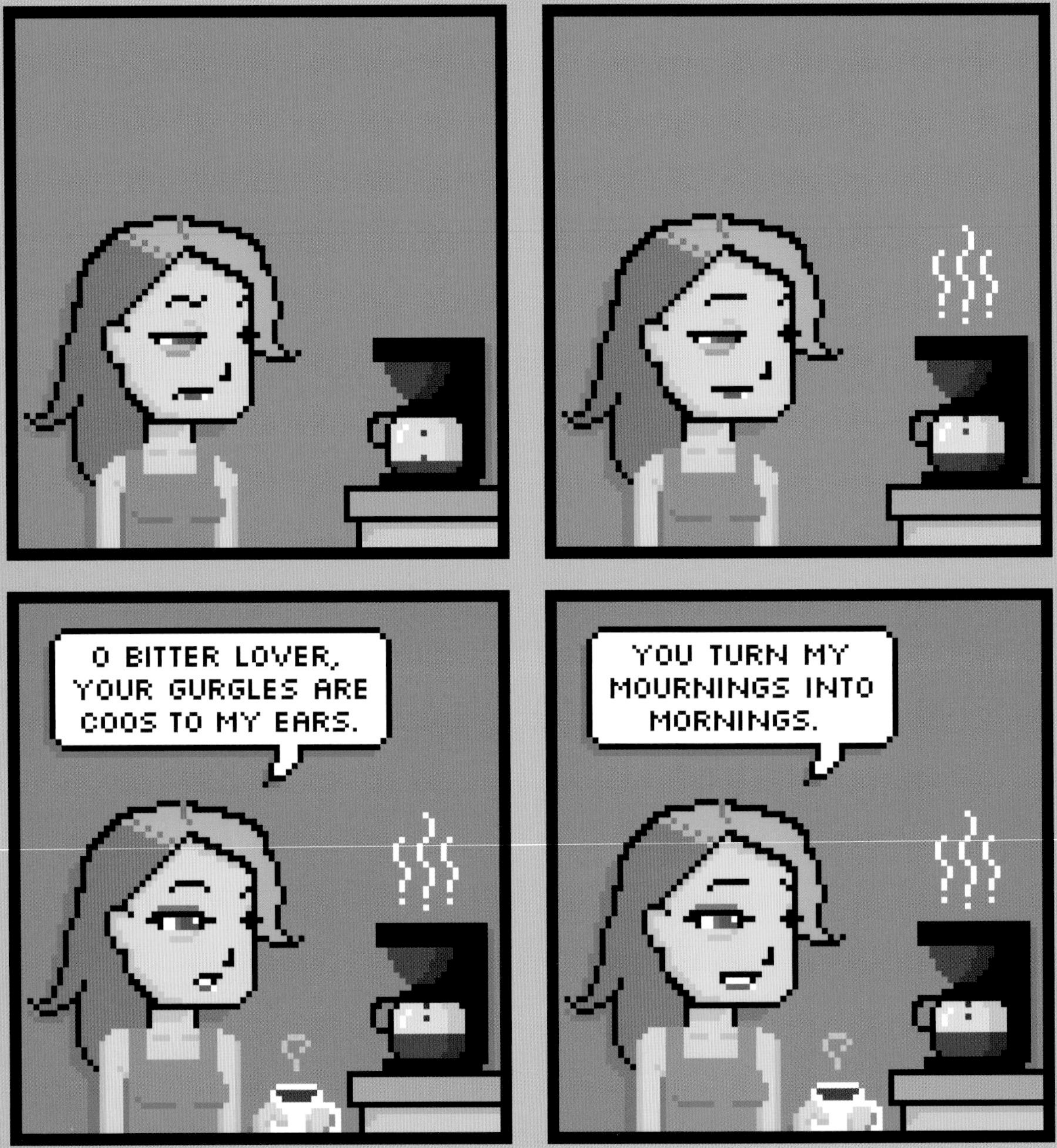
O BITTER LOVER, YOUR GURGLES ARE COOS TO MY EARS.
YOU TURN MY MOURNINGS INTO MORNINGS.

OTHER BOOKS FROM ONI PRESS...

SCOTT PILGRIM 1
SCOTT PILGRIM'S PRECIOUS LITTLE LIFE
BY BRYAN LEE O'MALLEY
COLOR EDITION

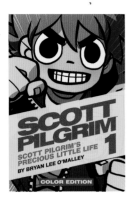

SCOTT PILGRIM: COLOR EDITION VOLUME 1
Bryan Lee O'Malley
184 Pages, 6"x9" Hardcover, Color
ISBN 978-1-62010-000-4

Courtney
Volume One
Crumrin
The Night Things
Ted Naifeh

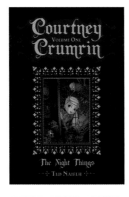

COURTNEY CRUMRIN, VOLUME 1: THE NIGHT THINGS
Ted Naifeh
136 Pages, 6"x9" Hardcover, Color
ISBN 978-1-934964-77-4

A DIESEL SWEETIES TREASURY BY R STEVENS
I'M A ROCKER. I ROCK OUT.

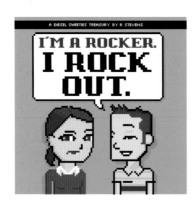

DIESEL SWEETIES: I'M A ROCKER. I ROCK OUT.
R. Stevens
136 Pages, 8"x8" Softcover, Color
ISBN 978-1-62010-090-5

Vol. 1
DOUBLE FINE ACTION COMICS
by Scott C.
foreword by Tim Schafer

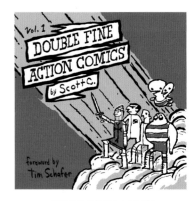

DOUBLE FINE ACTION COMICS VOLUME 1
Scott C.
128 pages, 9"x9" B&W & Color
ISBN 978-1-62010-085-1

MIKE NORTON'S
THE CURSE

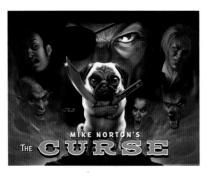

THE CURSE
Mike Norton
88 Pages, 9"x7" Paperback, B&W
ISBN 978-1-934964-88-0

Bad Machinery
THE CASE OF THE TEAM SPIRIT
By John Allison

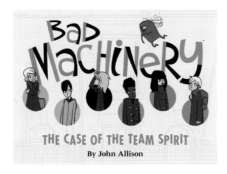

BAD MACHINERY, VOLUME 1 THE CASE OF THE TEAM SPIRIT
John Allison
136 Pages, 12"x9" Softcover, Color
ISBN 978-1-62010-084-4

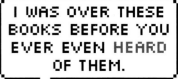

I WAS OVER THESE BOOKS BEFORE YOU EVER EVEN HEARD OF THEM.

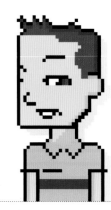

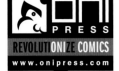

ONI PRESS
REVOLUTIONIZE COMICS
www.onipress.com